The American South in a Global World

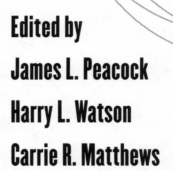

Edited by

James L. Peacock

Harry L. Watson

Carrie R. Matthews

 The University North Carolina Press

Chapel Hill and London

The American South

in a Global World

© 2005 The University of North Carolina Press
All rights reserved

Designed by April Leidig-Higgins
Set in Ehrhardt by Copperline Book Services, Inc.
Manufactured in the United States of America

The paper in this book meets the guidelines for permanence
and durability of the Committee on Production Guidelines
for Book Longevity of the Council on Library Resources.

Library of Congress Cataloging-in-Publication Data
The American South in a global world / edited by James L.
Peacock, Harry L. Watson, Carrie R. Matthews.
p. cm. Includes bibliographical references and index.
ISBN 0-8078-2924-2 (cloth: alk. paper)
ISBN 0-8078-5589-8 (pbk.: alk. paper)
1. Southern States—Politics and government—1951–
2. Southern States—Social conditions—1945– 3. Southern
States—Economic conditions—1945– 4. Globalization—
Political aspects—Southern States. 5. Globalization—Social
aspects—Southern States. I. Peacock, James L. II. Watson,
Harry L. III. Matthews, Carrie R.
F216.2.A455 2005
975'.043—dc22   2004016549

cloth   09 08 07 06 05   5 4 3 2 1
paper   09 08 07 06 05   5 4 3 2 1

Contents

Part Six. Tripartite Epilogue

Acknowledgments

We acknowledge support by the Rockefeller Foundation for three institutes pertaining to the globalizing South. The first was held from 1992 to 1995; the second, from 1998 to 2002; and the third, from 2002 to 2005. The first institute was sponsored by the Institute for Arts and Humanities (IAH); the second two were sponsored by the University Center for International Studies, with support from the Center for Study of the American South and the Institute of African American Research, all at the University of North Carolina at Chapel Hill. These institutes brought visiting fellows and supported seminars and workshops as well as conferences, all of which provided forums to research the topic addressed in this volume.

We give special thanks to Lynn Swazia and Thomas Santos of the Rockefeller Foundation and to Ruel Tyson, director of IAH, as well as to Donald Nonini, Leon Fink, David Moltke-Hansen, Gerald Horne, Chad Haines, Niklaus Steiner, and Beth Ann Kutchma, who were either coprincipal investigators or coordinators of the Rockefeller projects. We deeply thank David Camp, who was the organizer of the particular Rockefeller conference that resulted in this volume.

The American South in a Global World

James L. Peacock, Harry L. Watson, and Carrie R. Matthews

Introduction

Globalization with a Southern Face

For most of the twentieth century, observers and social scientists have seen the American South as locked in cultural isolation, first from the presumed mainstream of life in the United States and, even more, from the wider modern world beyond U.S. borders. Regional sociologist Howard W. Odum captured prevailing impressions exactly in his magisterial 1936 volume, *Southern Regions of the United States*. "Sectionalism itself has constituted a major crisis . . . ," he observed, "conditioning the South to isolation, individualism, ingrowing patriotism, cultural inbreeding, civic immaturity, and social inadequacy." Odum deplored the "homogeneity of the white people, with overwhelming ratios of native born and of prevailing early American stocks," that had created a "church going, Protestant, Sabbath observing, patriarchal folk, taking their honor, their politics, and their liquor hard." More than some other contemporaries (W. J. Cash comes to mind), Odum was prepared to see "many Souths" beneath the veneer of white homogeneity, but to his regret, the region's most compelling case of cultural diversity was still its "bi-racial civilization with its ever-present 'Negro problem' and dual drain on resources" (Odum 1936, 13, 15; Cash 1941, vii–x).

In truth, the legendary South of two isolated and homogeneous races was not entirely valid even in the 1930s, and variants like the Appalachian South and the Hispanic Southwest made their appearances in Odum's famous treatise. But even as a heuristic image, the isolated and homogeneous South was a limited historical phenomenon that was scarcely more than a century old when Odum wrote, and it now seems destined to vanish. As many early twentieth-century observers knew but saw no reason to emphasize, the colonial South had been called into existence by an early process of "globalization" that had created a worldwide demand for semitropical products like tobacco and rice and pulled together a remarkable mixture of peoples from around the Atlantic basin. Prior to the nineteenth century, a turbulent mix of three "races," each containing many different cultural groups within them, vied with one another in the area that came to be the U.S. South. Dozens of Indian tribes and European nationalities contended with one another for wealth and mastery, while an independent "black" identity emerged only slowly from the struggling welter of Coromantees, Mandingoes, Whydahs, Senegambians, Igbos, Calabars, Angolans, and Congolese held captive among them. Indeed, it was not until after the turn of the nineteenth century that the South's slave-based economy became unique within the United States, melding diverse groups into a (nearly) biracial civilization, repelling newcomers, and demanding white solidarity in defense of its "peculiar institutions." While the Civil War ended slavery in the United States, cultural isolation endured and may even have worsened in a New South based on cheap labor and social injustice, for blacks in the one-crop farm economy and for poorly skilled whites in the manufacturing plants that spread across its towns and upland regions (Wright 1986, 51–80).

At the dawn of the twenty-first century, the South described by Odum and Cash and their contemporaries is now disappearing. The civil rights movement did not end racial inequality but shifted its terms in ways unimaginable to previous generations. Aggressive development campaigns have brought new firms and new industries to the region's cities, and air conditioning has made its environment tolerable for their executives. Improvements in transportation and communication, the end of the Cold War, increased political stability in many developing countries, and the collapse of national trade barriers have ended the South's comparative advantage as a haven for low-wage industries. Recent decades have therefore seen the widespread migration of manufacturing jobs from the U.S. South to the global "South" of Latin America and southern Asia. At the same time, pervasive economic pressures have destabilized village economies, especially in Latin America, sending millions of migrants northward to the once "biracial" South. Caught up in the shifting currents of a rapidly changing world, the American South is once more subject to globalization.

The latest wave of globalization is thus a turning point in southern history, equal in importance to the earlier turning point that swiveled the South inward and inland for more than a century and a half. There is every reason to believe that the newest southern economy will stimulate the rise of yet another New South, closer perhaps than its earlier counterparts to an American or global mainstream or perhaps distinctive in ways that are only beginning to be apparent. It is now commonplace to observe that European regional identities have increased in importance as national identities have declined, amplifying Scotland and Sardinia while diminishing Britain and Italy and obliterating Yugoslavia and the Soviet Union (Von Hagen and Widgren 2001; Hönnighausen 2000). If that is so, the U.S. South may also be taking its place

✦ in a world of regions, not simply of nation-states. Since Odum's day and before, prevailing images of the American South have been framed in relationship to the nation, to the rest of the United States. The latest understanding of the U.S. South must be broader than that to take in the perspective of the world.

With the support of the Rockefeller Foundation, the University Center for International Studies and the Center for the Study of the American South at the University of North Carolina at Chapel Hill jointly explore the multiple meanings of the global or transnational South. This effort builds on earlier projects going back to a conference called "The Multicultural South" held in the late 1980s by our Institute for the Arts and the Humanities, which led to three Rockefeller Institutes from 1991 to 2004. Our participants began by investigating distinctive cases of southern people and southern communities touched by global change, assuming that the patterns and dynamics appearing in these disparate cases would become the elementary particles for larger generalizations. The studies in this volume present the first fruits of our investigations, treating Hispanic agricultural workers, Asian professionals, a rural mining community, new urban governance in a high-tech environment, and many other groups and issues.

These essays represent a variety of social science disciplines, including economics, history, sociology, and anthropology. While the humanities and the professional disciplines are less emphasized here, the case studies that are included raise new questions and provide a base for further exploration of the global South. What does this new world mean for arts and culture? What needs to happen in law, urban planning, and public health? Social and economic studies are not the end of analysis but the basis for further questions.

Surveying the transnational South as it emerges, our authors discover a multifaceted process of change. Their findings overlap and crosscut one another in a variety of ways, but we have grouped them into five convenient sections, followed by three concluding essays. We begin with a section called "Immigration" that focuses particularly on the experiences of newcomers from Latin America, the largest though certainly not the only source of the new southern population. As historian Paul Levengood's comparative analysis of Miami and Houston shows, not all immigrants from Latin America are alike, and their experiences vary considerably according to destination and country of origin. Barbara Ellen Smith and her coauthors explore how the market forces have reshaped the immigrant workplace in one key sector of the global economy, while Lucila Vargas delves into sensitive questions of identity that young Latinas find as they grow up in new environments. Sandy Smith-Nonini's essay explores how government policies supposedly designed to protect temporary workers have actually worked against them.

Drawing on the South's renowned sense of place, the second section takes up the connections between global movements and specific localities. Thaddeus Guldbrandsen discusses changes in city governance brought on by new population movements, while Bryan McNeil describes what international capital flows have done to the West Virginia landscape. Sections 3 and 4 describe the experience of workers in the South's new economic and social environment. Meenu Tewari and Rachel Willis show how global pressures, contrary to expectations, have revived certain sectors of southern industry, while Steve Striffler describes how a common work experience has helped to build a sense of solidarity across ethnic lines in an Arkansas chicken plant. Challenging the stereotype that the new immigrants are all low-skilled workers from Latin America, Peacock, Jones, and Brooks examine an Indonesian company's relations with the town of Mobile, Alabama, and Sawa Kurotani and Ajantha Subramanian explore the experiences of highly skilled Asian scientists and executives in North Carolina's Research Triangle.

Section 5 takes us from detached academic discussion to the perspective of activists in the transnational South. Gregory Stephens challenges the surviving tradition of biracialism in southern culture, asking southerners to respond to the arrival of Hispanic immigrants by rethinking long-held racial categories. Jennie Smith describes a teaching experiment that introduces mostly Anglo college students to Hispanic migrants in the changing society of Rome, Georgia, while Ellen Spears discusses the prospects for political collaboration between blacks and Latinos. We close with three concluding essays by Donald Nonini, James Peacock, and Harry Watson reflecting on the larger meaning of transnational change.

The authors of these essays have given intensive attention to one particular region and to many different localities within that region. Do their insights stretch any farther than the South itself? As we investigate what globalization has done to and for the South, we have tried to remember what the experience of the South may tell us about the larger meaning of the current wave of globalization to other places as well. In a world swept by global change, why is the experience of the U.S. South different from that of any other place? Or why is it as significant as the experience of southern China, northern India, or central Mexico?

One obvious answer is that the U.S. South is a large region in the world's wealthiest nation, now its only superpower, and the region's experience almost inherently influences other places. More subtly, the U.S. South has distinctive features that render it a telling example or "type." As historian C. Vann Woodward noted long ago, the distinct history of the U.S. South has given the region a "burden of history" with much in common with other nations, including the experiences of poverty, defeat, and a colonial economy (Woodward 1993). Though the South has changed a great deal and continues to do so, it claims tradition and sense of place, suggesting something in common with other Souths and, indeed, with many societies throughout the world that have seen themselves as reservoirs of tradition more than as engines of transformation. And finally, reflecting on these qualities, the U.S. South has long displayed a strong regional identity that many self-described southerners are reluctant to abandon (Reed 1975; Griffin and Thompson 2003). How this identity meets globalization is a question pertinent to most societies, certainly most Souths in a globalizing world. In this light, the experience of the U.S. South may illuminate not only its own scholars and specialists but those devoted to other regions as well.

References

Cash, W. J. 1941. *The Mind of the South*. New York: Knopf.
Griffin, Larry J., and Ashley Thompson. 2003. "Enough about the Disappearing South: What about the Disappearing Southerner?" *Southern Cultures* 9, no. 3 (Fall): 51–65.
Hönnighausen, Lothar, ed. 2000. *Regional Images and Regional Realities*. Tübingen: Stauffenburg.
Odum, Howard W. 1936. *Southern Regions of the United States*. Chapel Hill: University of North Carolina Press.
Reed, John Shelton. 1975. *The Enduring South: Subcultural Persistence in Mass Society*. Chapel Hill: University of North Carolina Press.
Von Hagen, Jürgen, and Mika Widgren, eds. 2001. *Regionalism in Europe: Geometries and Strategies after 2000*. Universitat Bonn Zentrum Fur Europaische Integrationsforschung. Boston: Kluwer.
Woodward, C. Vann. 1993. "The Search for Southern Identity." In Woodward, *The Burden of Southern History*, 3d ed., 3–25. Baton Rouge: Louisiana State University Press.
Wright, Gavin. 1986. *Old South, New South: Revolutions in the Southern Economy since the Civil War*. New York: Basic Books.

Part One

Immigration

Paul A. Levengood

Latino Migration to Miami and Houston

Transnationalism at Work in Two Southern Cities

As the South becomes increasingly integrated into the global economy, migration to the region from around the world has become the subject of significant comment, and some controversy as well. The rising tide of Latino migration to the South is perhaps the most striking of these transnational movements of people. Although this is a relatively new phenomenon in the heart of the South, on its southern and western edges, the "rim South," this influx has been occurring for decades. Not coincidentally, it is these parts of the South that have long been players in the interconnected framework of modern trade and cultural exchange. This study examines two major metropolitan centers of the rim South—Houston, Texas, and Miami, Florida—and asks several questions: What has Latino migration looked like in each city? How has the Latino presence changed the two cities? What challenges have faced Latinos in integrating into southern society? What role has this migration played in Miami and Houston becoming global cities?

Miami

Even by the standards of a young nation, Miami is a young city. Founded in 1896, it grew quickly in the early part of the twentieth century as a winter tourist destination. To meet the needs of the growing construction and tourist industries, thousands of migrants, mostly poor whites and blacks from other parts of the South, streamed into south Florida.[1] As might be expected with such a population, Miami developed in a southern manner. Racial segregation was absolute, and black residence was initially confined by law to two small areas. Violators of Jim Crow law or practice could expect harsh retribution from either law enforcement authorities or the strong local branch of the Ku Klux

Klan (Mohl 1991, 124). The only members of an ethnic group that migrated to Miami in any numbers from outside the South in the early twentieth century were northern Jews.

Miami had virtually no Latino population for the first forty years of its existence. The only notable concentrations of Cubans in Florida were in Key West and Tampa. Not until Miami reached a more advanced level of urban maturity in the 1920s and 1930s did it begin to attract even a modest number of immigrants from Cuba. Lured by the increased urbanity and amenities that Miami offered, many Cuban leaders found exile in the city, waiting for the chance to return to Havana when the political climate changed.

In addition to the small core of political exiles who took up residence, middle- and upper-class tourists from Cuba and other Latin American countries made Miami their primary destination throughout the 1940s and 1950s. Cuban customs estimated that in 1948 alone 40,000 Cubans visited Miami and spent more than $70 million dollars in Florida. This familiarity with Miami would be exceedingly important when exile of a more permanent sort forced many Cubans to settle in the United States beginning a decade later. Although tourism brought large numbers of Cubans and other Latinos to Miami to visit, by the end of the 1950s few had settled there. Events in Cuba would soon change that entirely.

The impact on Miami of Fidel Castro's revolution was immediate. Even before Fulgencio Batista was toppled, numerous members of the dictator's inner circle along with a few of the wealthiest members of Cuban society began to transfer capital, movable property, and in some cases themselves to Miami. Soon after Castro seized power, mass migration began in earnest. This first wave of refugees included many of the most skilled and affluent members of Cuban society. A 1968 study of this early wave of migrants found that those Cubans who arrived in Miami between 1958 and 1962 came disproportionately from the professional, semiprofessional, managerial, or clerical categories and had attained a significantly higher level of education than had the bulk of Cuba's population.[2]

The so-called Golden Exiles of 1958 to 1962 have achieved a mythic status in both southern Florida and American popular consciousness. A far larger number of exiles arrived between 1965 and 1973. However, the Golden Exiles provided a symbol of Cuba transplanted in foreign soil, and among them were many of the stalwarts who ensured that their new community retained its "Cubanness" and rallied to the cause of anti-Castroism.[3]

The success of these Golden Exiles was in many ways extraordinary. Legion are the stories of Cuban doctors busing tables and former lawyers digging ditches, only later to become wealthy in Miami. Though some of these tales might be fictional, by any measurement, Miami Cubans have been one of the most successful groups in U.S. immigration history. A very small but important number of Cubans transferred wealth to the United States either before the revolution or shortly thereafter. Combined with an uncommonly strong spirit of ethnic mutual aid, this allowed a sizable number of Cuban-owned businesses to emerge at an early date. As mentioned earlier, this group brought with it a high degree of education and what might be called cultural capital (professional, financial, and entrepreneurial skills). In some cases it was not long before this professional and business experience allowed Cubans to move out of menial labor and into more lucrative positions. Cubans' own efforts are only part of the story. Credit is also due to an unprecedented program of federal government aid, the Cuban Refugee Program. To ensure a black eye to the Castro regime, an estimated $2 billion was poured into the Cuban community in grants and loans, an unprecedented step by the federal government (Parks and Bush 1996, 136; Croucher 1997, 108–9).[4]

This seed money for Cuban exiles found fertile ground in Miami. By the 1960s the city was in an economic slump, brought on by competition for tourist dollars from Las Vegas and the Caribbean. In what would come to be called Little Havana—an area just southwest of downtown—Cubans found a down-at-heel but centrally located area in which to settle and work. Within less than a decade, a thriving business district would exist in this enclave that included numerous businesses established in Miami that had existed, with the same name and specialty, before the revolution in Havana or Santiago. Residents of this Cuban community re-created their homeland in South Florida in other ways. Some schools were refounded, employing the same teachers they had in Cuba. Similarly the Municipios de Cuba en Exilio was created to hold elections for the offices of the *municipios* back in Cuba.[5] As Cuban American academic Gustavo Pérez-Firmat wrote of this phenomenon of exile life, "'Exiles live by substitution. If you can't have it in Havana, make it in Miami. . . . Life in exile: memory enhanced by imagination'" (qtd. in Parks and Bush 1996, 146).

The lure of exile in Miami proved strong. The first wave, lasting from January 1959 until regular air traffic was halted by the tensions of the Cuban missile crisis in October 1962, saw 200,000 immigrants land in the United States, the lion's share ending up in Miami (Pérez 1986, 129). Between November 1962 and November 1965 immigration slowed dramatically and included some 74,000 persons. Another upsurge occurred from late 1965 to April 1973 via twice-daily "freedom flights" between Miami and Havana that brought more than 340,000 Cubans to the United States. The only dramatic increase in

Cuban migration since the flights ended in 1973 occurred in May 1980, when the northern Cuban port of Mariel was opened to U.S. vessels. The five-month Mariel boatlift resulted in the arrival of 125,000 "Marielitos" in Miami.[6] Since Mariel, migration has been limited to those few willing to brave the crossing from Cuba in small boats (Croucher 1997, 50).[7]

For most of the 1960s, Cuban exile politics was largely waged at the national level in an attempt to push Washington into ending Castro's rule. Not until the 1970s, when they realized that return to Cuba was not imminent, did significant numbers of exiles begin to become citizens and use the ballot box to affect events at the local level.[8] The first Cuban city commissioner of Miami was elected in 1972, and with significant Cuban support Miami elected its first Latino mayor in 1973 (Croucher 1997, 36). In 1985 Cuban-born Xavier Suárez was elected mayor, and in 1989 Ileana Ros-Lehtinen became the first Cuban to be elected to Congress. The trend continued in the 1990s with Cubans winning most of Dade County's state house and state senate seats, majorities in the Miami city council and county commission, and the office of county manager (Pérez 1992, 102–3).

As Cuban American politics has broadened, the theme of *el exilio* has grown slightly less prominent. Dissenting views are no longer punished by assassination as they occasionally used to be, but as the Elián González furor indicates, intense feelings lurk just below the surface of the Cuban community.[9] Despite stereotypes, all of Miami's Cubans are not virulent anti-Marxists. The community encompasses a broad range of politics, from reactionary right to the far left. However, a powerful and unifying sense of loss and anger seems to cut across political lines. Their degree of personal enmity for Castro notwithstanding, most Cubans agree that he is guilty of denying them their lives in Cuba and is responsible for the loss of a special "birthright" (Didion 1987, 17).

As the exile enters its sixth decade, the future of Cuban American politics is unclear. In a 1995 *National Review* poll, participants were asked if they would return to Cuba permanently if given the chance. Twenty-four percent answered yes; 64 percent said no; and 12 percent were undecided (Falcoff 1995, 43). Anecdotal evidence suggests that a change in attitude clearly falls along generational lines. Older and middle-aged Cubans retain personal bonds with Cuba; many under thirty-five do not. Miami architect Raul Rodríguez's family is illustrative. When the travel ban was lifted in the mid-1980s, the Rodríguez family took several trips to Cuba. Eventually Raul's twelve-year-old son Ruly told him that he "hated Cuba, that he never wanted to go there again." As author David Rieff puts it, even on the island, "Ruly had never left the United States, at least in his head" (1993, 205–6). The comparisons to the exiles in Miami who had long imagined themselves in Cuba are striking.

It would be surprising if Ruly Rodríguez or many of his generation would ever return to the island to live. Frankly, why would they? And should their reticence be a surprise? Ironically, the success of older Cuban exiles has inadvertently ensured that younger generations will probably lose interest in *la lucha*, "the struggle."

That success in Miami has been remarkable. By the 1970s, Cuban entrepreneurship had been largely responsible for revitalizing the city's economy focusing it on intrahemispheric trade. Cuban business leaders played to their centuries-old strength as merchants and used the extensive network of transnational contacts that existed among Cuban diasporic communities in Latin America and the Caribbean. As early as 1967 Miami was being recognized as "the gateway city to Latin America."[10] In the 1970s the city became a leading center of U.S. trade with the nations of the Western Hemisphere. The heavy Cuban presence lent the city a "Latino accent" that made it a comfortable location for Latin Americans to visit and do business, earning Miami the nickname "the capital of Latin America" (Croucher 1997, 35).[11]

The upward growth of international trade and finance in Miami continued in the 1980s with the establishment of dozens of businesses oriented toward commerce with Central and South America, including the branches of more than fifty foreign banks (Croucher 1997, 42–43). By the 1990s the city was clearly the leading U.S. center of export trade to the Western Hemisphere. According to 1998 Department of Commerce statistics, Dade County businesses accounted for exports of more than $11 billion to the nations of Latin America and the Caribbean—next was Detroit with less than $8 billion. In stark contrast, Miami exported only $854 million to Europe, $250 million to Asia, and $83 million to Africa. The 1998 breakdown of destinations of Miami exports to Latin America and the Caribbean was as follows: Mexico: $720,387,000; Caribbean and Central America: $3,731,312.000; and South America: $6,764,313,000. Interestingly, it seems that Brazil was the single largest trading partner of Miami exporters, signifying that Miami is not the capital of only Spanish-speaking Latin America. For interesting comparisons, table 1 contains the dollar values of other leading U.S. export centers to Latin America and the Caribbean. It is hard to imagine that this sort of trade would have been possible without the impact of Cuban exiles.

The strong ties to Latin America have made Miami a magnet for non-Cuban migration from the region. In 1960 there were approximately 50,000 Hispanic residents in Dade County, and they made up some 5 percent of the populace. In the 2000 census, that number mushroomed to 1.3 million, 57 percent of the entire population of Miami/Dade County. Cubans were trailed in numbers, in order, by Nicaraguans, Puerto Ricans, Colombians, Dominicans,

TABLE 1. Dollar Values of Leading U.S. Export Centers to Latin America and the Caribbean (in order of U.S. rank in total exports)

1. Seattle/Bellevue/Everett, WA	$1,469,482,000
2. Detroit, MI	$7,943,376,000
3. New York, NY	$3,649,569,000
4. San Jose, CA	$1,551.097,000
5. Los Angeles/Long Beach, CA	$4,043,728,000
6. Chicago, IL	$4,117,057,000
7. Houston, TX	$6,452,646,000
8. **Miami, FL**	**$11,216,012,000**
9. Minneapolis/St. Paul, MN	$1,605,279,000

Source: Office of Trade and Economic Analysis, International Trade Administration, U.S. Department of Commerce, "Metropolitan Merchandise Export Totals to Selected Destinations, 1993–1998" (retrieved from ⟨http://www.ita.doc.gov/td/industry/otea//metro/destinations⟩).

Mexicans, Hondurans, Peruvians, Guatemalans, and Ecuadorians. Although none can challenge the Cuban political and social hegemony in Miami, each nationality group fiercely defends its individual identity and bristles at being subsumed under a single heading. Many reject inclusive terms such as "Latino" or "Hispanic." Bumper stickers around Miami bear the legend, No Me Digas Hispano, Soy Cubano (Don't Call Me Hispanic, I'm Cuban) (Croucher 1997, 56). As one study asserted quite earnestly, "Miami is more a pluralistic society than an ethnic melting pot" (Cuban American Policy Center 1992, 35).

Houston

In contrast to Miami, Houston owes little of its existence as a global city to the contributions of a specific ethnic group; a converse relationship can, in fact, be postulated. Houston's role as a world center of materials processing, manufacturing, commerce, and medicine has, along with its location, served as a magnet for migration. On the other hand, the increased presence of Latinos, Asians, Europeans, and other immigrant groups has helped transform what was, a few decades ago, a traditional southern city. Today, with established ethnic and national communities that lend their customs, cuisines, religions, and cultures to the fabric of the city, Houston is an eminently more cosmopolitan and interesting place.

Founded in 1836, Houston proved no great attraction to migrants from outside the United States for the first eight decades of its existence. It served as a processing and marketing center of cotton and timber and offered few employment opportunities not filled by African Americans, who constituted the southern city's manual labor force. With the dawn of the twentieth century, however, Houston began to experience rapid industrialization.[12] According to Arnoldo de León, at this point there began the formation of a Mexican settlement large enough to be called a *colonia*. He estimates that by 1910 nearly 2,000 Mexicans resided in the city, attracted by new employment opportunities (de León 1989, 6–7). In addition to the pull exerted by Houston's booming economy, the revolution of the 1910s provided a push to many Mexicans. Immigrants found work in railroad yards and along the Houston Ship Channel — in oil refineries, cotton compresses, and textile mills and on the docks.

Besides the laborers who found work in industry, a few Mexicans of means made homes in Houston in the early twentieth century, and some opened businesses that catered to customers whose needs were unmet by the city's segregated commercial establishments. Following the dictates of Jim Crow, Mexican-only public schools were started in the 1920s, as were separate Roman Catholic churches (de León 1989, chap. 2).

Although buffeted by the Great Depression—which saw Mexican unemployment in Houston soar to 50 percent and forced deportations by state and federal authorities—by 1940 Houston's Mexican population stood at around 20,000.[13] Despite their numbers, Latinos were largely ignored by city government and earned hardly a mention in the press of the day. Only when living conditions in Mexican neighborhoods reached a state that threatened public health did many Anglos learn what life was like in the barrios. One social worker wrote, "No toilet, no running water, inadequate heat . . . structures in dangerous state of repair. . . . We see here the highest infant mortality rate in the city."[14] Although the descriptions shocked many, little was done to ameliorate conditions in the barrio. Not until 1952, more than ten years after it was opened to white and black residents, was any public housing made available for Latino occupancy.

In the postwar years, Mexican migration to Houston picked up significantly as the city's economy boomed from the 1950s through the 1970s with soaring demand for petroleum and petrochemicals. More Anglos entered white-collar positions, leaving opportunities for Mexicans and African Americans to move into higher-paying blue-collar work. Buoyed by their relative prosperity in the postwar period, some middle-class members of Houston's Mexican community became involved in economic, social, and political movements. Houston contributed important leaders to both the League of United Latin

American Citizens and the American GI Forum, both of which pushed civil rights issues such as bilingual education, the abolition of voting restrictions, and prosecution of discriminatory employment practices.[15]

Despite improvements in employment and education in the 1950s and 1960s, most Houstonians of Mexican origin remained among the city's poorest residents. Some gains were made in electoral politics: the state house, the office of city controller, and the school board all saw Houston Mexican holders in the 1960s and 1970s. But these advances were few and far between.

Gradual political gains increased in the 1980s with a slow but steady growth in the city's number of upwardly mobile Mexican Americans. At the top of the socioeconomic scale was a sizable group of entrepreneurs who took advantage of Houston's business-friendly climate to create enterprises that ranked with the most successful in the nation. By 1990, 14 of the largest 500 Hispanic-owned businesses in the United States were located in Houston. The number of middle-class Mexicans grew with access to white-collar jobs, although most were at the lower-paying levels of sales and clerical work (de León 1989, 205–6).

The flip side of this growth is the stark reality that Mexicans continue to be the poorest residents of Houston. This is at least partly due to the presence of large numbers of undocumented Mexicans in the city, perhaps 200,000. Illegal aliens can have the effect of depressing wages for Mexican Americans and legal Mexicans. Unfortunately the presence of large numbers of illegals can also have a negative effect on the prevailing image of the legal population. Some members of the Anglo community have marginalized the entire Latino population by mistakenly assuming that it is largely comprised of undocumented persons. This has led to resentment among some of the city's Mexican Americans who feel that all people of Mexican origin have been stigmatized by the presence of illegal aliens. Calling the illegals *mojos* (wetbacks), some blue-collar Mexican Americans deride their lack of sophistication and their inability to speak English and are indignant at competing with them for jobs.[16] Others in the Mexican American community see in the endless waves of migrants opportunities for renewing Mexican culture in Houston, a potent source of connection with their roots.[17] Most, however, probably fall somewhere between these two polar opinions.

Adding to the complexity of politics and social relations in Hispanic Houston since the 1980s has been the presence of large numbers of non-Mexican immigrants. Political upheavals have brought many Central Americans to the city. After Mexicans, Latin American national groups, in order of number, are Salvadorans, Colombians, Puerto Ricans, Cubans, Guatemalans, and Hondurans. Little study has been made of these groups, but anecdotal evidence suggests that the number of Central American immigrants has been greatly undercounted because many are undocumented. Central Americans also appear to be the very poorest members of the Latino community. Most work in the lowest-paying jobs available, as laborers in construction, as custodians, and on the landscape crews that are a ubiquitous feature of life in Houston. Central Americans have often earned the ill will of the Mexicans with whom they compete for jobs. As a result, many live outside the traditional Mexican barrios, opting for areas that were abandoned by whites beginning in the recession of the early 1980s. Thus small pockets of Latinos, often from the same country or even the same town, grew up in the 1980s, scattered especially on the southwest side of the city in the Chimney Rock/Gulfton and Sharpstown areas.

Among the few Central American groups to receive scholarly attention is the Maya from the *municipio* of San Pedro in the department of Totonicapán in Guatemala. In an amazing example of stem migration, all members of this Maya group can trace their presence in Houston to a single man, Juan Xuc, who arrived in 1978. He found work in the maintenance department of a local grocery store chain and eventually persuaded company managers to hire his fellow San Pedro Maya for similar positions. With this employment base, more than 1,000 of Juan Xuc's compatriots made the journey in the 1980s, and most settled in a number of neighboring apartment complexes in southwest Houston, speaking traditional Quiche and finding unity in evangelical Protestantism (Hagan 1994, chap. 1).

Despite growing numbers, Latinos in Houston have been unable to dominate local politics as they do in Miami. During the last two decades of the twentieth century, Houston was different from other big cities in at least one major way. Instead of being surrounded and economically strangled by a ring of affluent suburbs, the city annexed many of those surrounding areas, thus increasing its tax base and its population. This practice has had important repercussions on the Latino community. Unlike in Miami, where white flight gave control of the city to Hispanic politicians, in Houston Latinos have been unable to claim the political power that their large numbers might have otherwise given them. Structural factors have limited them as well. Largely a holdover of efforts to thwart African American political power, the Houston City Council was entirely elected at large until 1979, when it was forced by the Justice Department to adopt single-member-district voting. At the time of the writing of this essay, only two of the nine district-elected and one of the five at-large members of city council are Hispanic—in a county that in the 2000 census was home to 1.119 million Hispanics, 33 percent of its population.

By almost any measurement Latinos are not climbing the metaphorical ladder of success in the manner of either previous immigrant groups or, indeed, like those coming from Asia today. Roberto Suro, for one, posits in his provocative work *Strangers among Us* that the ladder itself is "broken," or at least "wobbly" (1998, 18). The case of Houston seems to prove this assertion. Despite some impressive gains in political and economic power, and with several generations of residence in the city under their belts, Houston Latinos still count relatively few of their number in the middle and wealthier classes. Their levels of education lag far behind, as does their per capita income. Of the nine councilmanic districts, the two with majority-Hispanic residents have the lowest income levels in the entire city (City of Houston 1996). With a lack of many prospects for economic betterment, the barrios of Houston function much like other poor neighborhoods in any large American city. Low wages coupled with a feeling of disfranchisement, especially among the young, give rise to endemic problems of violence, substance abuse, and broken homes.

Conclusion

Obviously, the experiences of the primary Latino immigrant groups to Miami and Houston have been different in numerous ways. Cubans came to Miami in large, distinct waves over a relatively short period of time. The demographic shift of Cuban migration to Miami coupled with white flight gave Cubans numerical dominance in that city by 1980. This has been followed by a political hegemony that is unchallenged in Dade County. Mexicans in Houston have faced far more substantial obstacles to political power and remain underrepresented in local government.

To this day, Mexicans are among the lowest income groups in Houston, while Cubans enjoy incomes at or higher than the average for Dade County. Cuban economic and political success, or the Mexican lack thereof, is also the result of what might be called ethnic focus. Miami has been the undisputed heart of the U.S. Cuban population for forty years, the focus of almost every aspect of that group's life in this country. In 1990 Dade County was home to 57 percent of all persons of Cuban origin in the United States. The oft-cited Cuban ethnic solidarity, it may be argued, has as much to do with concentration of population as it does with the unifying specter of the Castro bogeyman. Houston, in contrast, has been one of many centers of Mexican and Mexican American population and thus has had to share that group's best and brightest with Los Angeles, Phoenix, San Antonio, Chicago, and several other centers.

In spite of the many differences between Latino migrants in the two cities, commonalities exist as well. Despite the popular perception that they are all political refugees, it seems clear at this point that since 1965 most Cubans have fled to the United States for the same reason as Mexicans: a quest for economic betterment (Croucher 1997, 121). Just as their economic motivations are similar, in both cities Latinos faced the challenges of dealing with ingrained southern traditions of segregation and white supremacy. Both Miami and Houston featured barriers to any group from outside southern society, and Hispanics confronted hostility from local populations, preconceived notions of their racial inferiority, and at least initially, hurdles to political participation. Latinos in both locations also upset deep-seated patterns of southern biracialism. In Miami the perception among African Americans that Cubans, at least in the early stages of the migration, had robbed them of jobs and vaulted over them into a position of political and economic dominance resulted in several outbreaks of racial violence. Miami blacks rioted in 1968, 1980, 1982, and 1989, and each time frustration with status as third-class citizens was cited as a primary precipitating factor. Though such vivid spasms of racial conflict have been absent in Houston, members of the black community have on occasion complained about losing influence to Latinos at city hall and questioned the need for bilingual education in the public schools.

Interestingly, both Cubans in Miami and Mexicans in Houston have seen their role as sole Latino group challenged of late. There is now a dizzying array of peoples in each city, and this diversity has complicated what we mean when we speak of Hispanic Houston or Latino Miami. Both dominant groups have held these new and different immigrants at arm's length. Miami Cubans were also less than enthusiastic when the 1980 Mariel boatlift brought significant numbers of black Cubans to the city for the first time. The presence of these newcomers challenged the definition of Cubanness as a "white" identity and led to a good deal of debate as to how, and even if, the Marielitos should be accepted into the Miami enclave.

In conclusion, it might be useful to speculate as to the applicability of the experiences of Houston and Miami to the rest of the South. Obviously, the eventual scope of Latino migration to a place like North Carolina or Virginia remains to be seen. But almost assuredly, the future will resemble the Houston case far more than that of Miami. There is no reason to predict that one group with the unique qualities of the Cubans will relocate so heavily in one place. Far more likely is the Mexican pattern of dispersed settlement across the United States. The challenge is obviously for southerners to recognize both the difficulties of integrating a group whose language, culture, and historical experience are very different from their own and the promise of new cultural and economic opportunities that a diverse transnational society offers.

Notes

1. According to Mohl (1991), Miami ranked first of 100 large U.S. cities in the extent of its racial segregation between 1940 and 1960.

2. Feagan, Brody, and O'Leary (1968) used the 1953 Cuban census to show that though 23.5 percent of the Cuban population could be categorized as professional, semi-professional, managerial, or clerical, 68 percent of early (1958 through 1962) refugees were. Similarly, they illustrate that while only 4 percent of the Cuban population had achieved any postsecondary education, 36 percent of early refugees had.

3. Feagan, Brody, and O'Leary (1968, 112) report an irony that while the early wave of Cuban migrants would make up some of the most virulently anti-Castro elements in Miami, a significant number of them left the island before the revolution took its most radical turn and before Castro's conversion to Marxism-Leninism.

4. Interestingly, part of the Cuban Refugee Program's mandate was to encourage Cubans to settle in parts of the United States besides Miami, in hopes of easing some of the burden that the massive influx had brought upon the city. Numerous families took the additional inducements to locate elsewhere, concentrating especially in the New York metropolitan area. (See Proh'as and Casal 1973, 109.)

5. Cuban *municipios* do not refer to municipalities but, rather, to what might be compared to the county level of governance in the United States. In 1993, 114 of the 135 *municipios* of prerevolutionary Cuba were represented in the organization.

6. Portes and Bach (1985, 85) report that so great were the numbers involved in the Mariel boatlift that the state of Florida and the U.S. government had to set up temporary shelter for Marielitos under the stands at the Orange Bowl and under the elevated sections of Interstate 95 where it passes through Miami.

7. In 1994, in the wake of mounting public sentiment against unfettered immigration, the Clinton administration reversed thirty-five years of U.S. policy by declaring that it would return Cuban rafters picked up at sea and detain them at the U.S. base at Guantanamo, Cuba, until they could be sent home (Suro 1998, 27–28). Though this did not stop the flow, as evidenced by the Elián González imbroglio, it did drastically cut into the number of Cubans settling in the United States and Miami.

8. In 1971 the *Miami Herald* (November 21) estimated that between only 10 and 20 percent of the city's Cuban residents were citizens.

9. The aggressive suppression of dissent in the Cuban community in Miami has been the subject of significant attention through the years. As recently as 1992, human rights watchdog group Americas Watch published a damning report titled "Dangerous Dialogue: Attacks on Freedom of Expression in Miami's Cuban Exile Community."

10. See the *Miami Herald*, February 21, 1967.

11. Important as well was the relative safety of investments made in the United States compared with much of politically uncertain Latin America. Miami banks saw billions of dollars flow in through the 1970s and 1980s as many Colombians, Nicaraguans, and others attempted to safeguard their assets. This designation of Miami was apparently coined by Ecuadorian president Jaime Roldos in 1979 (Levine 1985, 48).

12. Through conscious effort, the city's commercial-civic elite had made Houston

the railroad center of Texas. They had also reached an agreement with the federal government to dredge Buffalo Bayou and create a ship channel that would connect the city with the sea. Thus when a massive oil strike occurred in 1901 near Beaumont, Houston was poised as a center of transportation and in position to seize control of the quickly growing petroleum business. Aiding Houston's rise to regional hegemony was the 1900 hurricane that almost entirely leveled Galveston, its longtime urban rival.

13. For more on this subject, see Rinehart and Kreneck 1988, 21–33.

14. See Handwritten Description of Conditions in the Second Ward 1944.

15. Houstonian Felix Tijerina, national president of the League of United Latin American Citizens from 1956–60, is best remembered for his "Little Schools of the 400" program in which five-year-old Spanish-speaking children were taught 400 key English words in hopes of easing their transition to early elementary school. This program was enthusiastically supported by Governor Price Daniel, who used state funds to expand its implementation across Texas. The federal government later used the Little Schools as a model for the Head Start Program (de León 1989, 135–36; de León 1993, 116).

16. Interestingly, new arrivals from Mexico often hold mirror-image negative views on Chicanos (Mexicans born in the United States). They view them as disconnected from their roots, made lazy and corrupted by the welfare state, inclined toward criminality, and unable to speak Spanish properly (Suro 1998, 4–7).

17. For this type of view, see de León 1989, 220–21.

References

City of Houston. 1996. "Per Capita Income by Council District." City Council district demographic information. Retrieved from ⟨http://www.ci.houston.tx.us/citygovt/council/demos.htm⟩.

Croucher, Sheila L. 1997. *Imagining Miami: Ethnic Politics in a Postmodern World*. Charlottesville: University of Virginia Press.

Cuban American Policy Center. 1992. *Ethnic Segregation in Greater Miami, 1980–1990*. Miami: Cuban American National Council, Inc.

de León, Arnoldo. 1989. *Ethnicity in the Sunbelt: A History of Mexican Americans in Houston*. Houston: Mexican American Studies Program, University of Houston.

———. 1993. *Mexican Americans in Texas: A Brief History*. Arlington Heights, Ill.: Harlan Davidson.

Didion, Joan. 1987. *Miami*. New York: Simon and Schuster.

Falcoff, Mark. 1995. "The Other Cuba." *National Review*, June 12, 43.

Feagan, Richard R., Richard A. Brody, and Thomas J. O'Leary. 1968. *Cubans in Exile: Disaffection and the Revolution*. Stanford: Stanford University Press.

Hagan, Jacqueline Maria. 1994. *Deciding to Be Legal: A Maya Community in Houston*. Philadelphia: Temple University Press.

Handwritten Description of Conditions in the Second Ward. 1944. Box 1, folder 2, Franklin I. Harbach Papers, Houston Metropolitan Research Center, Houston Public Library, Houston, Texas.

Levine, Barry B. 1985. "Miami: The Capital of Latin America." *Wilson Quarterly* 9 (Winter): 46–69.

Mohl, Raymond A. 1991. "The Settlement of Blacks in South Florida." In Thomas D. Boswell, ed., *South Florida: The Winds of Change*, 112–39. Miami: Association of American Geographers.

Moore, Deborah Dash. 1994. *To the Golden Cities: Pursuing the American Jewish Dream in Miami and Los Angeles*. New York: Free Press.

Office of Trade and Economic Analysis, International Trade Administration, U.S. Department of Commerce. 1998. "Metropolitan Merchandise Export Totals to Selected Destinations, 1993–1998." Retrieved from ‹http://www.ita.doc.gov/td/industry/otea//metro/destinations›.

Parks, Arva Moore, and Gregory W. Bush, with Laura Pincus. 1996. *Miami, the American Crossroads: A Centennial Journey, 1896–1996*. Coral Gables, Fla.: Institute for Public History, University of Miami, and Needham Heights, Mass.: Simon and Schuster Custom Publishing.

Pérez, Lisandro. 1986. "Cubans in the United States." *Annals of the American Academy of Political and Social Science* 487:125–37.

———. 1992. "Cuban Miami." In Guillermo J. Grenier and Alex Stepick III, eds., *Miami Now! Immigration, Ethnicity, and Social Change*, 102–3. Gainesville: University Press of Florida.

Portes, Alejandro, and Robert Bach. 1985. *Latin Journey*. Berkeley: University of California Press.

Proh'as, Rafael J., and Lourdes Casal. 1973. *The Cuban Minority in the U.S.: Preliminary Report on Need Identification and Program Evaluation*. Boca Raton: Florida Atlantic University.

Rieff, David. 1993. *The Exile: Cuba in the Heart of Miami*. New York: Simon and Schuster.

Rinehart, Marilyn D., and Thomas H. Kreneck. 1988. "In the Shadow of Uncertainty: Texas Mexicans and Repatriation in Houston during the Great Depression." *Houston Review* 10:21–33.

Schultz, Ronald. 1991. "Population Growth and Migration: Southeast Florida in Regional Context." In Thomas D. Boswell, ed., *South Florida: The Winds of Change*, 43–61. Miami: Association of American Geographers.

Suro, Roberto. 1998. *Strangers among Us: How Latino Immigration Is Transforming America*. New York: Knopf.

Barbara Ellen Smith, Marcela Mendoza, and David H. Ciscel

The World on Time

Flexible Labor, New Immigrants, and Global Logistics

The transnational dispersal of manufacturing, one of the most commonly acknowledged elements of economic globalization, requires a concomitant though less recognized capacity to integrate far-flung supply chains and transport products to their point of consumption. This essay examines emerging flexible labor practices in the logistics sector of Memphis, Tennessee, which is composed of a cluster of industries that contribute to the space–time compression achieved by global trade.[1] Anchored by the world headquarters of FedEx, logistics in Memphis also includes a burgeoning number of "distribution parks," or warehouses, through which diverse corporations move goods in response to global demand. Among employers in this sector, the drive to maximize space–time compression within the physical world of tangible objects and geographic distance is generating employment practices that take the concept of flexible labor, particularly the requirement of temporal flexibility, to new extremes. The workers of choice in this experiment are recent Latino immigrants, whose transnational movement also manifests and contributes to the spatial compressions of globalization. Moreover, their undocumented, immigrant status places them in a spatial and temporal limbo that employers exploit by aligning immigrants' working hours as closely as possible to the unpredictable tempo of global markets.[2]

The section that follows analyzes the linkages between space–time compression and flexible labor practices in the evolution of the Memphis logistics sector. The subsequent section theorizes these linkages; although the use of immigrants as flexible labor has been explored in a growing literature on the casualization of immigrant employment, we conceptualize this trend in new ways by relating it to space–time compression and temporal flexibility within the logic of global capitalism. Following the theoretical discussion we describe our methodological approach and summarize our empirical findings regarding Latino immigrant employment in the Memphis logistics sector. We conclude with a discussion of flexible labor as a new paradigm of work time.

Delivering the Goods: Space-Time Compression and Flexible Labor in the Logistics Sector

One of the things [Wal-Mart founder] Sam Walton told me several times . . . is that retail is about moving things. It's not about selling things.
—FedEx founder Fred Smith

The nanosecond of electronic transmission has become the temporal standard for movement through space. For corporations that operate in the clumsy universe of physical objects and real time, electronic instantaneity presents a fundamental contradiction. Television, cell phones, the Internet, and other forms of information and communication technology allow advertisers to market products simultaneously and instantaneously all over the globe. In return, buyers can communicate their orders with the same speed. Corporations can transmit this market demand to their suppliers, who in turn access their suppliers, and so on down the chain—all in a matter of minutes, if not seconds. However, in the end, goods must still be moved through time across the great distances of the globe in order for capital to realize any economic benefit. An important consequence of this spatiotemporal contradiction is the elevated significance of logistics, an economic sector that utilizes electronic communication to integrate all forms of transportation with systems of wholesale trade (or distribution) in order to deliver products immediately, if not instantaneously, in response to market demand. The packers, forklift operators, truck drivers, and other workers employed in logistics represent an important element in the economic infrastructure of globalization; by moving goods through space and time, they literally do the "heavy lifting" for global trade.

Memphis, "North America's Distribution Center," is the hub for a complex logistical system that integrates the decentralized supply chains of the global economy. Once a key link for the movement of regional products—above all, cotton from the Mississippi Delta—to national and international markets, the warehousing and transportation infrastructure of Memphis now funnels machine parts, furniture, pottery, and innumerable other goods all over the world. Today, Memphis warehouses and related industries employ close to 90,000 people, and the city has more than 130 million square feet of distribution space (Memphis Regional Chamber of Commerce 2003).

The appeal of Memphis as a global distribution hub is not simply its geographic location but also its transportation capacity, centered in the FedEx Corporation. Since its inception in 1972, FedEx has met a niche market for overnight delivery of small packages through an integrated air-ground transportation system (Sigafoos 1979). In 1979 the corporation expanded to Canada from its base of corporate customers in the United States, then moved into more global markets as well as home delivery service in the 1990s. Although FedEx now moves products through superhubs in Paris and Subic Bay, Memphis remains The Hub. For more than ten years Memphis International Airport has held the distinction of handling more metric tons of cargo than any other airport in the world (Airports Council International 2004).

FedEx's expansion to new destinations during the 1990s set off a frenzy of warehouse construction in Memphis. Within these sprawling structures, goods are off-loaded, repaired, assembled, packaged, wrapped, and addressed. The warehouse operators may be distributors in their own right, goods-producing corporations such as Cummins Engine, or retailers like Barnes and Noble. In addition, a host of subcontractors actually operates certain warehouses or leases space within them to perform small batch processing.

Speedup in the movement of goods through these warehouses is not just a function of the temporal standard of instantaneity. Other features of the trend toward flexible production are also at stake. Mass customization, that is, the specification of certain features within an overall product line, requires rapid movement along supply chains, as particular components are added to the basic product in response to customer demand. In addition, rapid turnover in the basic product line increases both the speed and the volume of products moving through the warehouses. Just-in-time inventory systems have the same effect. More generally, the global decentralization of production processes (both organizationally and spatially) requires speedy, sophisticated, and comprehensive logistical systems.

Essential to the profitable production of space-time compression by the logistics sector is the availability of flexible labor, that is, people who are willing to work on an as-needed basis. Although the pressure toward speed is relentless, the tempo of market demand is erratic. To take an example from mass consumption, Amazon.com requires an expanded labor force in its warehouses when *The Prayer of Jabez* unexpectedly becomes a best seller, but it also requires commensurate reductions when demand begins to wane. Logistics employers must access workers whose lives are not structured by the temporal obligations of a routinized workweek yet who are nonetheless sufficiently disciplined to be reliable—to show up promptly, work rapidly, and fill orders accurately—but only when needed.

FedEx initially set a high standard, designed to secure loyalty and reliability, for flexible labor in logistics. This corporation defined the terms of work for sorters, handlers, and other operatives at its enormous hub as part time, with variable schedules, but it also offered a basic fringe benefits package, relatively high wages, and a commitment to job security, that is, permanent employment. Within the southern labor market, in particular that of the Delta sub-region, characterized by low wages, weak to nonexistent unions (especially in the private sector), and meager fringe benefits, permanent part-time jobs with benefits were relatively appealing.

FedEx also encouraged loyalty among many employees by rejecting the rigidities of race and gender segregation that had long marked Memphis as a southern labor market. In a rare published account of FedEx's employment practices during its first decade of operation, Sigafoos (1983) noted, "Most of the 800 part-time handlers, keyers, and sorters inside the [FedEx] Hub are young college students who report in around midnight and work an average of just over three hours Monday through Friday. Their starting pay is $6.91 per hour. Experienced workers get $9.00 per hour. They are guaranteed 17 ½ hours of work a week. Not only is there an equal mixture of young men and women in the crew, but also there is an equal number of blacks and whites."

Today, FedEx maintains a similar employment strategy, albeit with a diversified and expanded workforce. Although wages for sorters and ramp workers have fallen in real terms, these employees still receive a benefits package that is unusual for part-timers. (The wages Sigafoos recorded would be worth $14.87 to $19.37 in 2001, adjusted for inflation, as opposed to the $10.00 to $12.00 per hour that entry-level workers currently report.) The corporation's expanded role in global trade during the 1990s fueled a tight labor market as its local workforce grew to more than 30,000.

FedEx's domination of the global overnight delivery market simultaneously drew more and more corporations, especially those for which speed of product delivery offers a competitive edge, to locate warehouses in Memphis. In accord with the "lean" management strategies of the 1990s—as opposed to the nascent form of flexible production that FedEx spearheaded in the 1970s —these distributors offer few of their packers, sorters, and other materials handlers job permanence, a minimum number of hours, fringe benefits, or relatively generous wages. Moreover, utilizing temporary labor supply agencies, they access many of their workers indirectly through a transaction that relieves them of all social obligation to and legal liability for their employees.

Attracted in part by this tight labor market and the prospect of employment, many new immigrants also arrived in Memphis during the latter half of the 1990s. At a very general level, the dynamics of globalization that the logistics sector was both responding to and propelling were at work in the lives of these new arrivals, most of whom came from Mexico, who headed to the United

States in the wake of the North American Free Trade Agreement, the devaluation of the peso, and other developments related to global trade. However,
although the global expansion of FedEx created the labor market conditions
that attracted these new immigrants to Memphis, most did not find employment with this corporation. Instead, the burgeoning distribution component
of logistics, both driving and driven by pressures toward space-time compression, moved quickly to hire these new immigrants indirectly, through temporary agencies, and to define them as completely flexible labor.

This conjuncture of interrelated trends—the growth of global trade, immigration, flexible production, and space-time compression—set the stage for
an experiment with flexible labor practices in Memphis that, although dramatic, is not unique. Distributors in the logistics sector are creating a labor
supply system that can respond flexibly but reliably to the intermittent but intensive labor demand of their worldwide distribution channels. In order to accomplish this, they are exploiting the spatial and temporal limbo of undocumented immigration by requiring that workers align the temporality of their
lives as closely as possible to the unpredictable tempo of global markets. These
employers achieve space-time compression in the material world of global trade
through the imposition of a regime of labor discipline that is marked by the
flexibility of time.

Flexible Labor and the Control of Workers' Time

Flexible labor, or as-needed, at-will employment, is part of the trend toward
nonstandard work. Although certain nonstandard arrangements, such as the
permanent, part-time jobs at FedEx, may guarantee at least a minimum number of hours in a set workplace, the flexible labor that we observe in Memphis
warehouses imposes on workers great spatial and particularly temporal unpredictability. In practice, this means

- temporal flexibility, wherein the days and hours of work are defined by
  the employer and may change at any moment, and the term of employment is short, and
- spatial flexibility, or movement from job to job (and workplace to workplace) as required by market demand.

Although the description above applies to many forms of casual employment, the flexible labor that we observe in logistics and seek to theorize is
driven by a specific and ominous logic. This variant of flexible labor may be
distinguished from other post-Fordist innovations not simply by its great spa-

tiotemporal unpredictability but, more importantly, by the dynamic that drives this unpredictability. A tight, direct linkage between global product markets and the local labor market, secured through the electronic transmission of information, defines the "flexibility" required of workers in logistics. This relatively unmediated linkage to globalization and its great pressure toward space-time compression yields a specific form of flexible labor that is extreme in its spatial and especially temporal irregularity.

Flexible labor in logistics also involves a new, post-Fordist relationship between the space and time of work. As David Harvey points out, Henry Ford and his imitators organized the space of the workplace in rigidly confining terms, epitomized by the assembly line, in order to control the pace of work. "Time could then be accelerated by virtue of the control established through organizing and fragmenting the spatial order of production" (Harvey 1989, 266). Paradoxically, even as flexible labor "releases" workers from the routinized temporal obligations of a forty-hour workweek and the spatial fixity of a single workplace, it also secures for employers more indirect but powerful forms of control. If, under Fordism, employers organized and fragmented the space of the workplace, in the post-Fordist context of labor power that is deployed according to the unpredictable tempo of global markets, employers indirectly organize and fragment workers' time. For employers in logistics, the goal is not temporal domination for its own sake, however, but a greater command of space. The control of workers' time enables corporations to compress and thereby better compete within the space of the globe.

Perpetual availability to work when an employer summons, with no guarantee of when that may happen or where that work may take place, is far from an appealing arrangement for most people. Flexible labor means not only unpredictable wages but also chaotic personal lives: last-minute appeals for transportation, undesirable child care arrangements, and disrupted households. To be sure, unstable employment has long been a fact of life for certain groups of U.S. workers, such as working-class African American women and men, who predominate in the Memphis labor market. They were only briefly, if ever, part of the Fordist social contract, and the employment circumstances of many such workers are now on the decline (Bernhardt and Marcotte 2000; Cobble and Vosko 2000; Wilson 1996).

However, for the regimen of flexible labor that they are institutionalizing in the Memphis logistics sector, employers are seizing upon new immigrants as workers of choice. Legal vulnerability due to undocumented status and the situational predisposition to work hard that is characteristic of first-generation immigrants are not the only factors accounting for this preference. A nuanced interaction between the insecurity of immigration and flexible labor is also at work. New immigrants live in a spatiotemporal limbo that articulates all too well with the irregularity of flexible labor. Transient and insecure within the space of the nation–state, they are also temporally dislocated—outside the history and sedimented cultural practices, including work ways, of the host country. This may be particularly true in locations like Memphis, one of several "new destinations" for immigrants in the South, where there is no ethnic enclave to ease immigrants' transition to new ways of life.

Methodology

The research on which this article is based began as a relatively innocent, descriptive effort to develop basic demographic and employment data on the Latino immigrant population of Memphis, whose growth during the 1990s was dramatically evident in the city's historically bipolar, black-white social milieu. Conversations and formal interviews with new immigrants accessed through ESL classes, Catholic churches, and other social contexts in Memphis alerted us to the significance of the distribution sector, accessed through temporary staffing agencies, as a key entry point into the local labor market for both women and men. We therefore undertook, beginning in May 2000, an ongoing investigation into Latino immigrant employment in local warehouses. This included a telephone survey of temporary agencies and distribution sector employers; personal interviews with bilingual agency staff, Latino immigrant workers, and employers; tours of local warehouses; and field observations at temporary agencies frequented by Latino immigrant workers.

Although this field research yielded rich and detailed qualitative data, we also sought other methods through which to quantify the use of Latino immigrants as flexible labor. These included analysis of standardized national data sources such as *County Business Patterns*, the *Census of Population*, the *Census of Wholesale Trade*, and the Equal Employment Opportunity Commission (EEO-1 data file). Unfortunately, all of these data failed to quantify reliably the overall Latino presence in Memphis, including Latino employment in the distribution sector. The U.S. Census indicates that the total Hispanic population of the Memphis metropolitan area is not large, but it increased by 245 percent from 1990 to 2000 (from 7,986 to 27,520). By contrast, calculations based on school enrollment records and other sources estimated that the local Latino population could be at least twice the official count (Burrell et al. 2001). National employment data are equally misleading. For example, the EEO data file, the most detailed national source on patterns regarding race/ethnicity in employment, indicates that Latinos have made no significant inroads into permanent warehouse employment. In 1997 a paltry 134 Latino workers were recorded in wholesale trade establishments with more than 100 employees. *County Business Patterns* data indicate that employment by personnel supply companies in Shelby County grew by 147 percent (from 7,854 to 19,423 workers) between 1989 and 1997. While neither the racial/ethnic nor industrial composition of this workforce can be discerned, these aggregate data are at least consistent with our hypothesis that the Memphis distribution sector is shifting toward flexible labor secured through temporary agencies.

Latino Immigrants and Flexible Labor

> We were hired for one week [in a small packing plant], but I did not last more than two days there. . . . The first day, the supervisor asked us to stay and keep working until 10:00 P.M. (We had started at 7:00 A.M.) I was telling my coworkers, "We shouldn't stay, they are being despotic (*muy despotas*)," but a woman replied, "I've been one month without a job, I have a child, my husband doesn't have a job either," so we stayed. They told us, "Come tomorrow morning [at 7:00 A.M.] to work until 11:00 A.M." I returned the next day, to be faithful to the temporary agency, but with the idea to call [the bilingual staff] to request a change. At 11:00 A.M., the supervisors told us that we should stay that day until 10:00 P.M. . . . I left, [but] many Latinos were still there and kept working. (Interview, April 22, 2002)

In Memphis, distribution sector employers increasingly use Latino immigrants to create new, flexible terms of employment. Typically hired by temporary staffing agencies, which assume all liability for wage payment, worker grievances, and quite importantly, proof of immigration status, Latinos (as well as African Americans and other immigrant and refugee groups) meet the distribution sector's demand for "spot market" labor. They may work at the same job for a few hours or as long as a year, but they are typically hired for the day or, at most, the week. Lacking fringe benefits such as health insurance and pensions, as well as those more customary benefits such as sick leave and paid vacations, Latino immigrants may be hired briefly, cheaply, and flexibly. The wage they receive is the federal minimum or slightly above—typically $6.00 to $7.50 per hour.

The temporary staffing agencies that connect these flexible workers with available employment tend to specialize by occupation, with more than 40 percent of their placements in the blue-collar sector (Brogan 2001; Gonos 1997).

On the bottom of their status and skill hierarchy are those agencies, which essentially represent the street-corner labor pool institutionalized and moved indoors, that place unskilled laborers by the day. "Work Today, Get Paid Today," they advertise. Although few immigrants seem to access them, other agencies offer more long-term placements and represent the top tier of the blue-collar sector of the industry.

Our survey of temporary agencies in Memphis suggests a strong trend toward the employment of Latino immigrant workers in the warehouses of the distribution sector: 53 of the 95 agencies that we surveyed actually referred workers for blue-collar jobs, and 44 (83 percent) of those 53 agencies hired Latinos. Moreover, 17 of the Latino-employing agencies had hired bilingual (English/Spanish) staff to communicate with applicants; another was in the process of hiring a bilingual staff member, and yet another was actively seeking Latino applicants though a church-sponsored ESL class. Agencies without fully bilingual staff typically had one employee able to converse in basic Spanish, and most had translated their applications into Spanish.

Twenty agencies provided estimates, ranging from 1 to 100 percent, of the Latino portion of their workforce; the median was 25 percent. Not surprisingly, agencies with bilingual staff tended to hire a larger proportion of Latino immigrants, but all reported an increase in such applicants. One interviewee estimated that the percentage of Latino immigrant workers hired by his agency jumped from 1 percent in 1999 to 25 percent in 2000. As of July 2001, one of the larger agencies (as measured by the number of Latino workers) was managing 900 Latino contracts, primarily with major warehouses; over the preceding two years, the agency had compiled a database of some 10,000 Latino applicants. Another agency that began employing Latino immigrants by the week three years ago had, as of July 2001, 2,900 Latino applications on file and estimated an average weekly employment of 250 Latino workers.

It is important to keep these numbers in context. Memphis is a predominantly working-class, African American city with a tiny (official) Latino population. According to the 2000 census, the entire Latino working-age population in the metropolitan area is approximately 17,000. Even the most generous population estimates (see our figures above) place the Latino population at 5 percent of the Metropolitan Statistical Area total. Nonetheless, 83 percent of temporary agencies specializing in blue-collar employment hired Latinos, and they represented one-fourth or more of the workforce at more than 20 percent of those agencies.

The relative significance of supply and demand—that is, whether Latino immigrants, as new and often undocumented entrants into the Memphis labor market, focus their job search on temporary agencies, or whether such agencies seek out Latino workers—is impossible to discern, but it is clear that both dynamics are at work. Agency staff who were willing to discuss racial/ethnic considerations in hiring typically referred to Latinos' temporal reliability and flexibility (see below) and/or to the ethnic-specific demand of contracting employers for Latino workers. It is clear that at least some, if not most, corporations are intentionally selecting for Latino immigrant hires. Three of the four warehouses that we toured were moving to create all-Latino workforces in their unskilled distribution operations, and the fourth had subcontracted these operations to a company that employed a workforce that was half Latino.

Employers cite an array of reasons, many of which involve explicit temporal considerations, for their interest in Latino immigrant workers. These include punctuality and good health, both of which were associated with reliability, willingness to work overtime (flexibility), and intensity of work effort (productivity, or output per unit of time). "Latinos are very dependable, very hard-working," commented one employer in a typical statement. "Mexican workers never get sick," said another. Recent research focused on employers' racial/ethnic hiring preferences in other cities has documented a tendency to emphasize intangible, attitudinal qualities, or "people skills," in hiring processes where level of education, prior experience, and other skill-based criteria are negligible (Kirschenman and Neckerman 1991; Lichter and Waldinger 2001; Waldinger 1997). These qualities function as euphemisms for worker tractability and manageability, which employers associate with specific racial/ethnic groups, particularly Latinos. We certainly heard such assessments in our interviews—for example, "The companies like to hire Mexican workers because they are humble"—but the greater tendency was to emphasize work habits and attitudes with temporal implications, particularly flexibility, reliability, and productivity.

The flexibility that distribution employers require involves not only an individual worker's willingness to tolerate spatiotemporal unpredictability, but also the employer's institutional capacity to summon a sufficient quantity of workers when global markets dictate. Employers clearly rely on immigrants' elaborate social networks to secure this latter form of flexibility. Information about job availability and the hiring process, including the extent of any document verification, circulates rapidly not only within the Latino immigrant networks of Memphis but beyond. One agency staff member reported that, when he needs additional workers for a specific client, he merely informs certain of his Latino employees; within forty-eight hours, their family members and friends from California and elsewhere arrive for work. In one recent instance, he needed 100 workers for immediate job openings and called 30 Latinos who had put their names on a waiting list; by the next morning he had 105 applicants waiting in line for the new jobs.

Flexibility at the individual level involves more than the willingness to work for short periods of time in different locations, possibly on different shifts, for modestly variable rates of pay—all of which are standard features of temporary employment arrangements. Latino immigrants are expected to be infinitely *available*—to go to a new job immediately, to work overtime on demand, and to move to a different shift. As one agency staff member commented, "Hispanics are valued because they are on time at the work site; they work hard, do not complain, and are always ready to do overtime." When jobs are available, workers are hired on the spot and sent to a warehouse immediately. In one instance, applicants were given maps showing where they needed to go for a drug test. They were also handed a map to the warehouse. They had to buy shoes with reinforced metal toes (they were advised to go to Payless or Wal-Mart) before showing up for work. They were required to wear short- or long-sleeved T-shirts and pants (for men and women). They had to report to work on the same day, carrying a picture ID and proof that they had taken the drug test. They also had to watch a thirty-minute training video (translated into Spanish by an agency employee) before leaving the agency.

In temporary employment, where work is by definition not reliable, neither are many workers. Agency staff and warehouse managers repeatedly praised the "reliability" of Latinos, meaning that they consistently and punctually showed up for work. One human resource manager at a large warehousing operation that contracts with three different temporary agencies for workers stressed that hiring Latinos is not a matter of complying with affirmative action or increasing diversity. "It is a business necessity," because Latinos are the kind of employees that the company needs. He asserted that they are reliable and highly motivated and do not miss work: "They are more than a body that shows up to work."

However, for Latino immigrants as for anyone else, life sometimes intrudes on work obligations in the form of illness, transportation problems, or lapses in child care. Temporary agencies and corporate employers have responded to Latinos' occasional "unreliability" with tactics ranging from helpful to coercive. For example, the spatial unpredictability of warehouse employment represents an obstacle for workers without independent and reliable means of transportation. Although a potential problem for all low-wage workers, it is particularly acute for immigrants, who may have insufficient documentation to obtain driver's licenses. The Latino applicants whom we interviewed and observed at temporary agencies invariably arrived in groups that either shared use of a single vehicle (through collective ownership or kin/friendship ties) or paid the driver-owner to transport them. Some of these drivers functioned as "labor brokers" who sold not only transportation but also job referrals. Once a job was secured, however, getting to and from work required other arrangements. Certain agencies actually provided transportation for workers, for which they charged $3.00 to $4.00 a day, to and from work sites.

Employers also enforced reliability through the manipulation of workers' wages. Several workers reported receiving lower hourly wages for an entire week after one episode of tardiness or absence. For example, one Latino worker telephoned his multinational employer to report that he would be absent that day. Because the person to whom he spoke could not understand Spanish, he was paid minimum wage ($5.15/hour, a $2.35/hour decrease) for the entire week. This worker escaped the more severe punishment for absenteeism, which is being fired.

Despite such treatment, "Los hispanos trabajan muy duro" (Hispanics work very hard). Repeatedly we heard testimonials from agency staff and corporate employers about Latinos' productivity and work effort. As one plant owner commented, "Immigrants come from a self-selected group that really wants to work." Workers who express reservations about working conditions or the intensity of required effort do not last. One Latina reported, "I told my supervisor that I shouldn't be lifting so much weight because I was pregnant, and she fired me the same day." One agency staff member commented that Latino immigrants worked so hard for so many hours, he wondered why they didn't "explode." He noted that the thousands of Latinos he has processed for employment are relatively invisible in the public spaces of Memphis—in part because they fear racism, crime, and deportation, and in part because they spend all of their waking hours at work: "Latinos are like ghosts; they come to work and then they go home."

Conclusion: The Price of Flexible Labor

The space-time compressions of globalization appear to be shifting the temporality of work. An extensive literature documents (although only recently has begun to emphasize) the temporal dimensions of contemporary employment trends related to economic globalization and flexible accumulation— the growth of nonstandard work arrangements, speedup in the pace of work, increased overtime, and the related erosion of leisure time (Epstein and Kalleberg 2001; Hinrichs, Roche, and Sirianni 1991; Hochschild 1997; Kalleberg and Epstein 2001; Schor 1991). However, critics tend to emphasize either the impermanence of nonstandard jobs and the insufficiency of nonstandard work hours or the imposition of higher workloads across a range of occupations, industries, and employment arrangements. Workers can meet the pressure for greater output only by intensifying the pace and/or extending the hours of their work. In these analyses the temporal problem is, in essence, either too few or too many hours of work.

This case study of Latino immigrant employment in the Memphis logistics sector points to a qualitatively different innovation: temporal unpredictability, or what we term flexible labor. Although the more commonly recognized temporal configurations of nonstandard employment and lengthy workdays violate the Fordist paradigm, they are not new. In the Memphis area, for example, episodic jobs off-loading barges (a "nonstandard" work arrangement) and more long-term but grueling labor from sunup to sundown in Delta cotton fields long predate the rhythms of Fordism. What appear distinctively new in the present era are work-time arrangements that collapse the distinction between work and leisure, or work and life, by requiring infinite availability to labor. The closest employment precedent in recent history is the on-call arrangement, confined primarily to skilled, emergency service workers such as nurses, firefighters, and paramedics; however, this diverges from newer, flexible labor arrangements in its greater job permanence as well as predictability in the duration of call. Moreover, the rationale for such on-call employment arrangements was and is the unpredictable nature of human emergency and need, not the vagaries of global capital. Today, it is the direct linkage between global product markets and local labor markets, made possible by the electronic transmission of information, that dictates the unpredictable tempo and potentially unremitting work requirement of flexible labor.

Notes

1. This form of flexible labor is sometimes referred to as "numerical" or "external" flexibility, to distinguish it from flexibility in knowledge and tasks required of workers in high-performance firms. (For a review, see Kalleberg 2001.)

2. When referring to our case study of Memphis, Tennessee, we use the terms "immigrants" and "Latinos" interchangeably. Although recent immigrants to Memphis/Shelby County originate from many different countries around the world, the majority of arrivals since 1990 have come from Latin America. In addition, although there have been people of Spanish-language heritage in the area for many years, most are recent arrivals (i.e., since 1990—see the text for relevant data). According to the 2000 census, 69 percent of Latinos in Shelby County are of Mexican nationality.

References

Airports Council International. 2004. Retrieved from ⟨http://www.airports.org⟩.

Appelbaum, Eileen, and Rosemary Batt. 1994. *The New American Workplace: Transforming Work Systems in the United States*. Ithaca, N.Y.: Cornell University Press.

Barker, Kathleen, and Kathleen Christensen, eds. 1998. *Contingent Work: American Employment Relations in Transition*. Ithaca, N.Y.: Cornell University Press.

Basch, Linda, Nina Glick Schiller, and Cristina Szanton Blanc. 1994. *Nations Unbound: Transnational Projects, Postcolonial Predicaments, and Deterritorialized Nation States*. Langhorne: Gordon and Breach.

Bayliss, John, and Steve Smith, eds. 1997. *The Globalization of World Politics*. New York: Oxford University Press.

Bernhardt, Annette, and Dave E. Marcotte. 2000. "Is 'Standard Employment' Still What It Used to Be?" In Francoise Carre et al., eds., *Nonstandard Work: The Nature and Challenges of Changing Employment Arrangements*, 21–40. Champaign, Ill.: Industrial Relations Research Association.

Branston, John. 1998. "Working Stiff." *Memphis* 23, no. 6: 34–40, 81–85.

Brogan, Timothy. 2001. "Scaling New Heights." *Staffing Success*, May–June, 1–8.

Burrell, Luchy, Steve Redding, Sonya Schenk, and Marcela Mendoza. 2001. *New 2000 Estimates of the Hispanic Population for Shelby County, Tennessee*. Memphis: Regional Economic Development Center and Center for Research on Women, University of Memphis.

Calavita, Kitty. 1998. "Immigration, Law, and Marginalization in a Global Economy: Notes from Spain." *Law and Society Review* 32, no. 3: 529–66.

Carre, Francoise, et al., eds. 2000. *Nonstandard Work: The Nature and Challenges of Changing Employment Arrangements*. Champaign, Ill.: Industrial Relations Research Association.

Cobble, Dorothy Sue, and Leah F. Vosko. 2000. "Historical Perspectives on Representing Nonstandard Workers." In Francoise Carre et al., eds., *Nonstandard Work: The Nature and Challenges of Changing Employment Arrangements*, 291–312. Champaign, Ill.: Industrial Relations Research Association.

Epstein, Cynthia Fuchs, and Arne L. Kalleberg, eds. 2001. *Time at Work: Implications of Changing Patterns of Time Use for the Sociology of Work*. Special issue of *Work and Occupations* 28, no. 1.

Featherstone, Mike. 1994. *Undoing Culture: Globalization, Postmodernism, and Identity*. London: Sage.

Glucksmann, Miriam. 1998. "What a Difference a Day Makes: A Theoretical and Historical Explanation of Temporality and Gender." *Sociology* 32, no. 2: 239–58.

Gonos, George. 1997. "The Contest over 'Employer' Status in the Postwar United States: The Case of Temporary Help Firms." *Law and Society Review* 31:81–110.

Gordon, David M. 1996. *Fat and Mean*. New York: Free Press.

Hardt, Michael, and Antonio Negri. 2000. *Empire*. Cambridge, Mass.: Harvard University Press.

Harrison, Bennett, and Barry Bluestone. 1988. *The Great U-Turn: Corporate Restructuring and the Polarizing of America*. New York: Basic Books.

Harvey, David. 1982. *The Limits to Capital*. Oxford: Blackwell.

———. 1989. *The Condition of Postmodernity: An Enquiry into the Origins of Cultural Change*. Oxford: Blackwell.

Hinrichs, Karl, William Roche, and Carmen Sirianni, eds. 1991. *Working Time in Transition: The Political Economy of Working Hours in Industrial Nations*. Philadelphia: Temple University Press.

Hochschild, Arlie. 1997. *The Time Bind*. New York: Metropolitan Books.

Honey, Michael K. 1993. *Southern Labor and Black Civil Rights: Organizing Memphis Workers*. Urbana: University of Illinois Press.

Kalleberg, Arne L. 2001. "Organizing Flexibility: The Flexible Firm in a New Century." *British Journal of Industrial Relations* 39, no. 4: 479–504.

Kalleberg, Arne L., and Cynthia Fuchs Epstein, eds. 2001. *Time and the Employment Relationship*. Special issue of *American Behavioral Scientist* 44, no. 7.

Kalleberg, Arne L., Barbara F. Reskin, and K. Hudson. 2000. "Bad Jobs in America: Standard and Nonstandard Employment Relations and Job Quality in the United States." *American Sociological Review* 65, no. 2: 256–78.

Kalleberg, Arne L., et al. 1997. *Nonstandard Work, Substandard Jobs: Flexible Work Arrangements in the United States*. Washington, D.C.: Economic Policy Institute.

Kelley, Robin. 1994. *Race Rebels: Culture, Politics, and the Black Working Class*. New York: Free Press.

Kirschenman, Joleen, and Kathryn Neckerman. 1991. "'We'd Love to Hire Them, but . . .': The Meaning of Race for Employers." In Christopher Jencks and Paul Peterson, eds., *The Urban Underclass*, 202–34. Washington, D.C.: Brookings Institute.

Lane, Julia, et al. 2000. *Low-Income and Low-Skilled Workers' Involvement in Nonstandard Employment*. Washington, D.C.: Urban Institute.

Lichter, Michael, and Roger Waldinger. 2001. "Producing Conflict: Immigration and the Management of Diversity." In John David Skretny, ed., *Color Lines: Affirmative Action, Immigration, and Civil Rights Options for America*, 147–67. Chicago: University of Chicago Press.

Memphis Regional Chamber of Commerce. 2003. "America's Distribution Center." Retrieved from ⟨www.memphischamber.com/economy⟩.

Mittelman, Guy. 1995. *Globalization: Critical Reflections*. Boulder, Colo.: Lynne Reinner.

Paulk, Michael. 2000. "2001 Holds Promise for Local Distribution, Logistics Industries." *Memphis Business Journal*, January 5.

Portes, Alejandro, Manuel Castells, and Lauren Benton, eds. 1989. *The Informal Economy: Studies in Advanced and Less Developed Countries*. Baltimore: Johns Hopkins University Press.

Rogers, J. K. 2000. *Temps: The Many Faces of the Changing Workplace*. Ithaca, N.Y.: ILR Press.

Ross, Andrew. 2000. *No Collar: The Humane Workplace and Its Hidden Costs*. New York: Basic Books.

Sassen, Saskia. 1988. *The Mobility of Labor and Capital: A Study in International Investment and Labor Flow*. New York: Columbia University Press.

———. 1998. *Globalization and Its Discontents*. New York: New Press.

Schor, Juliet. 1991. *The Overworked American: The Unexpected Decline of Leisure*. New York: Basic Books.

Sigafoos, Robert A. 1979. *Cotton Row to Beale Street: A Business History of Memphis*. Memphis: Memphis State University Press.

———. 1983. *Absolutely, Positively Overnight*. Memphis: St. Luke's Press.

Stark, Jeffrey. 1998. "Globalization and Democracy in Latin America." In Felipe Aguero and Jeffrey Stark, eds., *Fault Lines of Democracy in Post-Transition Latin America*, 67–96. Miami: North-South Center Press.

Thompson, E. P. 1967. "Time, Work Discipline, and Industrial Capitalism." *Past and Present* 38:56–97.

Thompson, Richard. 2002. "FedEx to Dedicate Toronto Facility." *Commercial Appeal*, September 19.

U.S. Bureau of the Census. 1988. *Census of Wholesale Trade, 1987, Tennessee*. Washington, D.C.: U.S. Government Printing Office.

———. 1991. *County Business Patterns, 1989, Tennessee*. Washington, D.C.: U.S. Government Printing Office.

———. 1998. *Census of Wholesale Trade, 1997, Tennessee*. Washington, D.C.: U.S. Government Printing Office.

———. 1999. *County Business Patterns, 1997, Tennessee*. Washington, D.C.: U.S. Government Printing Office.

U.S. Equal Opportunity Commission. 1967. *Job Patterns for Minorities and Women in Private Industry, 1966 (EEO-1 data)*. Washington, D.C.: U.S. Government Printing Office.

———. 1998. *Job Patterns for Minorities and Women in Private Industry, 1997 (EEO-1 data)*. Washington, D.C.: U.S. Government Printing Office.

Waldinger, Roger. 1997. "Black/Immigrant Competition Re-assessed: New Evidence from Los Angeles." *Sociological Perspectives* 40, no. 3: 365–86.

Wilson, William Julius. 1996. *When Work Disappears: The World of the New Urban Poor*. New York: Knopf.

Lucila Vargas

Media and Racialization among Young, Working-Class, Latina Immigrants

Russell King and Nancy Wood (2001, 1–2) suggest three main roles for the media in the migration experience. One is the potential for the global media, rich in images of northern wealth, to stimulate a desire to migrate in people from the South. Another is the role played by transnational media, such as the World Wide Web and satellite television originating in the home country, in the politics and cultural identity of immigrant individuals and communities. A third is the effect that the host country's media constructions of immigrants have on immigrants' own experiences of inclusion or exclusion. In this essay I study these roles at the level of everyday reception practices. My task is to shed light on how young, working-class, Latina immigrants[1] use media forms and meanings to accept, accommodate, or resist the subordinate place assigned to them in their host country. I am specifically interested in the part that media play in the emergence of racialized subjectivities among this youth.

Uprooted by war, political instability, and the international division of labor, the vast majority of immigrants from Latin America to the United States are assigned to the lower strata of their host society. For them, the reconstitution of identities that occurs in migration has often involved racialization—the process, as defined by Stephen Cornell and Douglas Hartman (1998, 33), "by which certain bodily features or assumed biological characteristics are used systematically to mark certain persons for differential status or treatment." Recognizing that racialization processes are overdetermined, I argue that, since the media are heavily implicated in the accelerated identity construction work that occurs during migratory processes, they have become mighty tools for the racialization of Latino immigrants. My observations are anchored on an action-research project on critical media literacy that I have been carrying out with immigrant young women who live in Durham, North Carolina. The project is far from complete, yet it gives me the opportunity to explore the issues at hand in a concrete situation. I suggest that Latino immigrant youth in North Carolina use various media cultures (the transnational media, the U.S. Latino media, and the Anglo media) and that these cultures compete to construct the subjectivity of Latino youth. Because media are one of the key sites of the broader struggle to construct Latino identity, the use of media by Latino immigrant youth in North Carolina should be contextualized within these broader struggles. Thus I review a few salient features of these struggles using Manuel Castells's proposal for the study of identity.

A Critical Media Literacy Project with Young, Working-Class, Latina Immigrants

My project draws on action-research, a methodology that combines outreach with qualitative or ethnographic research.[2] Accordingly, it has a twofold purpose. As an outreach effort, the project addresses a pedagogical concern: What is the potential of critical media literacy to empower young, working-class, Latina immigrants? How can media literacy skills empower them to reflect upon their own media use in order to transform the way they relate to media and engage more fully in the civic life of their host community? Simultaneously, as a research endeavor the project investigates how these young women use media to cope with the racialization process that Latino immigrants typically undergo. In the fall of 2002 I implemented a media literacy curriculum composed of twelve weekly sessions with a group of twelve young women (twelve to twenty-one years old). We held the classes at El Centro Hispano, the largest nonprofit, grassroots organization serving Latino immigrants in Durham.

The young women who participated in the project had a dual role in that they were both students and informants, but I refer to them as students. They had various levels of Spanish-English bilingualism, and their speech was characterized by constant code-switching. Four of them were second-generation immigrants, the U.S.-born children of Salvadoran immigrants. The remaining eight were born outside the United States: one in Puerto Rico, four in Mexico, one in Colombia, one in Honduras, and one in Venezuela. I follow a grounded theory approach to gathering and analyzing materials (Corbin and Strauss 1998). Such materials include the following: recordings of the two-hour, weekly sessions; follow-up conversations with individual students; and an array of classroom and homework assignments, including descriptions of students' use of media through their lives (life media stories) and collages describing their self-concepts. I also borrow from my own experience. As a Mexican immigrant of working-class origin who raised a child between two countries, I am familiar with many of the experiences, daily settings, and media practices of my students.[3]

By and large, the uses of media by immigrant young women remain to be investigated. According to King and Wood (2001, 2), "The migration studies literature—which has been growing extremely rapidly in recent years—is curiously silent on the role of the media." Empirical research on how immigrants use media to negotiate adolescence between cultures is extremely rare (Durham 1999). Marie Gillespie's ethnographic study with young Punjabi Londoners is a unique exploration of the uses of media by immigrant youth. Gillespie is concerned with the way everyday media reception practices help bring about what Stuart Hall (1998) and other cultural studies theorists have called "new ethnicities," a term that refers to the emerging cultural identities developed by postcolonial immigrants. Drawing on Gilroy's (1993) idea of the Black Atlantic, which posits that the framework for the study of black culture is the black diaspora, Gillespie argues that British Asian cultures should be investigated not as ethnic cultures bounded by local limits but as cultures that are part of transnational social formations. Accordingly, her study looks at how adolescents, as part of the British Punjabi diaspora, use media to deal with issues of cultural identity and to negotiate intergenerational conflict. Drawing on Gillespie's study, I think of Durham Latino youth as part of a transnational formation, but I am more interested in issues of working-class subjectivity and subordination. As opposed to Gillespie's study, a central working assumption in my research is that young, working-class, Latina immigrants negotiate and resist the dominant media's definitions of reality only to a certain extent. As much as I would like to celebrate their agency, my sense is that when it comes to media practices, they are in a weak position to overcome the formidable structural constraints that they face.

Race, Class, and Nation among Young, Working-Class, Latina Immigrants

Unlike in the American Southwest, where Latino settlement preceded Anglo settlement, significant numbers of Latinos did not begin to settle in North Carolina until 1980. Latino settlement represents the state's most significant local population change in a century (Johnson-Webb and Johnson 1996), and it has provoked a rapid redefinition of racial categories at the local level. Compared with other states, North Carolina has very large black and Native American populations, and race relations in the region have been characterized by discrimination and prejudice against both groups. In North Carolina, social stratification is closely linked to race (Wimberley and Morris 1997). Since 77 percent of the newcomers are younger than thirty-five years old, and 30 percent are younger than eighteen, schools and other educational institutions such as the media have become key to the ongoing reconstitution of the social hierarchy. Although a substantial number of Latinos in North Carolina work in military, construction, social services, and other occupations that pay moderate wages, Latinos have been assigned to a very low socioeconomic stratum, and they are overrepresented in low-wage occupations (Johnson-Webb and Johnson 1996, 32–35). In their home countries, most of my students' families were lower middle or lower class. In Durham, these families live in working-class neighborhoods and make a living in service or other working-class jobs. For most of them, the migration process involved some, but not drastic, changes in class status. For one of these families, however, migration also meant substantial downward mobility.

What a group brings from home is one of the factors that determine the group's outcome in their host society (Pedraza 1998, 3). It also affects the group's susceptibility to the media's hidden curriculum. Most Latino immigrants in North Carolina bring with them a working-class identity that has been constituted within the framework of the classism that characterizes Latin American societies. They also bring (post)colonial national identities. Especially in countries like Mexico, these identities have been forged with the remains of a glorious pre-Columbian past mixed with the wounds inflicted by defeat and colonization, first by European powers and, most crucially, by the very country that the immigrants are entering. Their colonial relationship with the United States is one of those pivotal historical facts that have made Latino immigrants' home countries what they are. Theorists of Latin American national identities, such as Samuel Ramos, have underscored that their prominent feature is what in Albert Memmi's terms would be the colonized mentality.[4]

Most of my students have Indian and/or black features, but they see themselves either as Latin American white (of European origin, but different from Anglos) or as *mestizas*.[5] Likewise, they do not seem to recognize the likely third, African root of their families. In their home countries, they (or their parents, in the case of second-generation youth) were full-fledged members of the dominant, Spanish-speaking society. Racism against blacks and indigenous people is rampant in the Spanish-speaking world, but many *mestizos* have a vague sense of the workings of systems of racial inequality; often they are unaware of their own racist attitudes and practices. The racism that my students and their families now experience in school and other settings of their daily life is a new experience for them. Renato Rosaldo and William V. Flores (1997, 94) note that "Mexican *mestizos* who cross the border into the United States move not only from one nation-state to another, but also from one side of the color line to the other." I believe that this experience is typical of *mestizos* not only from Mexico but from other countries. My students seem to be negotiating two different understandings of race, one stemming from their families' social locations in their home countries, and a second from their social locations in Durham. When I asked them to assign the characters of a Mexican *telenovela* (soap opera) into Latin American dominant racial categories, they were perplexed. However, when they talked about their current lives, they used four distinct categories: Americano/Americana, Hispano/Hispana, Chino/China,[6] and Moreno/Morena.[7] While there are numerous references to the term "racism" in the material that I gathered, and in my initial contact with young people at El Centro Hispano I was struck by what I thought was cultural insight regarding white privilege, I think that (perhaps with one exception) my students largely fail to grasp how many of their own media practices work to guarantee that they fit the racial category assigned to them. This does not mean, however, that they do not feel or do not resist racialization. Overt resistance to racialization was evident in the refusal of second-generation immigrant students to be labeled "Mexican," a term that in North Carolina schools and other settings of their everyday life has an unambiguously racist connotation.

Media Cultures of Young, Working-Class, Latina Immigrants

One of the organizing principles of the discourse on migration has been the dichotomy of home versus host country. In the literature on media and migration this dichotomy has been translated into home versus host culture (King and Wood 2001; Ogan 2001). The categories are used with caution by most authors, who recognize that cultures are not homogeneous. Nonetheless, the home-versus-host-culture dichotomy might obscure the media experience of Latino immigrant youth in the United States.[8] A decade ago, Federico Subervi-Vélez and Susan Colsant (1993) pointed out that Latino children live in a "dual television world." Following their lead, I inquired about the students' experiences with diverse cultural media traditions. Evidence of their participation in several media cultures was abundant. Take, for example, their television practices: by far, Univision (the major Spanish-language television network in the United States) was the students' top choice, but also high on their lists were MTV, Black Entertainment Television, and the Cartoon Network. In one of the class sessions, I asked the students whether they watch more English-language television or more Spanish-language television. Stephany's answer summarizes the group's response: "Both, because after school I watch in English but when it comes [time for] the *novelas*, I watch the *novelas*." They participate in the Anglo media culture and the U.S. Latino culture as well as the black media culture and the new transnational media culture.

The Durham Latino Youth Culture

Music is probably the media content that my students used most often, and music offers an excellent angle of entry for investigating processes of identity-building among transnational Latino youth. In the course of their migration, the students experienced a drastic change in musical tastes. The direction of such change was not so much toward the music of the dominant society, but toward Latin music. Most of the students reported in their homework that it was upon their arrival in Durham that they discovered the rich musical traditions of Latin America and the Caribbean. Here, for example, is how Isabel,[9] a student from Mexico, clarified her experience for me:

> Lucila: You put that you changed (your favorite music), that when you were sixteen you began to like *punta*.
>
> Isabel: I wasn't familiar with it [before migration], nor merengue, nor *bachata*, or reggae. In my house I seldom listened to it.
>
> Lucila: So, you became acquainted with more music here?
>
> Isabel: Yeah.
>
> Lucila: How come?
>
> Isabel: Because, there are several cultures here, and different, uh, people, they bring their traditions, their music, and all of that. That's why I became acquainted with *punta* from Honduras.

A local pan-Latino culture has emerged in Durham, and what could be called "Durham Latino youth culture" seems to have formed. The major sources of cultural forms and meanings for this formation are the transnational and the U.S. Latino media.

U.S. Latino Media Culture

The U.S. Latino media culture is entangled with, but different from, Latin American media. The U.S. Latino media tradition is bilingual and bicultural; part of its production is in Spanish, part is in English, and still another part mixes both languages. In contrast to the media traditions of Latin America, the U.S. Latino media culture borrows heavily from both Anglo and black media traditions. Its cultural specificity is rooted in the history of Latino set-tlement, which—as New Mexicans like to stress—preceded the English set-tlement; *El Misisipi*, the first Latino newspaper, began in 1808 (Wilson and Gutiérrez 1995, 175). It is also rooted in the failed record of incorporation of Latinos into the cultural institutions of the dominant society. Its distinctive features are most evident in alternative texts—for example, in the Chicano film—but they are also found in mainstream texts such as Univision's in-home productions. Both Latino resisting and project identities have been more clearly articulated in alternative texts, but mainstream texts such as Univision's Orgullo Hispano (Hispanic pride) campaign also articulate ele-ments of a project identity. Most important for the research on Latino immi-grant youth are the new offerings, specifically targeting Latino youth, that ar-ticulate both Latino resisting and project identities. In 2000, the cable channel Galavisión launched five youth programs targeting bilingual and bicultural urban youth:[10] *Galascene, Con Cierta, Intimidad, VideoMix, Al Desnudo*, and *¡Qué Locos!* These programs, characterized by constant code-switching, fea-ture many young Latino actors, comedians, and musicians with Indian pheno-types (González McPerson 2001, 34). Their inclusion contrasts with the media world of Latin America, where both Indians and blacks have been either ex-cluded or represented in stereotypical ways. Like many Latino families in North Carolina who have satellite television or, at least, have access to the local cable Spanish-language fare (which included nine channels in January 2002),[11] nearly all students reported having access to Univision at home, but only one had access to Galavisión; therefore, they are not exposed to these new youth shows.

U.S. Latino media texts directly address immigrant Latino youth and offer to them a large, symbolic repertoire for the construction of new, and not nec-essarily subordinate, racialized subjectivities. A case in point is *El Show de Cristina*, a popular Spanish-language talk show and certainly a program well regarded by several of the students. Hosted by Cuban exile Cristina Sarale-gui, the show (somewhat similar to the Oprah Winfrey show) mixes sensa-tional entertainment with serious topics, including issues of discrimination against Latinos. The students often talked about how much they learn from their preferred media texts. Here is what they said when I asked them why they like *El Show de Cristina*:

Carla: Because, mmm, I don't know, because sometimes, sometimes they
    show good things, and sometimes they show bad things, but sometimes
    they teach you something.

Lidia: I think that it's like everything else, no? It has its good parts and its
bad parts. They show something that is, that for you it's, it's something
good, but it's something bad. I mean, it's bad because of the way they are
living but it is shown as it really happens.

Carla: Uh, uh.

Natalia: Many times it leaves you with many lessons, many teachings.

Carla: Uh, uh.

Natalia: Not to do this, not to do that.

Lucila: *En Cristina*.

Natalia: Yes.

Lucila: Yes? Do you mean that it's an educational program?

Natalia: Yes.

Carla: Very much.

As my students said, the U.S. Latino media texts are contributing to their
education. These texts might be helping young Latina immigrants deal with
the racialization processes that they are undergoing. And they might be offering these women cultural resources to build their own Latina resisting and/or
project identities.

Transnational Spanish-Language Media Culture

Given that they live in a country with one of the highest rates of media availability in the world, the students are constantly exposed to transnational media
products that are available both through U.S. Spanish-language media and
through other outlets, such as television via satellite and audio/visual recordings produced in Latin America and available at local *tiendas*. Transnational
media are often intertwined with the U.S. Latino media, but they have their
own characteristics, many of which respond to the producers' need to cater to
supranational audiences. Spanish-language media in the United States have
often carried content produced in Latin America, and they have addressed an
audience composed, in part, of people who go back and forth between home
and host countries. Further, a new level of transnationalism emerged in the
mid-1980s, due in part to the processes of integration of the global economy,
particularly the global conglomeration and concentration of media ownership
that resulted in mergers and joint ventures by companies from two or more
countries, such as Mexico's Televisa and Murdoch's News Corporation (Thussu
2000). This new transnationalism was also due to the advent of new communication technologies, especially the convergence of digital and satellite tech-

nologies. Finally, it was due to the emerging political muscle of Latinos and the recognition, by major advertisers and media entrepreneurs, of the impact of the recent wave of immigrants on the buying power of the "Hispanic market." This market is now among the top twenty markets in the world. For advertising purposes, by the early 1980s the U.S. Latino population came to be seen as a niche market with three regional segments (Mexicans, Cubans, and Puerto Ricans). But by the early 1990s, Latino advertising agencies and Univision advanced the notion of a national, more or less homogeneous pan-Hispanic market (Rodríguez 1999). What many interested parties had in mind was a "greater Hispanic market" that would include all Spanish speakers in the world, regardless of place of residence. Media conglomerates have been exploiting this market for many years. Consumer magazines such as *People en Español*, for example, were designed as texts that would address middle-class readers from Latin America as well as U.S. Latinos. The flows of transnational media are bidirectional; while Mexico's Televisa, for example, exports television fare to the United States, Condé Nast Publications exports consumer magazines to Latin America. Latino youth are now seen as "the Hispanic youth market" and are becoming a most-wanted segment of the Hispanic market. As Juan Flores (2000, 12) rightly points out, the colonial subject is mostly visible as a consumer, and the Hispanic market constructs Latinos as consumers rather than as citizens. Still, it redefines their position in U.S. society, and thus it might advance the project identity of Latino political organizations.

Transnational media were salient for my students. *Telenovelas*, the staple of the two national Spanish-language networks Univision and Telemundo, were one of the transnational media offerings most attractive to my students. In fact, in the material that I gathered, *telenovelas* is the topic mentioned most frequently. Even the two students who repeatedly said that they do not watch television were quite familiar with *telenovelas*. They were, for example, able to relate the plots of *telenovelas* shown at the time of the class, and they displayed some understanding of the genre's structure. Their preference for *telenovelas* points to the significance of transnational Spanish-language media in their lives. In addition to *telenovelas*, their favorite transnational media products were CDs imported from Latin America, but they also consumed, for example, transnational magazines that originated in the United States, such as *Eres*, *Tu*, and *People en Español*. These media seem to be a source of cultural continuity for my students. When Natalia wrote about her reading practices, she noted that she used to read *Tu* magazine while in her home country and that she kept reading it after she moved to Durham. Like their use of transnational magazines, their use of transnational music suggests that some transnational media offerings may serve as a strand of continuity among the numerous disruptions that came with their migration. Not surprisingly, music was their preferred media content, and Selena was often mentioned as one of their beloved artists. Texan singer Selena was tremendously popular among both U.S. Latinos and some working-class audiences in Latin America. Her tragic death at the hands of one of her fans elevated her stature in the pantheon of transnational Latino artists. Carmen and Susana, who are originally from two different countries, reported in their homework that both used to like Selena when they were little. Here is what Carmen told me when I asked them to elaborate:

> Lucila: So, you became a fan of Selena.
> Carmen: Yes, and then when she died? It affected me so much! And then it was when her brother begun to sing, and it was then when I began to admire her brother too.
> Lucila: Also her brother? And how did her death affect you?
> Carmen: I mean, because I used to love her a lot, I mean, for me she was like a hero for me, because, how should I say this, I used to like her music, I used to like everything because she was pretty and everything . . . and she used to give advice, good advice.

Transnational media may also serve as bridges for the multiple transitions that immigrant young women have to negotiate. For instance, Selena may help Susana and Carmen to connect with Sabrina, a second-generation immigrant, who brought a CD of Selena to class as her favorite media sample. She explained to the class, "I brought a copy of a CD of Selena, because I used to listen to her a lot when I was little, because I was one of her number one fans, and I used, we used, to sing her songs, and I got her Barbie doll." But what makes a transnational media phenomenon like Selena germane to issues of racialization and Latino identity is that she embodied a Latino identity that rejects the legitimizing identity of U.S. dominant institutions, brings into play elements of Latino resisting identities, and puts forward another way of being a young Latina. Therefore, at least part of what both the transnational and the U.S. Latino media offer to my students might serve as resources for coping with processes of racialization.

The Anglo Media Culture

Despite the plethora of black and Latino cultural resources available to Latino immigrant youth, the Anglo media are still key providers of imagery and meanings for them. Language was not a barrier for accessing English-language media for my students. They said that they listened to popular Anglo artists, such as Metallica and Back Street Boys, and that among their favorite television shows are cartoons like *Scooby Doo, Courage the Cowardly Dog*, and *Rocket Power*. Some students said that they watch talk shows like *Sally* and *Jerry Springer*; others say that they enjoy sitcoms like *Friends*. Yet, from the Anglo media's fare, the texts that seemed to be especially significant for them were music videos (especially MTV) and films. *The Fast and the Furious* (Morris and Cohen 2001), an action film targeting adolescents, was released on video during the time of my fieldwork, and some of the students kept mentioning it. I used this film to probe the students on issues related to the representation of Latino youth in the media. I discuss their opinions below, but to provide some context, I first summarize the major findings of other research regarding the representation of Latinos in the Anglo media.

The two most consistent findings in this research are that Latinos have been nearly invisible in the Anglo media, and that when they have been included in news or entertainment content, their media portrayal has shared the racial stereotyping typical of the portrayal of African Americans.[12] Take, for example, a recent report on Latinos in primetime, which confirms the findings of other studies. Only 42 of the sample's 1,477 characters were Latinos, and only 8 played primary characters. Only 18 characters (1 percent) were Latinas, and two-thirds of them were nonrecurring characters. The secondary position of Latinos was also indicated by the low-status occupations held by the majority of the Latino characters. The majority of the Latina characters were cast as nurses or maids or as criminals or victims of crime (Children Now 2001, 2–7). The recent success of Latino crossover artists like Shakira and Gloria Estefan indicates that the racialized media construction of Latinos is not as uncontested as this research suggests, but the evidence for the Anglo media's contribution to the construction of racialized subjectivities for Latinos is nonetheless overwhelming.

Along with Latino advocacy organizations, Latinos working in the media industry have become more and more vocal in their demands for fairer representations. Cable networks like Showtime and Nickelodeon have aired a handful of Latino-themed programs. When Showtime was reconsidering its *Resurrection Boulevard*, a broad campaign to save the show was organized. Raúl Yzaguirre, one of the Latino political leaders behind the campaign, noted its significance: "Showtime's 'Resurrection Boulevard' is a show about a family living in East Los Angeles, California. There is nothing extraordinary about this family; they are loving, decent, and hard-working. But 'Resurrection Boulevard' is far from ordinary. It is historic—it is the first-ever drama series focusing on a Latino family on primetime television. It is unique—it is currently the only drama series about Latinos on television" (Yzaguirre 2002).

Yzaguirre's compelling statement gives a sense of the importance that the symbolic construction of Latinos has for the broader Latino struggle for social and economic justice. Having a Latino family appear on cable television is a historic event because, as opposed to the cable networks, the Anglo national television networks and Hollywood still consider it too risky to cast Latinos in primary roles. Hollywood cinema has contributed greatly to the racialization of Latinos. Charles Ramírez-Berg identified six enduring cinematic images of Latinos: the Bandito, the Half-Breed Harlot, the Male Buffoon, the Female Clown, the Latin Lover, and the Dark Lady. Ramírez-Berg (1997, 116–17) argues that "by and large, Hispanic stereotypes, and the traits that define them, essentially have not changed over the decades. Rather, they exist as repetitive variations played upon too-familiar themes. There have been numerous cinematic examples of combinations of these six stereotypes, but such stereotypic blends are still one dimensional, formulaic characters." Two of the female stereotypes are both highly sexualized and clearly racialized. The Dark Lady is sensuous but virtuous, an unusually erotic woman with light skin and European features; the Half-Breed Harlot cannot hide her Indian blood and her sexual drive. Writing about Chicanas in film, Carlos E. Cortés concurs with other film critics who have argued that the most obvious trait of the cinematic portrayal of Latinas is sexualization and thus racialization.[13] While light-skinned Latinas have played variations of the Dark Lady, the staple of dark-skinned Latinas has been the role of a highly sexualized woman, often a prostitute. The Chicana prostitute, Cortés (1997, 131) argues, is "a regular feature of the American Western." The typical portrayal of Latinas reveals a crucial mechanism of racialization because the inferiority implied by racial designations is "most importantly and almost invariably an inferiority in moral worth" (Cornell and Hartman 1998, 28). ↑ agree)

Representation of Latino Youth

The Latino gang film is emblematic of Hollywood's tradition of portraying Latinos as aggressive and hot tempered, and it also illustrates the role of the mainstream media in the dominant society's efforts to render void the resistance identities generated by Latino youth formations. Early films about Puerto Ricans, such as *The Young Savages* (1961), established a genre characterized by the demonization of Latino inner-city gangs, a representation that becomes even more salient against the backdrop of the otherwise near-invisibility of Latino youth in U.S. dominant popular culture. Cortés argues that the genre contributes to the cinematic tradition that equates Latinos with violent behavior. Numerous authors have written about the criminalization of minority youth and the racialization of youth violence in the United States (Cross 1993; Giroux 1995). Analyses of youth subcultures of the barrio stress that the media have played an instrumental role in shaping public opinion and in legitimizing the heavy-handed policing of Latino youth. The most remarkable example of the representation of youth subcultures of the barrio as evil is the coverage of the so-called Zoot Suit Riots. Historical analyses of the events that took place in Los Angeles in 1943 have shown that the media demonized *pachucos* and twisted the facts to create a story of the incidents that fit such demonization (McWilliams 1949; Wilson and Gutiérrez 1995). This typical representation of Latino youth has also been documented in analyses of more recent formations, such as California's lowriders, the Chicano student movement, and the Young Lords Organization of Puerto Rican street gangs (Brake 1985, 129–32). In an essay on the shameful representation of public schools and students of color in a series of Hollywood films of the late 1990s, Henry A. Giroux reviews *187*, a film set in a Los Angeles high school where most students are Latinos. He says that films like *187* "carry the logic of racial stereotyping to a new level" by presenting denigrating images of Latino youth and inner-city schools while ignoring the political and economic factors that bring forth the social maladies portrayed. Giroux (2000, 77) explains: "Decontextualized and depoliticized, Hollywood portrays public schools as not only dysfunctional, but also as an imminent threat to the dominant society. Students represent a criminalized underclass that must be watched and contained through the heavy-handed use of high-tech monitoring systems and military-style authority."

In a similar vein, in a study of the representation of youth gangs in Santa Cruz, California, Tim Lucas quotes from a local student publication that commented sharply on the stereotypes of Latino youth circulated in the local media: "They are everywhere: hanging out in front of coffee shops on Pacific Avenue, violating city law by sitting on curbs, smoking cigarettes around the corner, having unprotected premarital sex, spraying graffiti all over the place, and pretty much heading for a quick trip to nowhere. Nowhere, that is, if you look at them through a lens of mainstream media negativity" (cited by Lucas 1998, 145).

Lucas points out that the demonization of Latino subculture at the local level is achieved by associating it with issues that are already problematized at the national level: "drugs, gun violence, graffiti, and gangsta culture"—and one should add teen pregnancy. (I should note here that young Latinas have been largely neglected in the research on Latino youth subcultures.)

The Fast and the Furious

The text that I used to probe my students about Hollywood cinematic construction of Latinos is a B-grade film that tries to reach the youth-of-color market without offending Anglo audiences. It has many black, Asian American, and Latino characters, but it simultaneously reproduces the Anglo media stereotypes of youth subcultures and their resistant identities. It is about the drag-racing subcultures of Los Angeles and caters to adolescent boys with its theme (on-street racing), its fast action scenes, its soundtrack and special effects, its stars, and its male gaze (the camera often pans on scantily clad female bodies). The film has been a commercial success, and it has sprung a sequel (2 Fast 2 Furious). It is also an excellent example of an intriguing trend in the recent media construction of race in the dominant culture's texts, in which racial ambiguity is mixed with traditional racial stereotypes. The main characters are an undercover detective (played by Paul Walker) and a leading racer, Dominic Toretto (played by Vin Diesel). The detective is an extremely flat character, and his race seems equally obvious, with his blond hair and blue eyes functioning as unequivocal signs of his whiteness. Toretto is a bit more complex as a character, and his race is ambiguous. His name identifies him as Italian or white ethnic, but his looks may confuse viewers. Toretto's sister (played by Jordana Brewster), who becomes the detective's love interest, looks less racially ambiguous, but she could pass for Latina. When I asked my students to identify the race/ethnicity of the characters, their answers strengthened my sense of the racial ambiguity in the film. Natalia asked, "What race was Diesel?" and Lidia thought that many characters "looked like Hispanic." She said, "Some [characters] looked like Hispanic, I mean, most, most looked like, the bold one [Diesel] looked like Hispanic. . . . Both girls looked like Hispanic, his wife or something like that. . . . His girlfriend, they were like Hispanic."

As I mentioned above, Toretto and his sister are ethnic white or Italian, but Toretto's girlfriend, Letty, is clearly marked as Latina by her name, her Indian phenotype, and her makeup and clothing style. Played by Michelle Rodríguez, a Latina actress, Letty comes across as a tough gang girl involved in an abusive relationship with Toretto, who seems to cheat on her at every opportunity. Although hers is a secondary role, it is nonetheless important in that she is the only woman who races in the film (something that my students pointed out), and thus she complicates the film's androcentric story. Moreover, Rodríguez is the only Latina/Latino actor whose name appears in the credits. Other minor Latina characters are clearly depicted as sexually available, and Hector, the leader of the Latino gang, is portrayed as stupid. In one scene, Toretto asks

Hector to watch over the money for a bet. Someone asks, "Why Hector?" Toretto replies, "Because he is too slow to run away with the money." Hector looks puzzled but says nothing. The large number of racialized bodies shown on the screen may make the film's denigration of Latinos (and, indeed, of other groups, especially Asian Americans) difficult to see. Here is what one reviewer thought about the film's ethnic diversity: "We also see the marketing of the film in how it is cast, portraying ethnic diversity. Lance Nguyen and Johnny Tran lead a polished but ruthless Asian motorcycle gang called a 'wolf-pack,' that is in competition with Dominic. Not only has a business deal gone sour but Dominic slept with Tran's sister. In one of the drag race sequences, Ja Rule, as Edwin, an African-American driver, has a cameo scene. Add to the mix Michelle Rodríguez and an uncredited Latino actor as Hector, and we have a politically correct movie" (Singleton 2000).

Like this reviewer, my students seemed to have missed the denigration of youth of color. They said that the film was quite popular among Durham Latino youth and talked about how their male Latino friends imitated on the Durham highways the races depicted in the film. The students explained that they liked the film because it caters to youth and because it is about cars and racing. They also said that they liked it because it has Latino characters. Lidia put it this way: "They represent Hispanics, I mean, they do not represent them so badly." The relative abundance of clearly racialized but nonetheless racially ambiguous characters in music videos and films targeting youth may obscure the contribution of the hidden media curriculum to the racialization of Latino immigrants. Young women like Lidia may feel that the inclusion of Latinos (even when they are stereotypically portrayed and Latino actors are not even credited) in Hollywood youth films is a sign of progress.

Conclusion

During migratory movements people undergo rapid processes of identity reconstruction. In the case of people migrating from Latin America and the Caribbean to the United States, such reconstruction has entailed racialization. Racialization of Latino immigrant youth is necessary to ensure that they are in accord with the needs of the global economy and international division of labor. In a broader sense, this essay is concerned with Paul Willis's question about why working-class kids let themselves get working-class jobs. More specifically, this article explores the role of the media in the construction of a dominant Latina immigrant identity—that is, the way the media contribute to a Latina identity in accord with the working-class jobs that the dominant society expects these young women to get. While numerous institutions of the dominant society act in tandem to transform Latino immigrants into a lower race, as the major storytellers in U.S. society, the media play a fundamental role in processes of racialization of Latino immigrants. Unraveling the complexity of such a role at the level of everyday reception practices poses fresh theoretical challenges and opens uncharted topics. My main suggestion in this essay is that we begin by looking at the four media cultures from which Latino immigrant youth draw cultural forms and meanings to build their identities and to accept, accommodate, or resist racialization processes. There are multiple overlaps and interactions among these four media cultures, and the distinctions among them are at times very subtle. Yet these categories provide an angle of entry into the intricate dynamics of the use of media by transnational Latino youth.

My sense is that, on one hand, the Anglo media's hidden racializing curriculum disciplines Latino immigrant youth to accept the inferior status assigned to them, and by so doing, it contributes greatly to the emergence of a dominant, racialized identity among Latino youth. But on the other hand, the transnational, the U.S. Latino, and perhaps the black media culture may offer this youth resources to resist such curricula. The combination of differing and often contradictory meanings that circulate in the multiple media worlds of Latino youth adds one more layer to the bewilderment that often comes with adolescence. Such meanings may become important factors in the emergence of an ultimately self-defeating resistance identity. As Willis (1981, 3) showed, oppression is deeply rooted in identity, and people often experience their compliance with their own subordination as resistance. Still, the possibility exists for Latino youth to use media critically and selectively to cope effectively with their new environs. Such a possibility points to media literacy for Latino immigrant youth as an urgent field of intervention. Transnational critical media literacy has the potential to assist these youth in the difficult task of using media to build project identities, so that they can redefine the position of Latinos in North Carolina.

Notes

1. My use of the term "immigrant" corresponds to the term "foreign stock," as used by the U.S. Census Bureau (Schmidley 2001, 22). Thus I employ the term "Latino/Latina immigrant" to talk about both foreign-born individuals and natives of foreign-born or mixed parentage (one parent native and one parent foreign-born). It is important to distinguish between the terms "Latin American" and "Hispanic/Latino." The former denotes inhabitants of Latin America, but the latter designates persons who are

U.S. residents (both natives and immigrants) and who trace their origins to Latin America and the Caribbean.

2. There are numerous approaches associated with the term "action-research." I have borrowed from many of them but have drawn most heavily from the Southern Cross University website "Action Research Resources" (available at ‹http://www.scu.edu.au/schools/gcm/ar/arhome.html›).

3. I am not claiming an insider's view, but, rather, I wish to clarify that my experience and participation in the local Latino immigrant community has shaped all aspects of this research.

4. Samuel Ramos (1951) was a Mexican philosopher who used Alfred Adler's psychoanalytic theory to interpret Mexican collective identity. He convincingly argued that Adler's inferiority complex explains Mexican character at the level of both individual and collective action. The inferiority complex, said Ramos, is rooted in the experience of Spanish conquest and colonization and is a constitutive element of the national identity that emerged after the independence of 1810. The notion of the colonized mentality seems to fit better with outdated conceptualizations of the audience as an aggregate of passive receivers than with trendy images of readers who actively resist dominant meanings. I am aware of this contradiction.

5. Literally, the term refers to the offspring of Spaniards and Latin American indigenous people, but it is also used to discuss the hybridity that characterizes the cultures of these people. The term also has a class connotation, linking *mestizo* to the cultural production of peasants and the urban poor.

6. Literally, "Chinese," meaning Asian/Asian American.

7. Literally, "dark-skinned," meaning black.

8. As Benedict Anderson (1991) pointed out, community and home are always entities more imagined than real. The collective home of Latin American immigrants is a notion with a rather fuzzy territorial referent because "home" can refer to any place south of the U.S.-Mexico border or to the border itself. The situation is even more complex for immigrants who are members of the numerous ethnic minorities of Latin America. It is only through the process of immigrating to the United States that one comes to regard the collectivity of all those places—Latin America—as home. It is only in the United States that one becomes Hispanic or Latina.

9. All students' names have been changed.

10. Galavisión is owned by Univision.

11. Recognizing the growing Latino population in the local market, Univision opened an affiliate in Raleigh in June 2003.

12. Like other youth, my students did not prefer news programs. Given space limitations, I do not discuss here issues related to news programming. It is worth mentioning, however, that by and large the representation of Latinos in news content is consistent with their representation in popular culture texts (Navarrete and Kamasaki 1994). Carveth and Alverio (1996; 1997) found that Latino-oriented news was largely ignored, that Latinos rarely appeared on camera, and that most news stories mentioning Latinos were about crime, drugs, welfare, immigration, and affirmative action. In my own research on the coverage of Latino news by the major newspaper in North

Carolina, I argue that the coverage genders Latino news as feminine and (re)produces the stereotype of Latinos as an underclass (Vargas 2000).

13. Interestingly, in his essay on Chicanas in film, Cortés notes the conspicuous absence of major female characters in films produced by Chicanos.

References

Anderson, B. 1991. *Imagined Communities*. New York: Verso.

Brake, M. 1985. *Comparative Youth Culture*. New York: Routledge.

Carveth, R., and D. Alverio. 1996. *Network Brownout: The Portrayal of Latinos in Network Television News*. Washington, D.C.: National Association of Hispanic Journalists.

———. 1997. *Network Brownout 1997: The Portrayal of Latinos in Network Television News*. Washington, D.C.: National Association of Hispanic Journalists and the National Council of La Raza.

Castells, M. 1997. *The Power of Identity*. Malden, Mass.: Blackwell.

Children Now and National Hispanic Foundation for the Arts. 2001. "Prime Time for Latinos." Report 2, "2002–2001 Prime Time Television Season." Retrieved March 16, 2002, from ‹www.childrennow.org/media/fc2001/fc2001›.

Corbin, J. M., and A. Strauss. 1998. *Basics of Qualitative Research: Techniques and Procedures for Developing Grounded Theory*. Thousand Oaks, Calif.: Sage.

Cornell, S., and D. Hartman. 1998. *Ethnicity and Race: Making Identities in a Changing World*. Thousand Oaks, Calif.: Pine Forge Press.

Cortés, C. E. 1997. "Chicanas in Films: History of an Image." In C. E. Rodríguez, ed., *Latin Looks: Images of Latinas and Latinos in the U.S. Media*, 121–41. Boulder, Colo.: Westview.

Cross, B. 1993. *It's Not About a Salary . . . : Rap, Race, and Resistance in Los Angeles*. London: Verso.

Durham, M. G. 1999. "Out of the Indian Diaspora: Mass Media, Myths of Femininity, and the Negotiation of Adolescence between Two Cultures." In S. R. Mazzarella and N. O. Pecora, eds., *Growing Up Girls: Popular Culture and the Construction of Identities*, 193–208. New York: Peter Lang.

Flores, J. 2000. *From Bomba to Hip-Hop*. New York: Columbia University Press.

Freire, P. 1999. *Pedagogy of the Oppressed*. New York: Continuum.

Gilroy, P. 1993. *The Black Atlantic: Modernity and Double Consciousness*. New York: Verso.

Giroux, H. A. 1995. "White Panic." *Z Magazine*, 12–14.

———. 2000. "Disposable Youth/Disposable Futures: The Crisis of Politics and Public Life." In N. Campbell, ed., *The Radiant Hour: Versions of Youth in American Culture*, 71–87. Exeter, Devon: University of Exeter Press.

González McPerson, J. 2001. "Targeting Teens." *Hispanic*, September, 33–36.

Hall, S. 1988. "New Ethnicities." In K. Mercer, ed., *Black Film, British Cinema*, 27–31. London: Institute for Contemporary Arts.

Havens, T. 2001. "Subtitling Rap." *Gazette* 63, no. 1: 57–72.

Johnson-Webb, K. D., and J. H. Johnson. 1996. "North Carolina Communities in Transition: An Overview of Hispanic In-migration." *North Carolina Geographer* 5 (Winter): 21–40.

King, R., and N. Wood, eds. 2001. *Media and Migration: Constructions of Mobility and Difference.* New York: Routledge.

Lucas, T. 1998. "Youth Gangs and Moral Panics in Santa Cruz, California." In T. Skelton and G. Valentine, eds., *Cool Places: Geographies of Youth Subcultures,* 145–61. New York: Routledge.

McWilliams, C. 1949. *North from Mexico.* New York: Greenwood Press.

Morris, N. H. (producer), and R. C. Cohen (director). 2001. *The Fast and the Furious.* Los Angeles: Universal Pictures.

Navarrete, L., and C. Kamasaki. 1994. *Out of the Picture: Hispanics in the Media.* Washington, D.C.: National Council of La Raza.

Ogan, C. 2001. *Communication and Identity in the Diaspora.* Boulder, Colo.: Lexington Books.

Pedraza, S. 1998. "The Contribution of Latino Studies to Social Science Research on Immigration." JSRI Occasional Paper 36. Julian Samora Research Institute, Michigan State University.

Ramírez-Berg, C. 1997. "Stereotyping in Films in General and of the Hispanic in Particular." In C. E. Rodríguez, ed., *Latin Looks: Images of Latinas and Latinos in the U.S. Media,* 104–20. Boulder, Colo.: Westview.

Ramos, S. 1951. *El Perfil del Hombre y la Cultura en México.* Buenos Aires: Espasa-Calpe.

Rodríguez, A. 1999. *Making Latino News: Race, Language, Class.* Thousand Oaks, Calif.: Sage.

Rosaldo, R., and Flores, W. V. 1997. "Identity, Conflict, and Evolving Latino Communities: Cultural Citizenship in San Jose, California." In W. Flores, V. Benmayor, and R. Benmayor, eds., *Latino Cultural Citizenship: Claiming Identity, Space, and Rights,* 57–96. Boston: Beacon Press.

Schmidley, D. A. 2001. *Current Population Reports: Profile of the Foreign-Born Population in the United States, 2000.* Washington, D.C.: U.S. Census Bureau.

Singleton, G. O. 2000. "Superb Action Carries Weak Plot and Pedestrian Acting." Reel Movie Critic.com. Retrieved June 22, 2003, from ‹www.reelmoviecritic.com/2000/id1066.htm›.

Subervi-Vélez, F., and S. Colsant. 1993. "The Television Worlds of Latino Children." In L. B. Gordon and J. K. Asamen, eds., *Children and Television,* 215–28. Newbury Park, Calif.: Sage.

Task Force on Latino Issues. 1994. *Willful Neglect: The Smithsonian Institution and U.S. Latinos.* Washington, D.C.: Smithsonian Institution.

Thussu, D. K. 2000. *International Communication: Continuity and Change.* London: Arnold.

Vargas, L. 2000. "Genderizing Latino News: An Analysis of a Local Newspaper's Coverage of Latino Current Affairs." *Critical Studies in Media Communication* 17, no. 3: 261–93.

Willis, P. 1981. *Learning to Labor*. New York: Columbia University Press.

Wilson, C. C., and F. Gutiérrez. 1995. *Race, Multiculturalism, and the Media*. Thousand Oaks, Calif.: Sage.

Wimberley, R. C., and L. V. Morris. 1997. *The Southern Black Belt*. Lexington: TVA Rural Studies, University of Kentucky.

Yzaguirre, R. 2002. *Help Save the Showtime Drama Series*. National Council of La Raza. Retrieved May 22, 2002, from ‹http://nclr.policy.net/proactive/newsroom/release.vtml?id=17540›.

Sandy Smith-Nonini

Federally Sponsored Mexican Migrants in the Transnational South

One of the defining features of neoliberal globalization has been the polarization between haves and have-nots. This theme has been prevalent in recent writings about the U.S. South, as many observers have noted that even as the South becomes more urbanized with an influx of high-tech industry and tourism, a wider gap has emerged between cities and rural areas where social programs and public infrastructure remain greatly underfunded. Further, labor-intensive industries have moved abroad since the North American Free Trade Agreement (NAFTA), leaving a wave of unemployment behind that disproportionately affects rural areas. Interestingly, Mexico, the country in which so many formerly southern factories have relocated, is experiencing a similar polarization, as free trade policies create new forms of rural poverty that help drive migration north.

Ironically, as rural southerners lose manufacturing jobs, another phenomenon since the 1990s has been a shift of Mexican immigrant flows from traditional migrant destinations—Texas, the West Coast, and Florida—to the mid-South. North Carolina, the state that has lost the most manufacturing jobs since NAFTA, actually led the nation for Hispanic immigrant population growth from 1995 to 1999.[1] Many Mexican migrants first come to the South as farmworkers and then move into other low-wage sectors such as poultry processing, construction, and service work. By the late 1990s, nearly all North Carolina farmworkers were Latino migrants, and the state was importing more Mexican "guestworkers" than any other state under the federal H2A program, which allows agents for agribusiness to recruit Mexican workers who receive seasonal visas. This essay will focus on the H2A program in North Carolina as a way of examining the politics and economics of new migrant labor flows in the transnational South.

Although it is not widely known, since 1990 a company called the North Carolina Growers Association (NCGA), housed in a rural warehouse in the tiny hamlet of Vass, North Carolina, has been importing around 40 percent of all federal H2A workers that enter the United States. The NCGA is run by Leroy Dunn (a pseudonym), a former state rural manpower employee, who now has a license from the federal government to import more than 17,000 Mexicans into the country each year. Of these, about 12,000 work for farmers affiliated with the NCGA in North Carolina, and the remainder come in through a separate company Dunn runs that supplies workers to nearby states. Despite a stream of adverse publicity, numerous complaints of labor violations, several legal suits, and the occasional heatstroke death of a farmworker, Dunn's multimillion-dollar operation continues, a set of orders for new workers rubber-stamped by the U.S. Department of Labor each winter.

The role of the state in this process raises interesting questions, in that a central theme of many writings about the neoliberal changes is the diminished role of the state vis-à-vis the private sector. In contrast, this essay recognizes the state's continued involvement in economic regulation. What has changed in recent decades is not state intervention in the market per se so much as the relationship between the state and its citizenry with regard to the "public good." At both the federal and regional levels during the neoliberal period (roughly post-1980) the U.S. government has abandoned many aspects of the social contract that characterized the post–World War II era.

This study also shifts the analytical lens from trade and capital flows to labor. Numerous observers have pointed out that free trade agreements such as NAFTA deregulated the flow of capital across borders but did not liberalize laws on labor flows. Sassen (1998) observed that NAFTA differs from the free trade agreement in the European Union, where unions successfully fought for a relaxation of immigration restrictions as part of the unification process. In agriculture, a labor-intensive industry that depends on land—a non-exportable resource—labor relations become paramount. The U.S. government has long played a role in regulating the supply of foreign farm labor on behalf of agribusiness, and that role has become more critical as the industry has restructured itself in the competitive climate of the last twenty years. Yet relations between the state and agribusiness are more complex than a purely functional economic alliance; state elites weigh factors such as security of the borders against demands for foreign labor, and there are electoral implications where politicians have constituencies with interests in labor or immigrant rights issues.

In this essay I argue that the H2A program establishes a mode of contractual labor relations that constitutes a case of "government by proxy" (Holland, Nonini, and Lutz in press). In this arrangement the state delegates responsibility for labor supply manipulation, control of workers, and oversight of labor regulations directly to private brokers representing growers. While this practice opens some areas to public scrutiny, it also creates new invisibilities and legitimizes forms of labor control that replicate some of the same abuses associated with private labor brokerage and the discredited bracero program of the 1950s.

This study began as a documentary project with the Institute for Southern Studies in 1998 (see Smith-Nonini 1999) and grew into a postdoctoral research project.[2] I remain active with a Unitarian Universalist educational outreach project on farmworkers. Some research at labor camps was done in collaboration with nonprofit organizations working on behalf of farmworkers' civil and labor rights. These findings were based on visits to 16 North Carolina migrant labor camps in eastern tobacco-belt counties and more than 85 interviews between 1998 and 2002, including 32 farmworkers, 9 members of the agribusiness community, 12 state employees or officials, and 30 volunteers or staff of nonprofit organizations working on farmworker issues. I also attended 16 conferences or forums on North Carolina farmworker issues.

The Historical Role of the State in Shaping the Farm Labor Market

The NCGA labor brokerage opened its doors in 1990, but the current H2A program is part of a long history of government mediation in agricultural labor relations. State subsidies for American agriculture have always included either a tacit or an official license to exploit the labor of marginalized populations—from the days of slavery to post–Civil War freedmen to the Mexican braceros and H2A guestworkers of today.

The federal bracero program of imported Mexican farm laborers, which lasted from 1942 through the mid-1960s, is testimony to the long history of economic integration between Mexico and the United States in the area of agriculture. The program, under which more than 5 million braceros (literally, "strong arm men") were contracted to Western growers and ranchers, was prompted by a purported shortage of rural labor during World War II. Yet, as recent work by Hahamovitch (1999) has shown, there was no data to support a labor shortage; rather, the legislation was a response to staunch resistance within the agricultural sector to paying more than depression-era wages to workers. The Farm Security Administration initially attempted to use mobile work camps to redistribute migrants within the United States to address local shortages in specific crops. But southern growers resisted federal agents' recruitment of local labor for out-of-state farms, calling it "labor piracy," and they complained of militancy by workers in federal migrant camps who were no longer at risk of being evicted or losing the landowner's aid if they refused to work for low wages (Hahamovitch 1999).

Today the bracero program is mainly remembered for *Harvest of Shame*, the CBS documentary that exposed the program's widespread abuses and which, together with pressure from the United Farm Workers (UFW), led Congress to discontinue it. Although the bracero contracts had clauses guaranteeing levels of wages, housing, duration of employment, and even health insurance, these protections were poorly enforced, and growers routinely circumvented them. The temporary workers, lacking legal standing, were in a poor position to negotiate better conditions.

Today's effort by the agribusiness lobby to maintain a surplus of cheap labor has precedent in the lobby of growers that kept farmworkers excluded from New Deal labor protections of the 1930s. The vulnerability felt by workers in today's H2A program, in which their legal status is controlled by their employer, is not unlike that of the bracero workers. The objections of today's growers to proposals from labor unions for amnesty for immigrants (in which workers carry their own identity cards) must be interpreted in light of a history of farm labor in which post–Civil War growers felt threatened by a workforce of free blacks who could migrate at will in search of the best wages. Instead growers found legal and other means to restrict workers' mobility and keep them isolated on labor camps under the control of foremen or labor bosses.

Immigration Reform, Farm Labor, and Agricultural "Rationalization"

There is historical precedent in the responsiveness of federal immigration policy to economic changes. During war economies (e.g., World War II and the Korean War), immigrants were welcomed, but during the 1960s economic boom or after a national security incident such as September 11, 2001, "close the border" ideologies gained traction. In fact, the revitalization of the H2A program (a successor to a smaller H2 guestworker program) came about in response to the 1986 Immigration Reform and Control Act (IRCA). The reform simultaneously put in place a legalization process open to immigrants who could prove long-term U.S. residence and introduced employer sanctions for hiring illegal immigrants. Interestingly, the sanctions have proven largely symbolic, as the law brought about a flourishing of underground businesses producing false documents. In the booming economy of the 1990s, the Immigration and Naturalization Service (INS) made raids on workplaces a low priority (Heyman 1998).

As in the 1940s, growers saw drop-offs in the supply of cheap migrant labor after IRCA as a labor shortage. Rather than pay competitive wages, California growers, facing the neoliberal marketplace of the 1980s, led a new round of lobbying in Congress to gain approval for the H2A program that began in 1990. Today the H2A program imports about 40,000 Mexican workers to the United States each growing season (Bacon 2001).

Importantly, the reality of the current agricultural labor "shortage" that justifies the H2A program is in dispute and so warrants clarification. A 1997 General Accounting Office study found no national labor shortage in agriculture, while noting that local shortages may occur periodically. The report did find that few unemployed Americans are willing to take jobs as farm laborers. Philip Martin, an agricultural economist, recently estimated that in California there has actually been a labor surplus, with 700,000 farmworkers chasing about 400,000 jobs. In some California counties unemployment among farmworkers in the late 1990s was in double digits (Hubner 2000). These figures are supported by U.S. Department of Labor surveys but disputed by growers (e.g., see Cleeland 1999).

A new influx of Latino migrants into the American Southeast began to transform farm labor in the early 1980s. In North Carolina the migrant population doubled between 1990 and 1997, one of the fastest growth rates in the country. Latinos moving into agricultural jobs largely replaced blacks leaving for service and retail jobs (Skaggs and Tomaskovic-Devey 1999). Rather than raise wages to compete better for workers, growers looked south of the border for a cheaper and more pliable workforce. Today more than 90 percent of farm labor in the state is Spanish speaking.

In interviews with immigrants the consistent refrain is that it is no longer possible to make a living wage in rural Mexico. Unskilled and semiskilled jobs pay at best $2 a day, with wages only slightly higher in urban centers. Trade legislation and nationalist agrarian reforms are, in the words of Roger Bartra (1993), forcing Mexican campesinos into "extinction." Increasingly, studies show that NAFTA has favored transnationals and U.S. brokers to the disadvantage of Mexico's agro-export industry and small farmers (Gledhill 1998; Raghaven 2000). New imports of cheaper U.S. corn and sucrose into Mexico are undermining the market for many domestic producers. The Mexican banking crisis and the 1994 devaluation of the peso added insult to injury. The major strategy rural families use to cope is migration of men to the United States for low-wage work. Due to an extensive network of agricultural recruiters with ties to "coyotes," the easiest job for new migrants to find is farmwork.

To understand the recent changes, it is necessary to look beyond the increased supply of labor to the demand side of the equation. Vertical integration in agribusiness, in which food processors have gained control over the growing of crops, has hurt small farmers. The decline of small farms goes back three decades in North Carolina. Thanks to tobacco and income from textile factory jobs, North Carolina's rural families were able to hold on to their land longer than small farmers in many southern states. State policies of developing a rural industrial working class with families depending on both factory and farm incomes have remained intact to the present day, although meatpacking operations—mainly poultry and pig processing—have gradually replaced textile mills in many areas, as that industry moved overseas.

In North Carolina the number of farms smaller than fifty acres declined by 35 percent from 1982 to 1997, while the median size of farms grew by 24 percent in the same period, according to the state Department of Agriculture. The average tobacco farm actually doubled in size between 1987 and 1997 (U.S. Department of Labor 2002). Total farm acreage has stayed relatively stable, but the survivors in agriculture tended to be larger and more mechanized farmers, who benefited from the sale of farmland by smaller farmers going out of business. These are also the main employers of farm labor. Sixty percent of North Carolina farmworkers in 1997 were employed on farms that hired ten or more workers. Farmers who survived tended to be those with the means to develop side operations such as on-site packing or processing facilities that improved capital flows. In general, processors and integrators have captured a much larger share of the food income dollar in the last twenty years than have growers, whose 30 percent share has declined. Meanwhile, the share of food dollars paying for farm labor has remained flat, at 8 to 9 percent since the mid-1970s, and farm wages have lost value due to inflation.[3]

Likewise, increasing reliance on global trade, including imports of foreign produce (in many cases grown abroad by U.S. companies) has heightened competitiveness within the industry. The new industry leaders tend to be companies that have diversified, expanded their markets, and maximized production while minimizing labor costs. For example, Mt. Olive Pickle Company, a North Carolina food processor that is being boycotted by the Farm Labor Organizing Committee (FLOC) for its growers' farm labor practices, is one of the winners in the global trade game. Mt. Olive has rapidly grown to become the second largest U.S. processor of supermarket shelf pickles and has expanded its market outside the South while increasing its purchases of pickles from abroad. This geographical breadth gives the company greater leverage, both in capturing new markets and in its efforts to resist the efforts of FLOC, an Ohio-based farm labor union, to organize cucumber pickers. Before its subcontracting practices for farm labor were brought into the public eye by the FLOC campaign, Mt. Olive had been active in lobbying Congress on behalf of the local H2A program run by Leroy Dunn's NCGA. Today more than 70 percent of the workers that supply Mt. Olive pickles come through Dunn's H2A guestworker pipeline.

Working and Living Conditions of Brokered Farm Labor

Farmers' efforts to cut labor costs have been facilitated by INS policies of quietly scaling back raids on workplaces; by migration from the West Coast, where farm unemployment is high; and by the H2A program, which, for the first time, is serving a wide range of southern states.[4] In addition, the rise of labor brokers for both H2A and illegal immigrants has radically transformed the nature of farmwork in the last decade, creating a system that in many ways resembles the treatment of blacks in the Jim Crow South. The difference is that today's "sweatshops in the fields" exist in a postreform era, in which minimal standards to improve pay and conditions are in place but lack enforcement. With today's quasi-legal system of labor brokers, the middleman has replaced the plantation boss as "patron."

A *San Jose Mercury News* investigation of farm labor brokers concluded, "Thirty years ago, 80 to 90 percent of seasonal farmhands in California worked directly for growers. Today, as few as half do. The rest are employed by about 1,200 farm labor contractors, or *contractistas*, who maximize their profits by paying laborers as little as possible" (Hubner 2000).

The middlemen not only deliver crews to the fields, but they supply everything from work gloves to fake Social Security cards—for a price. The more unscrupulous brokers also gouge workers on housing, transportation, and food and intimidate them into working longer hours than their paychecks reflect, according to interviews with farmworkers and farmworkers' advocates. The rise of quasi-legal labor brokers in the 1990s has increased the incidence of cases like that of Ramón, a farmworker I interviewed who came to North Carolina in 1996:

I paid the coyote $800 to come and then had a debt on top of that with the crew leader. So the crew leader took out $50–$100 or more out of each paycheck for those debts. They take money out for Medicare, Social Security, taxes. And then there are deductions of $25 for rent and $20 per week for transport and trips to the grocery store. So the money you get to keep is nothing; I'd have maybe $40 left each week. . . . And the work wasn't steady. In one two-month period I only earned about $280. . . . Most of us didn't dare try to leave. We didn't have any cars. [The crew leader] had spies who reported on us if we talked to visitors. Sometimes . . . they even put guards on people with guns to keep you from escaping. I worked for one and a half years before I had paid off enough debts that I had something saved to send my family in Mexico. They had a small store, but they lost it because I couldn't send them any money.

A U.S. Department of Labor study found that farmworkers hired directly by growers earn about 20 percent more than workers hired by middlemen.

Reforms since the bad old days of the 1960s should mean that farmworkers get a better deal today than they did in the past. Minimum-wage laws went into effect in 1966, migrant housing reforms were passed in 1986, and new pesticide regulations date to 1993. But North Carolina has a poor record of enforcing even these minimum standards.

Many farmworkers interviewed in both H2A and non-H2A jobs have reported being cheated by piecework wages and long workdays. A majority of laborers report working ten- to twelve-hour days at the height of the tobacco and cucumber harvests. On non-H2A farms some growers convert those long days into eight-hour days at minimum-wage rates for federal reporting and weekly paychecks. By law higher overtime pay is not required for farmwork, yet many workers do not object to long hours. Some do this because they know full-time work is scarce between harvests, and others fear losing their jobs if they do not put in the overtime. A generous minimum-wage exemption exists in North Carolina law allowing many "small" farmers to pay less than the federal minimum.[5] Wage and hour oversight by the state Department of Labor is almost nonexistent due to a shortage of inspectors and a "complaint-driven" system of enforcement that is unresponsive to the realities of farm labor (Smith-Nonini 1999).

Only about 16,000 of the state's estimated 150,000 farmworkers live in inspected housing, and housing standards are minimal.[6] Housing for most of the 22,000 farms that hire farmworkers (or for about 85 percent of all farmworkers hired) remains unregistered and uninspected, much of it likely substandard. Many workers that I have interviewed rent from farmers or crew leaders, paying premium rents for decrepit house trailers or rundown farmhouses that are shared with ten or fifteen workers. H2A workers more often live in barracks-style housing that is supposed to be inspected prior to occupation.[7] Only one of the state's eight housing inspectors was bilingual in 1999, and state officials acknowledge that inspectors rely primarily on interviews with farmers.

Pesticide education is now available at many migrant clinics, but once again the realities of power relations in farm labor mean that workers are often not in a position to put recommendations into effect. (E.g., a worker should wash work clothes daily; yet regulations require only one washtub per thirty workers, and crew leaders only take the workers to laundromats on weekends.)[8] Fines for pesticide violations are rare and rarely exceed $300. At the current rate of inspections, it would take forty-three years for the state's (monolingual) field inspectors to visit all farms using "restricted use" pesticides (Smith-Nonini 1999).

Although it is difficult to study the epidemiology of farmworkers, there is little doubt that the estimated 300,000 injuries and 1,000 pesticide deaths per year as well as the short life expectancy (estimated at forty-nine years in one study) of this population are tied to these working conditions. While other hazardous industries, such as mining and construction, have improved their injury and death rates in recent decades, farmwork remains the nation's most dangerous occupation. Every summer there are one or two deaths of farmworkers in North Carolina fields, usually cases of dehydration and heatstroke that occur after a worker has put in many days or weeks of long hours during hot weather.[9]

H2A in Practice: When Your Boss Doubles as Immigration Officer

Leroy Dunn of the NCGA touts his H2A program as a humanitarian alternative to unscrupulous labor brokers like the one who enslaved Ramón in the example above. Dunn's colorful brochure and promotional video describe the NCGA, which has a $5 million revenue flow, as a nonprofit organization, although the company has dropped its nonprofit status and pays taxes on income. Dunn claims the NCGA functions "like a union" for the workers, offering "worker protections without labor union dues." At a recent conference, Dunn described himself as "a farmworker advocate." Certainly in some ways the H2A program has created a degree of visibility for farmworker conditions on participating farms. H2A guestworkers are entitled to workers' compensation coverage, free housing, and transportation from Mexico. H2A housing is supposed to be inspected prior to occupation. The 12,000 workers in the state H2A program today occupy more than three-quarters of all inspected housing in the state.[10]

Now the NCGA orientations of large groups of H2A workers provide a venue for the state's only bilingual pesticide specialist to give a talk on safety and show workers a video. Unfortunately, his video, which focuses on West Coast crops, contains no information on the agents used in North Carolina agriculture, and the brochures, while translated into Spanish, are highly technical and poorly designed for workers with limited literacy.

Mexican men who wish to work in the program pay an entry fee of up to $500. Many of them take out a loan in Mexico at high interest rates to cover these costs. In return they receive the right to earn up to $350 a week from labor on a North Carolina farm, as well as a free trip home if they stay until the end of their contract. H2A workers are recruited by private firms in Mexican agricultural areas such as Guanajuato and Michoacan. They are bused to the Texas border, where NCGA agents arrange their seasonal visas, then they continue on buses to Vass. They initially arrive in small numbers for the planting season in early spring; in May and June the program hits its busiest season, with huge orientation sessions of up to 400 workers who crowd into the warehouse's open space (there are no seats) to hear talks and receive workplace assignments.

Three sides of the NCGA warehouse are bare metal walls. A large banner in Spanish on one wall reads, "Legal Services Wants to Destroy the H2A Program," and a concession stand in one corner sells tacos. But one wall has been perversely transformed into a sort of Disney World of contract labor. There is a coral-colored stucco facade of a Latin American hacienda. On one side is an altar to the Virgin Mary; on the second story a Mexican blanket hangs over the rails of a wooden balcony from which NCGA staff address the men below. A dry fountain and rustic furniture can be seen in air conditioned offices behind teller-style windows where clerks process workers' documents. After the orientation session the men are trucked to labor camps on the farms where they will work.

Farmers pay $498 to NCGA for each worker provided and an additional $200 for annual membership in the association. Most farmers pay H2A workers using either a piece rate or a set price for a share of production, which is not supposed to fall below an adjusted minimum-wage rate that is slightly higher than the federal minimum—a provision that is intended to prevent guestworkers from routinely outcompeting domestic farmworkers for jobs.

The high costs for obtaining workers through the program have deterred many farmers, and some larger farmers, such as Bob Harris (a pseudonym), who runs a multimillion-dollar farming enterprise in Nash County, have opted out. Instead, Harris now runs his own labor brokerage in collaboration with a private contractor who imports around 600 workers into North Carolina annually.

To find farm labor camps for the first time, I usually have had to ride with farmworker advocates or service workers. We try to avoid confronting farmers or crew leaders, who often object to visitors. Many camps are hidden down long dirt roads marked with "No Trespassing" signs. Many workers in these camps know only the first name of the farmer or of the crew leader. Some pay weekly sums to camp managers for meals, but in many H2A camps each worker buys supplies on weekend trips to town and cooks for himself in a common kitchen.

The rapid growth of the H2A program in North Carolina, which added about 2,000 new imported laborers to its work orders annually during the 1990s, has been subject to very little state or federal oversight. Despite dozens of reports from workers of abuses, ranging from low pay to long hours and poor treatment, few are willing to speak out for fear of deportation and being blacklisted by the NCGA.[11]

In 2002 the North Carolina Department of Labor investigated a foreman from a Lenoir County farm accused of practicing pay irregularities, forcing a crew to put in a fourteen-hour day, and ignoring a worker who became ill. Farmworker advocates criticize the NCGA for only rarely dropping a grower with a record of abuses from eligibility for H2A workers.

I encountered another labor dispute on an H2A camp in Greene County shortly after the floods from the hurricanes of September 1999. This camp was completely flooded, and neighbors in rowboats rescued workers as the waters rose. They spent several days in a Red Cross shelter until the farmer went looking for his workforce to salvage what was left of his sweet potato harvest. Already angry from what they had endured and the farmer's failure to show any interest in their situation, the workers became dismayed after beginning work in the waterlogged fields. About half the sweet potatoes they dug up were rotten. Under the piecework system, they were being paid 35 cents per bucket for the good potatoes and nothing at all for the rotten ones. They held a short work stoppage (*paro*) and complained to the farmer that their pay was working out to less than half the minimum wage. When he did not offer any increase, the workers called the NCGA office to complain. In interviews a few days after this incident, they insisted that the NCGA representative told them to take what the farmer offered if they wanted work. Given the option of a complaint with Legal Services, the workers declined, citing fear of "the consequences." Asked about the incident later, Leroy Dunn claimed he could find no record of the complaint from that farm.

A few weeks later, at a press conference called about the farmwork situation during the floods, North Carolina Legal Services lawyers played two tape recordings from their phone machines in which H2A workers at different camps who had filed complaints about abuses said they had been harassed by other workers who feared NCGA retaliation and wanted to withdraw the complaints. Here is a transcription of one of the recordings:

Hello, we're calling from Camp. . . . Some of you from Legal Services were here with us, and we made a complaint against the [company] about the bad living conditions. Unfortunately, later on, our companions started trouble with us and almost hit us. Due to the fact that other farmworkers (*compañeros*) from Spring Hope got into trouble for making a complaint, . . . our companions demanded that you withhold the complaint or, if not, that you come tomorrow to straighten things out with our companions that don't agree and who don't want to file this complaint for fear that they will lose their jobs or be sent back to Mexico. Good evening.

The fear is well based. Dunn acknowledges keeping a list of workers who fail to complete the H2A contract who are not allowed to return with the program the following year. In any camp the existence of this "blacklist" (*lista negra*) is common knowledge among the workers, who are convinced that they will lose their jobs and be deported if they complain about anything. In interviews, it is the first-timers in the program who are the more fearful ones (and these are usually the majority), while the more outspoken workers are often those who have gained a little experience in prior seasons. The NCGA was sued for blacklisting in 1995 and settled out of court. One worker interviewed during this research claimed in a legal affidavit that he had been fired and blacklisted when he complained about irregularities in pay. In a rare move, the North Carolina Department of Labor recently announced that it was investigating an improper deportation of an H2A worker by a Sampson County grower.

Another way the NCGA selects for highest productivity at least cost is by hiring mostly young men. Almost no women are hired, and a recent survey showed H2A workers to be slightly younger than other migrants (Cravey 2002). In June 1999 an older man told a delegation visiting his camp that he would not return with the H2A program the next year because he was too old. He said that recruiters in his hometown posted a sign reading, "Jobs available for men between ages of 18 and 25 years." Dunn claims the NCGA does not discriminate for reasons of gender or age in hiring.[12]

One of the biggest objections to the NCGA program cited by farmworker advocates and workers is the long contract period. H2A workers are expected to remain on the farms where they are assigned through the first week in November. However, an estimated 75 percent of all farmwork employment ends by mid-September. In October only about 2,000 jobs (mostly in sweet potatoes) remain, and the majority of the NCGA's 12,000 workers are working only part time or are idle. In 1997 the U.S. General Accounting Office found that around 40 percent of H2A workers abandon their H2A farms in search of work in this period. Dunn maintains that the total number of employees who leave is closer to 15 percent. He declines to allow public scrutiny of the program's records, but statistics reported to the North Carolina Agricultural Services office show that typically 25 to 35 percent of H2A workers abandoned their farms early from 1995 through 2002. The year 1999 stood out, with 60 percent of workers abandoning their contracts early due to hurricanes that cut the growing season short (Yeoman 2001; Fann 2003).

In theory workers are compensated for slack periods. A clause in the H2A contract guarantees workers pay for at least three-quarters of their days in the country. Yet interviews reveal that most H2A workers are unaware of this provision. In mid-October 1999 I visited an H2A camp in Duplin County with an FLOC member. We brought a trunkload of donated blankets, since nights had gotten chilly, and in unheated camps the thin coverlets most workers have provide little protection. We found a group of forty workers impatient to find work. A man I will call Pablo told me he had earned about $3,000 since he arrived in July, most of which had been sent home to his family of four in Guanajuato. But he had only worked twelve days in the preceding month and was tired of sitting idle. He said he had never heard of the guarantee that H2A workers would be paid for three-quarters of their time in the country, explaining, "We get up each morning hopeful, ready to work, but many days no one comes. If no one comes by midday, most workers just put on their flip-flops and relax. I'm not sorry I came, because there was no work in Mexico. No way to earn this much money. But I'm disappointed that there's no work, nothing to do. I'm going to think twice before coming back to the United States to work."

In an interview later Dunn said that the only time the NCGA had needed to make the three-quarter guarantee payments was in the aftermath of the September 1999 floods, when the association paid sixty workers (out of 12,000 in the program) extra checks. At the time the NCGA was under scrutiny by the U.S. Department of Labor in Atlanta after a series of unfavorable news reports. Dunn said the NCGA did not usually calculate workers' total hours until they were on the bus returning to Mexico, although he acknowledged that mailing checks to workers in Mexico was not the best approach (several checks had already been returned undelivered).

Invisibilities in the Information Age: How H2A Brokers Avoid Scrutiny

Several analysts note that rhetoric from employers and the state tends to focus on magical marketplace outcomes. For example, some sectors are designated "hyper-competitive" and others are "backwards" (Holland, Nonini, and Lutz in press). Such discourses and related policies enact a "regime of disappear-ance" to erase the poor from public debates and visibility (Goode and Ma-skovsky 2001).

The mechanisms through which these invisibilities are maintained take many forms, from intimidation to oversights and unfunded mandates, often rein-forced through subtle forms of racism and class discrimination. The NCGA re-lationship with North Carolina and federal authorities is a case in point, as there is no single agency accountable for oversight of the H2A program but, rather, a myriad of subdivisions within agencies, which have inadequate bud-gets and lack both the capacity and political will for proper oversight.

Although farmers in the NCGA are supposed to hire domestic workers or migrants with green cards, if they are available, North Carolina agricultural field agents (locally known as ag reps) say they have stopped referring work-ers to H2A farms. One reason, they report, is that domestic workers "don't last more than a day on the job," due to the working conditions and low pay. An-other reason is that the agents feel they are unable to follow up on domestic workers assigned to a farm that also hires guestworkers. One staff member, who is deeply suspicious of Dunn's operation, said, "When we go onto an H2A farm [Dunn] raises hell. Why would he raise hell if he wasn't afraid we'd dis-cover something?"

The NCGA actively warns its workers away from consulting with federally funded Legal Services lawyers, whom Dunn has publicly described as out to destroy his program. In case workers entering the NCGA's warehouse miss the banner disparaging Legal Services, a similar warning not to trust the labor rights lawyers scrolls across a black electronic display in glowing red letters, and a poster details why workers should "avoid being a Legal Services puppet." At an orientation session in March 1999, Dunn's associate Wayne Graham (a pseudonym) told workers a moralistic story in Spanish of how the federally funded Legal Services of Florida put that state's guestworker program out of business by harassing growers with frivolous lawsuits, thereby depriving work-ers of needed jobs. In a July 1999 orientation session, workers who had received Legal Services brochures outlining their civil and labor rights at the border were told to line up and throw the brochures in the trash can as they passed in front of the table handing out the H2A work contracts.[13]

Dunn forbids entry to Legal Services attorneys and FLOC union organizers during worker orientations. After a 1999 *Charlotte Observer* series criticized the NCGA, he further restricted visitors. These policies are troubling because farm-workers—lacking transportation, knowledge of English, unmonitored mail, or even a telephone at most labor camps—face enormous barriers getting information on what rights they are entitled to or contacting outsiders when they need help. This is especially important with the complaint-driven system of state regulations in North Carolina, where the burden falls on farmworkers to report violations.

Some growers count on "No Trespassing" signs and sympathetic local sheriffs to keep unwanted visitors away from workers. I was present when four FLOC union organizers were arrested in August 1998 for holding a meeting with farmworkers at a migrant camp on Rainbow Farms, in Nash County. The magistrate threw the case out, but the intimidation effects remained. Another group I accompanied on a June 2003 visit to a Greene County camp was threatened with arrest after informing the grower of abuses we had documented.

Farmers justify these practices by citing the H2A contract, which waives tenancy rights for farmworkers housed on their property. This effectively denies farmworkers the right to receive visitors at their camps. The Institute of Southern Studies undertook a letter-writing campaign in early 2000 to convince the U.S. Department of Labor to remove this denial of tenancy rights from H2A contracts. When institute representatives visited the Department of Labor in Washington, officials claimed to be shocked by the photos of the NCGA banner attacking Legal Services and agreed to remove one clause denying tenancy rights in the H2A contract, but they left another similar clause untouched, despite appeals by Legal Services attorneys.

"Seeing No Evil": Failed Enforcement of State Regulations

The H2A guestworker program generates a set of unique cultural relations in straddling the line between the public and the private sectors. In some ways the state involvement has institutionalized housing reforms and mitigated extreme forms of exploitation such as indentured servitude. But close study of the role of the state reveals more than purely bureaucratic inefficiencies, where agencies sometimes inadvertently work at cross purposes. Strong political interests shape farm labor policy.

For most of the twentieth century federal and state authorities subsidized private agribusiness by facilitating a steady supply of "super-exploitable" migrant labor. The strategy has worked. Low wages for labor helped explain how North Carolina's ranking for net agricultural income rose to second in the nation at the beginning of the 1990s, even while the state ranked relatively lower —in ninth place—for production expenses.[14] Farms, like meatpacking plants, have discovered that for low-skill jobs for which there is a steady supply of workers, high turnover is preferable to the expense and concessions involved in retaining experienced workers.

While there is constant pressure to streamline those regulations that interfere with profitability, there is a remarkable tolerance for bureaucratic irrationality in other areas, such as the lack of state appropriations of funds to enforce regulations, the U.S. Department of Labor's rubber-stamping of H2A work orders (99 percent of which are approved), the two-faced policy on tenancy rights, or loopholes that allow abuses such as the overcrowding that occurs in many North Carolina camps in July after state housing inspectors have come and gone.

Under the existing system, the quasi-legal status of H2A workers and the cultural (or racial and political) complications of these cases have become excuses to ignore complaints. An agency with the political will to enforce the laws for Latino migrants would have put in place the kinds of practices that are routine at Legal Services (and implemented on a shoestring budget), such as hiring bilingual staff, protecting identities of clients during investigations, and employing field staff with some sensitivity to the daily routines and sensibilities of immigrant workers.

More frank criticisms of state policies come from Leroy Dunn, who claims that state inspectors rarely fine non-H2A farmers for their substandard housing. Here Dunn has a point. For example, the 1,328 farms with inspected housing in 1998 accounted for less than a third of the workers (H2A and non-H2A) that the state estimated had migrated here from out of state that year.[15] One former ag rep said it is common practice in the department to sidestep the requirement for inspected housing by registering undocumented migrant workers as day laborers, even though the field agents know the farmer will be renting them housing to make it feasible for workers to work on the farm. Supervisors acknowledge that those practices may take place but insist they are not common. Turf battles with the NCGA aside, the state ag reps are serving the same farmer clients and have little incentive to enforce federal housing regulations if it will anger farmers, who wield political influence in rural areas.

New Forms of Local and Global Solidarity

Despite the problems with H2A, from one perspective state involvement in migrant labor opens possibilities for solidarity. Even in a globalized economy, the ideal of a government that serves the public good remains alive in public consciousness. Unlike the underground economy of migrant crew leaders, state-sanctioned labor brokerage contains mechanisms for public visibilities and intervention.

Changes in policy can have enormous consequences. It was not coinciden-tal that the gains of the UFW in the 1960s came after the public scrutiny that led to the shutdown of the abusive bracero program, which had created a sur-plus of farm labor. In the next seven years organized farmworkers in Califor-nia achieved a 156 percent increase in their wages (Hubner 2000). And intel-lectuals have an important role to play. Importantly, the gains by both the UFW and FLOC in recent decades depended not on strikes (which were easily broken by growers) but on solidarity with students, educators, and religious organi-zations who enforced boycotts and engaged in public education about the hid-den exploitation at the heart of American agriculture.

The campaign has taken some surprising turns. In the spring of 2003 both the NCGA and Mt. Olive Pickle Company spokesmen sat alongside farmworker advocates at a state legislative hearing to speak in favor of extending workers' compensation coverage to non-H2A farmworkers. (The NCGA notes that re-quiring only its member growers to provide the insurance hurts their ability to compete with non-H2A growers.)

Increasingly, efforts to legalize migrant workers are central to the organiz-ing. On May 11, 2002, FLOC members joined delegations from around the coun-try in Washington, D.C., to march for amnesty for immigrant workers. Al-ready some Republicans are taking note of blocs of Latino and union voters in key states that support amnesty and oppose the expansion of the current H2A program (Bacon 2001). Intellectuals should also support calls from organized labor and from the Mexican government for amnesty. Not only the disembod-ied capital of business but also working people should be able to cross the bor-der to earn a living while retaining the dignity and rights of human beings.

Notes

1. North Carolina's Hispanic population grew by 73 percent in this period, accord-ing to statistics from an Urban Institute study cited by Dr. Nolo Martinez, Hispanic liaison, Office of the Governor, North Carolina.

2. During 1999–2000 I received support for research as a Mellon-Sawyer Post-Doctoral Fellow through the University Center for International Studies at the Uni-versity of North Carolina at Chapel Hill. I also have been active since 1999 as a founder and member of the Farmworker Action Team at the Eno River Unitarian Universal-ist Fellowship (ERUUF) in Durham, N.C, which has received funding from the Uni-tarian Universalist Funding Program to help educate North Carolinians about farm-worker issues. In both the Institute for Southern Studies documentary project and the ERUUF project we have worked in collaboration with the National Farm Worker Ministry, the Farm Labor Organizing Committee, Student Action with Farmworkers (at Duke University), and the North Carolina Legal Services Farmworker Division in

organizing camp visits and compiling documentation and information on farmworker issues.

3. According to North Carolina Agricultural Statistics published by the North Carolina Department of Agriculture, 1998.

4. Prior to 1990 the only southern state receiving a large number of foreign guest-workers was Florida.

5. Any farmer who employs fewer than eight workers on a full-time basis in any quarter is exempt from minimum-wage laws, according to the North Carolina Department of Labor Wage and Hour Division.

6. There are no requirements for heating, fans, or air conditioning, which makes much farmworker housing barely habitable during hot summer days or at night during early April or after mid-October, when temperatures can drop to freezing. Nevertheless, the season for some crops and for workers in the H2A program extends into these months. Despite requirements that houses include a stove and beds, I interviewed several workers who described sleeping on floors and cooking over campfires.

7. Despite inspections of H2A housing, in some camps workers report overcrowding in midseason. The state of the housing is a main complaint cited by workers in interviews; old, moldy mattresses and disgusting bathrooms are typical.

8. In interviews workers often expressed concern about being sent into tobacco fields shortly after spraying, or having to harvest leaves behind a truck spraying a ripening agent on the crop. Some claimed they had become sick after getting sprayed.

9. In its statistics the North Carolina Department of Labor does not separate farmworker deaths from other worker deaths, so it is difficult to obtain comprehensive reports on farmworkers who die in the state. According to state employees, many go unreported. The most well-known cases include those of Raymundo Hernández, who died after a possible pesticide poisoning in 1995 (the sick man went missing, and his skeleton turned up months later), and Carmelo Fuentes, who fell into a coma and was pronounced brain dead after a heatstroke in 1998. Both were H2A workers. In 2001 Urbano Ramírez, a non-H2A farmworker on a farm supplying cucumbers to Mt. Olive Pickle Company, died after heatstroke. In the latter two cases, foremen did not call for an ambulance until it was too late. In 2002 a foreman on a Wayne County farm reportedly refused to take a worker with acute appendicitis to the doctor (forcing his coworkers to pool their funds to hire a taxi).

10. Initiation of the H2A program coincided with a reform of the state's housing oversight following several lawsuits over abuses.

11. For further documentation of controversies surrounding the H2A program in North Carolina, see also Ward 1999, Schrader 1999, Glascock 1999, and Yeoman 2001.

12. One news reporter visiting a recruiting station in Mexico has seen such a sign. But certainly some recruiters do hire older men (I have interviewed men in the program as old as fifty), and an anthropologist based in Puebla, Mexico, reports older men are recruited for the H2A in that region (Leigh Binford, personal communication 2002).

13. The speech was videotaped and transcribed by a visitor who attended the orientation session and later shared the material with reporters attending a Legal Services press conference in the fall of 1999. The July incident was witnessed by visitors to that orientation session who reported on it at a meeting of farmworker advocates.

14. The 1992 North Carolina Census of Agriculture reports that hired labor accounted for only 10 percent of production costs, about the same amount spent on fertilizer and chemicals.

15. The North Carolina Department of Labor's Employment Security Commission statistics on the farmworker population, which are on the low end compared with estimates made by other researchers, showed a total of 124,762 farmworkers in 1998, including both migrants and those who live in the state all year. (North Carolina Legal Services put the number at 142,000.) When family members are included in this population, rough estimates by the North Carolina Office of Rural Health placed the total population at 334,000.

References

Bacon, David. 2001. "Braceros or Amnesty." *Dollars and Sense*, November/December, 10–37.

Bartra, Roger. 1993. *Agrarian Structure and Political Power in Mexico*. Baltimore: Johns Hopkins University Press.

Burawoy, Michael. 1976. "The Functions and Reproduction of Migrant Labor: Comparative Material from Southern Africa and the United States." *American Journal of Sociology* 81:1050–87.

Ciesielski, Stephen, John Seed, Juan Ortiz, and J. Metts. 1992. "Intestinal Parasites among North Carolina's Migrant Farmworkers." *American Journal of Public Health* 82:1258–62.

Cleeland, Nancy. 1999. "Immigration Policies Threaten U.S. Growth; Economy: A Decade of Restrictions Has Compounded Severe Labor Shortages in Many Fields." *Los Angeles Times*, April 11.

Collier, George. 1994. *Basta: Land and the Zapatista Rebellion in Chiapas*. Oakland: Food First Books.

Comaroff, Jean, and John Comaroff. 1991. *Of Revelation and Revolution*. Vol. 1, *Christianity, Colonialism, and Consciousness in South Africa*. Chicago: University of Chicago Press.

Cravey, Altha. 2002. "Harvesting Labor in the U.S. South." Manuscript.

Fann, Neal. 2003. "Report on the Overstay Problem of the H2A Program." Sanford Institute for Policy Studies, Duke University. Manuscript.

Glascock, Ned. 1999. "Foreign Labor on Home Soil." *Raleigh New and Observer*, August 29.

Glasmeier, Amy K., and Robin M. Leichenko. 2000. "From Free-Market Rhetoric to Free-Market Reality: The Future of the U.S. South in an Era of Globalization." In Richard Tardanico and Mark Rosenberg, eds., *Poverty or Development? Global Restructuring and Regional Transformations in the U.S. South and the Mexican South*, 19–40. New York: Routledge.

Gledhill, John. 1991. *Casi Nada: A Study of Agrarian Reform in the Homeland of Cardenismo*. Austin: University of Texas Press.

———. 1998. "The Mexican Contribution to Restructuring U.S. Capitalism." *Critique of Anthropology* 18, no. 3: 279–96.

Goode, Judith, and Jeff Maskovsky. 2001. Introduction to Judith Goode and Jeff Maskovsky, eds., *The New Poverty Studies*, 1–34. New York: New York University Press.

Gouveia, Lourdes. 1994. "Global Strategies and Local Linkages: The Case of the U.S. Meatpacking Industry." In A. Bonanno et al., eds., *From Columbus to Con-Agra: The Globalization of Agriculture and Food*. University of Kansas Press.

Griffith, David. 2000. "Work and Immigration: Winter Vegetable Production in South Florida." In Richard Tardanico and Mark Rosenberg, eds., *Poverty or Development? Global Restructuring and Regional Transformations in the U.S. South and the Mexican South*, 139–78. New York: Routledge.

Hahamovitch, Cindy. 1999. "The Politics of Labor Scarcity: Expediency and the Birth of the Agricultural 'Guestworkers' Program." *Backgrounder*, Center for Immigration Studies, December, 1–5.

Hall, Bob. 1986. *Who Owns North Carolina? Report of the Landownership Project*, pt. 2. Durham, N.C.: Institute for Southern Studies.

Heyman, Josiah McC. 1998. "State Effects on Labor Exploitation." *Critique of Anthropology* 18, no. 2: 157–80.

Holland, Dorothy, Donald M. Nonini, and Catherine Lutz. In press. "Social Landscapes of North Carolina, the South, and America as the Century Opens." Chapter 2 of D. Holland, D. Nonini, C. Lutz, L. Bartlett, M. Frederick, T. Guldbrandsen, and E. Murillo, *If This Is Democracy: Public Interests and Private Politics in a Neoliberal Age*. New York: New York University Press.

Hubner, John. 2000. "Farm Workers Face Hard Times; Middlemen Maximize Profits by Paying as Little as Possible." *San Jose Mercury News*, July 7.

Martin, Philip. 1999. "California's Farm Labor Market and Immigration Reform." In B. Lindsay Lowell, ed., *Foreign Temporary Workers in America*, chap. 8. Westport, Conn.: Quorum Books.

Meillassoux, Claude. 1981. *Maidens, Meal, and Money: Capitalism and the Domestic Community*. Cambridge: Cambridge University Press.

Otero, Gerardo. 1996. *Neoliberalism Revisited: Economic Restructuring and Mexico's Political Future*. Boulder, Colo.: Westview.

Raghaven, Chakravarthi. 2000. "Mexico: NAFTA Corn Liberalization Fails Farmers, Environment." *South-North Development Monitor (SUNS)*. Distributed through Third World Network. Retrieved from ‹www.twnside.org.sg.›.

Runsten, David, and Sandra Archibald. 1992. "Technology and Labor-Intensive Agriculture: Competition between Mexico and the United States." In Jorge Bustamante, Clark Reynolds, and Raul Hinojosa Ojeda, eds., *U.S.-Mexico Relations: Labor Market Interdependence*, 449–76. Palo Alto: Stanford University Press.

Sassen, Saskia. 1998. "America's Immigration 'Problem.'" In *Globalization and Its Discontents*, 31–55. New York: New Press.

Schrader, Esther. 1999. "Fielding a Legal Team of Workers." *Los Angeles Times*, August 26.

Scott, James C. 1985. *Weapons of the Weak: Everyday Forms of Peasant Resistance*. New Haven: Yale University Press.

Skaggs, Sheryl, and Donald Tomaskovic-Devey. 1999. "Increased Latino Employment in North Carolina: Ethnic Displacement or Succession Processes?"
Manuscript.

Smith-Nonini, Sandy. 1999. *Uprooting Injustice: A Report on Working Conditions for
North Carolina Farmworkers and the Farm Labor Organizing Committee's Mt. Olive
Initiative*. Durham, N.C.: Institute for Southern Studies.

Tardanico, Richard. 2000. "Conclusion: Poverty or Development?" In Richard Tardanico and Mark Rosenberg, eds., *Poverty or Development? Global Restructuring
and Regional Transformations in the U.S. South and the Mexican South*, 255–80.
New York: Routledge.

U.S. Department of Labor. 2002. Bureau of Labor Statistics. Retrieved from
⟨http://www.bls.gov/⟩.

Ward, Leah Beth. 1999. "Desperate Harvest: N.C. Growers' Trade in Foreign Farm
Workers Draws Scrutiny." *Charlotte Observer*, October 31.

Wood, Philip. 1986. *Southern Capitalism: The Political Economy of North Carolina,
1880–1980*. Durham, N.C.: Duke University Press.

Wright, Gavin. 1996. *Old South, New South: Revolutions in the Southern Economy
since the Civil War*. Baton Rouge: Louisiana State University Press.

Yeoman, Barry. 2001. "Silence in the Fields." *Mother Jones*, January/February. Retrieved from ⟨http://www.motherjones.com/mother-jones/JF01/farm.html⟩.

Part Two

Global/Local Conjunctions

Thaddeus Countway Guldbrandsen

Entrepreneurial Governance in the Transnational South

The Case of Durham, North Carolina

The story of Durham, North Carolina, resonates with the story of many "second tier cities" in the United States that have been redefined by late twentieth-century political economic transformations (Markusen, Lee, and DiGiovanna 1999). Durham's trajectory resembles most closely that of those cities in the American South whose economic competitive advantage was built partly on the lasting legacy of some aspects of their southernness, including low property values and low labor costs, as well as on massive public investment in universities, roads, telecommunications, and other infrastructure. It is thus useful to compare Durham and the Research Triangle region to the cities that many corporate leaders considered when they looked at Durham as a potential city to which to relocate operations. Athens, Austin, Dallas, Lexington, Louisville, Memphis, Richmond, and the Research Triangle were all places with good "business climates," which included not only cheap land and labor but also a highly educated sector of the population and other benefits associated with university towns.

Once known as the City of Tobacco or Bull City, Durham officially changed its nickname in 1988 to the City of Medicine to reflect its new face and the fact that one in three of its residents works in medicine or a related field.[1] Throughout the 1990s Durham and the broader Research Triangle area of North Carolina had one of the fastest-growing economies in the United States, and it was one of the centers of the late twentieth-century Sunbelt Boom. A medium-sized city of nearly 200,000 amidst a region of 1 million inhabitants, Durham provides a useful case study of the impact of political economic changes that redefined the urban South. The move from an agricultural and industrial economy toward a high-tech and service-oriented economy and a reorientation toward refashioned global markets is only part of the story of the Research Triangle in the 1990s. Equally important to daily life in the region are the reorganization of the built environment and shifts in systems of governance, which developed alongside economic shifts.

With its strong orientation toward transnational capital and global markets, high technology, and a booming real estate market, Durham and the Research Triangle embodied the economic prosperity so celebrated in the late 1990s. However, at the same time, the city's persistent rift between rich and poor and its areas of squalid living conditions and outright despair gave a view of the mixed fortunes of postindustrial America. Shifts toward flexible, postindustrial, and high-technological economic organization were associated with unprecedented prosperity for some people, while many others were structurally excluded from the promise of "the new economy." Per capita income had risen significantly in the second half of the twentieth century. However, this overall rise in incomes did not seem to mitigate economic inequality or alleviate poverty. So while Durham had one of the highest per capita incomes in the state, it also had one of the highest disparities between rich and poor. African Americans tended to be affected by poverty more than whites did, and the wealthiest people in Durham still tended to be white. This would seem to suggest the persistence or intensification of factors that privilege those with wealth and power at the expense of those who are, by comparison, less privileged.

At the time of my research, entry-level service-sector (such as fast food and janitorial services) jobs had become prolific, but wages in those jobs were considerably lower than in the industrial jobs of the past.[2] This affected Durhamites of all genders and racial/ethnic affiliations and helped reconfigure Durham's class structure and economic opportunities.

Gender relations in Durham had been refashioned since the 1970s. Women had taken more powerful positions in the new dominant fields of research and development, real estate, finance, education, and medicine and had put themselves at the center of economic life in Durham as well as taking low-end service-sector jobs. Women had far greater representation in government and the nonprofit sector than was the case a decade earlier. However, as I show elsewhere (Guldbrandsen 2001, 118–47, 172–80), men tended to dominate the market-oriented partnerships and economic development, which were notably more influential than female-dominated social service work. In short, there was a mixed but patterned set of opportunities for men and women in that women were more visibly active as wage earners and community leaders, but in general, substantial barriers to political equality persisted in Durham in the late 1990s.

Closely tied to other economic and political changes, that emergent social order can be summarized in the following ways: A new professional class of people associated with Research Triangle Park (RTP), Duke University Medical Center, and the high-end service economy had moved into the center of economic, political, and social life in Durham, replacing a previous generation of tobacconists, textile capitalists, and their affiliates. As racial inequality persisted and had become, in some ways, more pronounced, race relations in Durham had been reconfigured. Thirty years earlier the black middle class was partly defined by constraints and opportunities of the legacy of Jim Crow laws and conventions. In the late 1990s, middle-class African Americans worked in high-tech firms, owned their own small businesses that served firms in RTP, and worked in long-established professional positions as preachers, teachers, attorneys, accountants, and small business owners. More and more black business leaders were joining the chamber of commerce and allying with the dominant business leadership, while the once-thriving Business and Professional Chain (the "black chamber of commerce" in Durham) was diminished in its importance, in comparison with its Jim Crow heyday. Whereas black professionals of previous generations lived in Hayti or the area around North Carolina Central University, fair housing laws had facilitated greater integration of suburban neighborhoods. As a result, affluent African Americans had left black neighborhoods for newer houses in more affluent subdivisions such as Hope Valley, near RTP. This contributed to greater class divisions among black Durhamites, who no longer attended segregated neighborhood schools or relied on racially segregated businesses.

With the integration of black and white professionals in suburban neighborhoods and workplaces and the influx of new immigrant populations (see Kurotani's and Subramanian's contributions to this volume), sometimes racial boundaries appeared to be no longer a problem. However, poorer black Durhamites were concentrated in central city neighborhoods or out-of-the-way rural areas, and poverty among African Americans was as extreme as ever. With significant high school dropout rates, many black Durhamites were not faring well under the city's late twentieth-century economic restructuring. The situation became truly desperate for a great many people who lacked relevant skills to make a living in a time of rising costs and declining resources in poorer neighborhoods.

This reconfiguration was creating two tiers of service-sector employment: affluent professionals and a class of people who served them. That part of the story was fairly well known. However, the implications of the growing divide between rich and poor extended beyond purely economic concerns and had important ramifications for governance and the possibilities of democracy.

Public-Private Governance

Durham used to be a place where a small group of corporate leaders had enormous influence and a sense of paternalism for the city and some of its inhabitants that is now difficult to grasp fully. It was a place where, in the name of progress, federal agencies along with local leaders demolished large sections of the city, including the famous Hayti African American business district and adjacent residential zone, in the hopes of constructing an efficient urban freeway and to make way for modern buildings. The unfinished project of post–World War II urban renewal in Durham left piles of rubble, weedy lots, and other visible scars on the urban landscape; it also left bad feelings, distrust, and scars of civic alienation among many Durham residents, especially African Americans. Out of the cauldron of political protest of the 1960s, 1970s, and early 1980s an emergent regime of governance characterized by public-private partnership and entrepreneurialism took hold. It was still a system characterized by political exclusion and the privilege of relatively elite interests, even if the operations of exclusion and privilege were somewhat harder to discern.

Among the many political changes that had occurred at the end of the twentieth century to alter the conditions of local politics in Durham, the American South, the United States, and around the globe was the growth of the nonprofit sector and the increasing partnership between government, private entities, and other nongovernmental organizations. In connection with decreasing federal funds earmarked specifically for cities and increasing availability of federal moneys for nongovernmental entities, the nonprofit sector had become especially important to political relations in American cities. At every level of government, agencies fundamentally altered the way they interacted with other agencies and the private sector. This resulted in a blurring of the boundary between public and private sectors. Under the rhetoric of "political devolution," local governments were faced with more opportunities for autonomy and more responsibilities to meet the needs of the populace. At the same time, prevailing sentiments of fiscal conservatism made it difficult to fund these new "opportunities," so the city and county governments of cities such as Durham had, in effect, outsourced these new opportunities to the private and nonprofit sector.

Some of the most important political work in Durham—in terms of governing the city, providing services, planning the future, allocating public resources, and defining public good—was not necessarily managed by public (government) institutions or defined as political. Instead, when nonprofit organizations did the work of government, their efforts tended to be construed as voluntary or philanthropic activity. When government agencies outsourced work to private for-profit organizations, it was construed as good business. In either case, such public work was not construed as political per se.

In order to illustrate the impact of political restructuring and the importance of nongovernmental organizations in local governance, this essay focuses on one of the several nonprofit organizations that I studied in the late

1990s. It was an organization that acted as a quasi-governmental organization and collaborated in numerous public-private partnerships oriented toward urban development in Durham. The case shows how government reorganization and new forms of activism offered a range of possibilities available to residents of the city. However, capitalizing on these opportunities took significant time, resources, and knowledge. Ultimately, political restructuring privileged economic development interests, displaced social justice programs, and had some antidemocratic tendencies.

A Municipal Entrepreneur: Community Development Ventures

Frank Valek was the chief executive officer of Community Development Ventures (CDV), a nonprofit organization that was devoted to urban development in central Durham and operated through a set of overlapping public-private partnerships.[3] One of CDV's primary responsibilities was to help other people, particularly investors, implement their visions for particular properties or entire sections of the center city. I examine CDV and Valek here because CDV was successful, and it provides a model for understanding how public-private partnerships work. In fact, under Valek's tutelage other partnerships and non-profit organizations prospered by emulating CDV's organizational strategies. While CDV was not representative of nonprofit organizations in Durham, other cities throughout the United States had similar urban development organizations. Lastly, the work of CDV represents the possibilities for, and challenges to, local democracy posed by public-private partnership and nongovernmental organizations. Valek was good at what he did, and CDV has been relatively successful in achieving its goals, but I want to problematize the work of CDV and the conditions that made its approach possible and intelligible, though not utterly predetermined.

Early in my field research, I met with Valek in order to learn more about urban development in Durham and CDV's vision for how to develop the urban core. When I asked Valek to explain the details of CDV's vision for future urban development in Durham, he rose from his chair, stepped over a dozen or so manila folders of "work-in-progress," and indicated some very general plans as he drew circles around sections of town depicted on a laminated four-foot Planimetrics map of Durham fastened to the wall.

Well, there are basically five parts of downtown. [1] Within the loop is the office center where banks and institutions are located; I don't think we're likely to see any retail in there. [2] There's the Inner Village area that will probably be the biggest mixed-use area. [3] There is the Brightleaf area, which has retail, restaurants, and entertainment. Increasingly that is being considered [the center] of downtown. . . . Brightleaf is going to continue growing. [4] There's the Liggett and Myers [cigarette factory] area that will probably be mixed use, but you might see a major investor come in and do a lot with that property. We really don't know what is going to happen with that. . . . [5] Then there is the Ballpark area, which will probably have some retail right next to the Ballpark. Then the rest, anything can happen. We've already planned some office space, but we don't know what will happen with the American Tobacco buildings. . . . This is all dependent on private interests and what they want to do with the properties. This is what we envision for the best-case scenario.

One point to be made about this five-part vision pertains to the notable lack of industrial development or opportunities for blue-collar employment with livable wages and the predominance of service or consumer-oriented development. In fact, later in the conversation Valek explained the need to be selective about the kind of development that does take place. He noted the undesirability of the potential development of new warehouses or adult entertainment venues. "Mixed-use," articulated as the most desirable kind of development, in its ideal form was imagined as a mix of upscale residential development (e.g., loft apartments) along with professional offices, boutiques, cafés, restaurants, and entertainment venues. (The Brightleaf Square area—on the western edge of downtown, not in the geographical center—was a good example of this.) So it was not, as Valek said, "all dependent on private interests and what they want to do with the properties" but, rather, a process of encouraging certain kinds of investment while discouraging others.

The more significant issue to explore regarding this ethnographic encounter pertains to the basis of CDV's and Valek's authority and ability to influence urban development, particularly since CDV's plan for downtown coincided with, if not defined, the dominant vision for downtown revitalization in Durham in the 1990s. This raises a set of questions that need to be considered within the context of broader political trends of the last thirty years of the twentieth century. When Valek said, "*We* really don't know what is going to happen" or "*We've* already planned some office space, but *we* don't know what will happen," who was being invoked by the reference to *we*? How was that *we* connected to other institutions and the broader community? And what was the basis of their authority and influence?

Durham's experimentation with governance needs to be considered within the context of America's long-standing tradition of economic liberalism and the propensity of the U.S. government to cater to the desires of private enterprise above other goals. These tendencies can be summed up with the term "privatism." (Neoliberalism is a recent manifestation of privatism.) Urban sociologist Gregory Squires suggests that the central ideology of privatism is that the public sector should play a supporting role to private interest in an attempt to enable capital accumulation in the private sector. Public-private partnerships are a way in which new relations between private capital and state agencies are managed in an age of flexible accumulations. Although they may seem to be new innovations, they are more accurately new names for old relationships between the two sectors. Indeed, neither privatism nor public-private partnerships were new ideas in Durham but were amplified as part of a new schema for managing political processes that developed in relationship to a changing political terrain and material shifts in Durham's urban landscape (Squires 1989; Harrison and Bluestone 1988).

Public-private partnerships and the work of some nonprofit organizations are often cited as innovative ways to solve the social problems where an inefficient government has failed. Harrison and Bluestone, scholars of political economy and urban planning, take issue with such sentiments and offer these insights for making sense of the kinds of partnerships in which CDV is involved:

> Leaders may call these deals "public-private partnerships" and attempt to fold them under the ideological umbrella of laissez-faire. But they must be seen for what they are: the reallocation of public resources to fit a new agenda. That agenda is no longer redistribution, or even economic growth as conventionally defined. Rather, that agenda entails nothing less than the restructuring of the relations of production and the balance of power in the American economy. In the pursuit of these dubious goals, the public sector continues to play a crucial role. (1988, 107–8)

Elsewhere Bluestone and Harrison (1982) describe the trend of increasing use of subsidies, reduced taxes, and other incentives to support private investment, particularly in regard to "speculative ventures" in real estate development and other service-sector economic activity (Harrison and Bluestone 1988). So it is not simply a matter of economy becoming restructured or the service sector "just happening." Following from the work of scholars like Bluestone and Harrison is an understanding that economic restructuring (i.e., the shift from an industrial to a postindustrial economy) is largely a product of public policy and activist projects and *not* simply a product of the "invisible hand" of "the market."

Changes in federal public policy are an understated force structuring urban development and the nature of local democratic engagement. The past thirty years of changes in federal urban policies have had profound effects on every aspect of urban life, and this was visible in Durham. Magit Mayer summarizes the redefined relationship between the federal government and local actors by arguing that the role of the municipality "has changed from being the local arm of the welfare state to acting as the catalyst of processes of innovation and cooperation, which it seeks to steer in the direction of improving the city's (or community's) economic and social situation" (Mayer 1994b, 326).

Building on this rough conceptual framework, the U.S. urban policy can be summarized as a long, steady increase in federal funding for urban infrastructure and services until about 1978, when greater market-oriented "experimentation" became increasingly important. The late 1960s and early 1970s backlash against large-scale, federally funded urban renewal projects applied political pressure to rethink the way that urban development would be funded and executed. After the dismantling of urban renewal programs in the early 1970s, municipalities lost much of their federal support when the Nixon administration put in motion policy changes that would revitalize the commitment to privatism and leave the fate of cities in doubt. In 1974, federal agencies redefined urban policy with such initiatives as the Community Development Block Grant, which wrested funds from federal agencies and made them more flexible and more accessible to local actors. These policy changes continued with the Carter administration, which instituted Urban Development Action Grants, another form of block grants (Frieden and Sagalyn 1989). Throughout the 1970s the public-private sector was considered an important part of federal urban policy recommendations in an attempt to find alternatives to letting the government bureaucracy deal with problems (U.S. Department of Housing and Urban Development 1978). With these shifts in policy, public-private partnerships became a more important part of urban development that has become even more pronounced in recent years. Partnerships promised financial returns with shared risk and profits. In return, businesses and other nongovernmental organizations sought direct relationships to federal dollars, circumventing local governments and becoming important to local municipal politics in new ways. In the Reagan era, the urban policy of the 1980s favored "market solutions" to urban development and social problems even more (Frieden and Sagalyn 1989). According to Robertson and Judd,

> Overall spending dropped from $6.1 billion in fiscal year 1981 to $5.2 billion in fiscal year 1984. The $5.2 billion spent for the fiscal year 1984–1985 amounted to a decline of almost 20 percent when corrected for inflation. By

the 1989 budget year, money for urban programs was cut to $4.4 billion—a further reduction of about 40 percent when effects of inflation are considered.

Nearly all subsidies for the construction of public housing were ended. . . . Urban mass transit grants were reduced 28 percent from 1981–1983 and were cut another 20 percent by 1986. CETA [Comprehensive Employment and Training Act] funds were eliminated after 1983. (Robertson and Judd 1989, 314, cited in Gottdeiner 1994, 325)

This decline in urban funding and changes in the way that public resources are allocated left cities to fend for themselves in providing municipal services. Cities had concentrated their remaining resources in economic development (Gottdeiner 1994, 326). However, promoting economic development was an especially daunting task in the competitive environment of trying to attract increasingly mobile capital. When cities attempted to attract outside investment (through plant relocations, for example), place was pitted against place in a process that tends to favor low wages, low costs, low taxes, and decline in human and municipal services in order to offer various subsidies for business development—all factors that favored Sunbelt cities like Durham.

With the rollback of social welfare initiatives, it became apparent that the emphasis on privatism in the logic of urban development undermined the promotion of social justice. To borrow an idea from Bruce Shulman, a historian of the South, economic development strategies (when they are successful) tend to enrich places but not people. Increases in investment, even when per capita income increased, did not necessarily translate into benefits for local residents.

As a result, greater emphasis on privatism through partnership and greater commitment to private and nongovernment interest changed urban development and the possibilities for democratic civic engagement. These conditions of political restructuring made organizations like CDV possible and influential. While Frank Valek often complained that city government's inefficiency was one of his greatest obstacles to accomplishing his work, CDV's work was predicated on the relative weakness of local government.

Valek illustrated this in the following way: "It is hard to get things done in Durham because the city is not effective. If there is a dead tree downtown, you have to get four agencies to do anything about a tree box. So we just go and cut the tree down. . . . City government is just too complicated. There is too much dead wood."

Valek proposed that city government could be more streamlined by having a "point person" or an agency that serves as a "one-stop shopping center" for business leaders who want to work with the city on economic development.

He said, "We want to make [the county economic development officer] in charge of city deals too. He takes care of deals with the county, and we would like to see that all consolidated." In fact, the city did institute a new office for economic development in 1998. This had the effect of strengthening the position of nongovernmental interests by making city government more responsive to private interests and nongovernmental organizations.

During our conversation, Valek drew attention to a municipal government that lacked resources to accomplish its ever-expanding demands, as well as the process in which agents of public-private partnership circumvented government procedures. This did not, however, imply that such circumvention was unsanctioned by city government. In fact, CDV and other organizations were authorized to act as quasi-governmental institutions, which was highlighted by the fact that the loose collaboration among nonprofit organizations concerned with the downtown area defined the vision for future urban development.

In an interview with me, the city manager confirmed this. When I asked him about visions for downtown redevelopment, he suggested that I talk with Valek, explaining that Valek had a clearer idea of what was happening in the urban core. However, not everyone in city government—and certainly not all of the city councillors—consented to the centrality of nongovernmental organizations in acting as a catalyst of urban redevelopment, as was apparent on many occasions.

Valek himself described an ongoing conflict with one city councillor. He claimed, "Council makes it difficult for revitalization. They say they are for it, but . . . [there is one city council member who] always asks, 'What does this do for Northeast Central Durham?'"[4]

Thus there was a perception, and indeed a reality, that the privatist tendencies of government and the strength of nongovernmental organizations did not serve all residents of the city in the same way and neglected entire neighborhoods. Northeast Central Durham, for example, was not considered to be in the domain of CDV, even though it was as close to the central business district as Brightleaf Square. That neighborhood had its own community associations and nonprofit organizations, however ineffective and ill-equipped they may have been at promoting community improvement.

If CDV was authorized to act on behalf of the public good but was not answerable to all residents of Durham, to whom was CDV accountable? The question of accountability can be answered in three parts. First, the organization's operating budget was funded with public monies (from both city and county government) as well as through private donations, all of which varied from year to year. That funding was contingent on the success and agreeability of the organization's work. This was an era of government that has been defined as "empowering rather than serving" (Osborne and Gaebler 1992); some oversight came from government and elected officials, but CDV was inspired largely by its relationship to other nongovernmental organizations and private interests (which also had strong influence in city and county government).

Second, the organizational structure of CDV was in place, in part, to liaise with other community members. CDV, like many nonprofit organizations, was comprised of a board of directors, an executive board, and a chairperson who oversees the operating staff (including Valek). Though the board was not exclusive, it was almost entirely comprised of business leaders and prominent members of related nonprofit organizations (with ex officio members from city and county government). The chairperson received input from the community and acted on behalf of the board to direct Valek and the other CDV staff.

Third, since CDV was a 501(c)(3) tax-exempt organization, its actions were monitored by the Internal Revenue Service, which sets limits on how nonprofit revenues may be used. For example, the revenue service stipulated that nonprofit organizations should not operate for the financial benefit of individual stakeholders and that revenues may not be used for certain kinds of political lobbying (U.S. Code 1996). Both of these stipulations, however, are ambiguous and not strictly adhered to. In the matter of financial benefit, some of the board members of CDV were property owners in the downtown area, bankers, and real estate agents. It was precisely the intent of CDV to benefit these interests. As far as lobbying was concerned, advocating for certain kinds of development in the central city was another stated goal of CDV. Yet these actions were often seen as somehow being apolitical, in that CDV was trying to be sensitive to market demands or to operate successfully within the market. Here, "the market" is construed as being outside the realm of politics.

This highlights the way that, under privatist regimes, economic interests were often taken for granted as an integral part of the public good, an understanding that rendered opposing perspectives political as it elevated business interests to a supercitizen status (Guldbrandsen and Holland 2001). While Frank Valek benefited from a logic that defined economic development as an unquestioned good, his less influential counterparts in Northeast Central Durham, for example, were typically construed as special interests, political, and lacking the ability to partner with city government or other organizations. Social justice and human service organizations had the same political status and, as such, were not able to operate as freely or raise funds as effectively as economic development organizations.

Furthermore, operating a successful nongovernmental organization required some expertise in addition to financial and symbolic resources. What little oversight that was in place to monitor the actions of nongovernmental organizations was a disproportionately onerous burden for some small organizations. Maintaining an organization took time, some business acumen, and/or administrative resources. That put many social justice and human service organizations at a further disadvantage in relation to economic development organizations.

Privatism and political restructuring also privileged people and organizations that had clearly stated goals and measurable outcomes. In numerous meetings of different nongovernmental organizations, this was often stated in terms of the difference between being process-oriented and product-oriented. Whereas some people with whom I did research articulated a commitment to open, deliberative dialogue, others (like Valek) criticized them for taking too much time and energy with long, drawn-out debate. Conversely, product-oriented people (like Valek) favored a more no-nonsense style of decision making that expediently brought measurable outcomes. As Valek put it, "So we focus on the questions, What's the problem and how do we solve the problem?" Unlike the process-oriented people, who were willing to spend time questioning the broader implications of whether some goal, project, or investment should be valued, for Valek, value was assumed and pursued in a no-nonsense manner, even at the expense of democratic deliberation.

Entrepreneurial Governance by Partnership

To better understand the arrangement of urban governance that structured political relations in Durham, this section will further conceptualize the terrain of what I call entrepreneurial governance by partnership. The above case study suggests that there was no clear division between government and nongovernmental agents (e.g., nonprofit organizations, community development corporations, public-private partnerships, and quasi-governmental bodies), which were increasingly called upon to do the work of government (use public resources and act on behalf of the public good). Rather, there seemed to be a continuum between official government agencies and emergent decentralized agents. At one end of the spectrum, centralized, bureaucratic agencies were subject to a relatively high degree of public oversight, as they were (at least theoretically) accountable to a broad group of stakeholders. These agencies had many rules and regulations that had developed over years to hold those agencies accountable to the people they were supposed to serve. At the other end of the spectrum, decentralized, nongovernmental agents, such as CDV, were more experimental and maintained greater autonomy from public oversight. As a result, community-based organizations, nonprofit organizations, and to a lesser extent public-private partnerships were able to work more expediently, less encumbered by governmental red tape.

In considering the intent of different agencies, there was another spectrum that ranges between an extreme market orientation (perhaps self-interest or private interest) and the extreme social service orientation (public interest). Market orientation is akin to the set of theories and practices that fit within the realm of neoliberalism (Barry, Osborne, and Rose 1996; Navarro 2000) and hold closely to the long-standing tradition of privatism (Squires 1989). A stronger social services orientation is comprised of a kind of communitarianism, which relies on such mechanisms as redistribution of wealth, public funding, and official government oversight of services. I do not mean to imply that market-oriented agencies were not concerned with communitarian issues. In fact, most neoliberal actors held strong beliefs that market orientation was in the best interest of the community and the best way to achieve social justice.

An important part of this system was that much of the work that was done on behalf of the public was considered to be voluntaristic and apolitical. As such, voluntarism often was not held to the same level of scrutiny as the work of government agents, though both forms of work were important to the governance of the city and drew on public resources. In short, an emergent form of governance, connected to global economic transformation, altered the terms of local governance in Durham and elsewhere in the United States at the end of the twentieth century. New governmental partnerships with private and nonprofit entities have blurred boundaries between the state, the market, and civil society and effectively redefined government and the possibilities for political engagement. I term this arrangement entrepreneurial governance by partnership.

This political restructuring appears to offer new possibilities for different people to participate in guiding the future of their communities. However, the same mechanisms that grant possibilities for proactive engagement simultaneously undermine the promise of democratic debate and tap resources from social justice initiatives. With increasing emphasis on economic development and the concentration of resources for those ends, economic interests have become ever more central to local governance, subordinating the perspectives of those who are more concerned with social justice and vital local democracy.

Experimentation with governance has continued into the twenty-first century and has become even more entrepreneurial. Cities in the American South, such as Durham, exemplify this trend. Between 1997 and 2004, Durham continued on its path of political and economic transformation. At the federal level, the George W. Bush administration has championed the cause of entrepreneurial governance, and the work of nonprofit organizations has been the centerpiece of Bush's vision for political reform. If current political trends continue, the case of Durham and the Research Triangle will provide ever more relevant insights for understanding governance throughout the transnational South and the United States. The late 1990s were a time of relative economic prosperity. In times of economic hardship the challenges that entrepreneurial governance poses to social and political equality may become even more pronounced.

Notes

1. By the end of the 1990s, the largest private sector employers in Durham were medical, pharmaceutical, high-technology research and development, and other "service" sector corporations. In 1999 the list of top employers included Duke University Medical Center, International Business Machine (IBM), Duke University, Northern Telecommunications, Glaxo-Wellcome, Duke Health System, Research Triangle Institute, and Labor World (North Carolina Employment Securities Commission 1999). Each of the ten companies employed more than 1,000 people. Labor World was a temporary labor agency. Research Triangle Institute was a consulting firm employing highly educated researchers. Nortel is a telecommunications research, development, and manufacturing firm. Glaxo-Wellcome was a pharmaceutical company. IBM was, of course, a computer company.

2. There is a danger here of reflecting nostalgically on Durham's former textile and tobacco jobs. These jobs were difficult, wages were often low, and racist segregation defined Durham's workforce (Davidson 1996; Hall et al. 1987; Tullos 1989). Clearly, there are differing perspectives on what was lost and what was gained by Durham's economic shift. However, many people (including some people that I knew well) with little formal education were able to make a living in the mills and factories of Durham.

3. Community Development Ventures and Frank Valek are pseudonyms.

4. Northeast Central Durham is a largely underserved and relatively poor part of the city.

References

Amin, Ash, ed. 1994. *Post-Fordism: A Reader*. Cambridge, Mass.: Blackwell.
Barry, Andrew, Thomas Osborne, and Nikolas Rose, eds. 1996. *Foucault and Political Reason: Liberalism, Neo-Liberalism, and Rationalities of Government*. Chicago: University of Chicago Press.
Billings, Dwight B. 1982. "Class Origins of the New South." In Michael Burawoy and Theda Skocpol, eds., *Marxist Inquiries: Studies of Labor, Class, and States*. Chicago: University of Chicago Press.

Bluestone, Barry, and Bennett Harrison. 1982. *The Deindustrialization of America: Plant Closings, Community Abandonment, and the Dismantling of Basic Industry.* New York: Basic Books.

Cartron, Kimberly. 2000. "The Grim Side of North Carolina Economy: Income Inequality and Persistent Poverty." *Newsletter of the North Carolina Budget and Tax Center* 6, no. 4.

Coble, Ran. 1996. "The Nonprofit Sector in North Carolina: Trends and Key Public Policy Challenges." *North Carolina Insight*, 16, no. 4: 66–96.

Conlan, Timothy. 1996. *From New Federalism to Devolution: Twenty-Five Years of Intergovernmental Reform.* Washington, D.C.: Brookings Institute Press.

Davidson, Osha. 1996. *The Best of Enemies: Race and Redemption in the New South.* New York: Scribner.

Fainstein, Susan S., and Dennis R. Judd. 1999. "Global Forces, Local Strategies, and Urban Tourism." In Dennis R. Judd and Susan S. Fainstein, eds., *The Tourist City*, 1–17. New Haven: Yale University Press.

Finger, Bill. 1996. "Making the Transition to a Mixed Economy." *North Carolina Insight* 17, no. 2–3: 4–18.

Frieden, Bernard J., and Lynne B. Sagalyn. 1989. *Downtown, Inc.: How America Rebuilds Cities.* Cambridge, Mass.: MIT Press.

Gottdeiner, Mark. 1994. *The New Urban Sociology.* New York: McGraw Hill.

Guldbrandsen, Thaddeus Countway. 2001. "Bull City Futures: Transformations of Political Action, Inequality, and Public Space in Durham, North Carolina." Ph.D. diss., University of North Carolina at Chapel Hill.

Guldbrandsen, Thaddeus Countway, and Dorothy C. Holland. 2001. "Encounters with the Super-Citizen: Neoliberalism, Environmental Activism, and the American Heritage Rivers Initiative." *Anthropological Quarterly* 74, no. 3: 124–34.

Hall, Jacquelyn Dowd, James Leloudis, Robert Korstad, Mary Murphy, Lu Ann Jones, and Christopher B. Daly. 1987. *Like a Family: The Making of a Southern Cotton Mill World.* Chapel Hill: University of North Carolina Press.

Hall, Peter Dobkin. 1999. "Blurred Boundaries, Hybrids, and Changelings: The Fortunes of Nonprofit Organizations in the Late Twentieth Century." In George E. Marcus, ed., *Critical Anthropology Now: Unexpected Contexts, Shifting Constituencies, Changing Agendas.* 147–202. Santa Fe: School of American Research Press.

———. 2001. "Philanthropy, the Welfare State, and the Transformation of American Public and Private Institutions, 1945–2000." Paper presented at Twenty-First-Century Activism: Governance, Political Action, and the Nonprofit Sector. University of North Carolina at Chapel Hill, March.

Harrison, Bennett, and Barry Bluestone. 1988. *The Great U-Turn: Corporate Restructuring and the Polarizing of America.* New York: Basic Books.

Harrison, Faye. 1995. "The Persistent Power of 'Race' in the Cultural and Political Economy of Racism." *Annual Reviews of Anthropology* 24:27–74.

Hubbard, Phil, and Tim Hall. 1996. "The Entrepreneurial City and the New Urban Politics." In Tim Hall and Phil Hubbard, eds., *The Entrepreneurial City: Geographies of Regime and Representation.* New York: Wiley.

Leitner, Helga. 1990. "Cities in Pursuit of Economic Growth: The Local State as Entrepreneur." *Political Geography Quarterly* 9:146–70.

Logan, John, and Harvey Molotch. 1987. *Urban Fortunes: The Political Economy of Place*. Berkeley: University of California Press.

Luebke, Paul. 1981. "Activists and Asphalt: A Successful Anti-Expressway Movement in a New South City." *Human Organization* 40, no. 3: 256–63.

———. 1998. *Tar Heel Politics 2000*. Chapel Hill: University of North Carolina Press.

Markusen, Ann R., Yong-Sook Lee, and Sean DiGiovanna, eds. 1999. *Second Tier Cities: Rapid Growth beyond the Metropolis*. Minneapolis: University of Minnesota Press.

Mayer, Magit. 1994a. "Politics in the Post-Fordist City." *Socialist Review* 91, no. 1:105–24.

———. 1994b. "Post-Fordist City Politics." In Ash Amin, ed., *Post-Fordism: A Reader*, 316–37. Cambridge, Mass.: Blackwell.

MDC, Inc. 2000. *The State of the South 2000: A Report to the Region and Its Leadership*. Chapel Hill, N.C.: MDC, Inc.

Navarro, Vincente. 2000. *The Political Economy of Social Inequalities: Consequences for Health and Quality of Life*. Amityville, N.Y.: Baywood.

North Carolina Employment Security Commission. 1999. "North Carolina's Largest Employers by County." Retrieved from ⟨http://www.ncesc.com/⟩.

Osbourne, David, and Ted Gaebler. 1992. *Reinventing Government: How the Entrepreneurial Spirit Is Transforming the Public Sector*. Reading, Mass.: Addison-Wesley.

Putnam, Robert. 2000. *Bowling Alone: The Collapse and Revival of American Community*. New York: Simon and Schuster.

Salamon, Lester. 1996. *The Emerging Nonprofit Sector: An Overview*. Johns Hopkins Nonprofit Sector Series 1. New York: Manchester University Press.

Squires, Gregory, ed. 1989. *Unequal Partnerships: The Political Economy of Urban Redevelopment in Postwar America*. New Brunswick, N.J.: Rutgers University Press.

Tullos, Allen. 1989. *Habits of Industry: White Culture and the Transformation of the Carolina Piedmont*. Chapel Hill: University of North Carolina Press.

U.S. Code. 1996. 26 § 501(c)(3).

U.S. Department of Housing and Urban Development. 1978. "The President's National Urban Policy Report." National Urban Policy Report. Washington, D.C.

Zukin, Sharon. 1991. *Landscapes of Power: From Detroit to Disney World*. Berkeley: University of California Press.

Bryan McNeil

Global Forces, Local Worlds
Mountaintop Removal and Appalachian Communities

Though globalization has come to mean many things, I use the term to describe economic and social trends that facilitate and encourage communications and trade across national borders. The growing academic literature on globalization highlights shifting political and economic priorities as distinguishing characteristics of this often vague and elusive topic. Typical discussions of globalization focus on highly mobile production centers and patterns of flexible production and accumulation, as well as the increasing competition between nations and states to attract companies with incentive packages and favorable regulation. The most often cited examples of transnational corporations changing the rules of business in the American and global Souths are the fierce competitions between states to lure assembly pants for BMW (eventually won by South Carolina) and Mercedes (Alabama). Also, manufacturing centers are moving from the United States and other industrialized nations to offshore export-processing zones, particularly the maquiladora region of Mexico as well as regions of Central America and South and Southeast Asia.

Expanding globalization depends on restructuring the social contract between industry, government, labor, and communities in the United States to emphasize efficiency, cost-effectiveness, and mobility across borders. The new configuration relieves industry of its obligations to organized labor, its previous level of investment in the social reproduction of the workforce, and its traditional attachments to particular places and regions (Harvey 1989). Usually mentioned alongside these features is globalization's expanding reach both across the face of the earth and deep into the everyday workings of our lives. Trends identified by globalization theorists,[1] as well as specific cases identified by scholars studying the effects of globalization in the United States (notably Dudley 1994; Dudley 2000; Modell 1998), indicate that as political and economic priorities are rearranged, the cultural legacies of those changes are left to be managed by the communities they affect. Confronted by the local effects of shifting relationships with industry, citizens in many communities are developing new structures and practices that reflect the complex set of interests at stake in negotiations between industry and community.

The contemporary struggle over the future of Appalachian coal mining in the United States provides a good example of the complexity that often accompanies globalization issues. Illustrating the coal industry's participation in the trends associated with globalization and describing the contours of the mining conflict within a specific community creates a picture of tangled environmental, economic, and social goals. Attention to the cultural and community issues that arise from the collision of global forces and local worlds will contribute to a discussion of how the negotiation of these conflicts will define the emerging global era. Efforts to frame and negotiate these issues within the coalfields may provide useful examples for other communities seeking to confront the globalization juggernaut.

Coal Mining and the Global Economy

The southern coalfields of West Virginia are full of communities whose pasts, presents, and potential futures are intimately intertwined with the coal industry. At first glance, West Virginia coal mining may not seem like a typical example of globalization at work. While the examples of transnational capitalism most often discussed involve companies moving their operations to take advantage of cheaper production costs, technologies, or tax incentives, historical and geographical circumstances have made the coal industry highly immobile and forced it to make changes that bring these benefits to the areas where it already operates.

The Coal River region of West Virginia winds south from Charleston through the middle part of the state. Throughout this area, large underground and surface mines operate in one of the state's most productive coalfields. While these mines are independently operated under several apparently local companies, two large corporations own many of the mines and their production capacity. Massey Energy and Arch Coal, Inc., are two of the small handful of companies that dominate the U.S. coal industry. While coal mines have always been affiliated with large corporations, a brief overview of the histories of Massey and Arch gives an indication of how today's mining corporations are involved in corporate restructuring trends associated with global capitalism.[2]

After beginning as a family-owned operation, Massey grew as a regional coal producer for most of the twentieth century. The Fluor Corporation purchased Massey in 1981. A transnational construction and energy giant, Fluor

Corp's other notable subsidiaries included Royal Dutch Shell. While involved in this transnational corporate relationship, Massey's coal operations remained concentrated in central Appalachia. By the time it split with Fluor, Massey had become the nation's fifth largest coal producer. Ostensibly, the company split with Fluor to improve Massey's ability to maneuver in highly competitive coal markets. People familiar with coal industry economics, however, interpreted the move to be in anticipation of large-scale consolidation among coal producers competing for shrinking profits.

Another legacy of Massey's long history is a reputation for nonunion operating practices. The United Mine Workers (UMWA) has tried for decades to organize Massey workers and has, in most cases, failed. Union miners were familiar with Massey's practices based on the company's track record in other West Virginia regions when they protested the opening of Massey's first Coal River mine in the early 1980s. Massey bought several area mines and redesigned the operations. While the first Massey mines were being built, antagonism grew between union miners and the company building the first nonunion mine in the county. Locals tell of armed guards with dogs patrolling the perimeters of the new mines and of Massey bringing nonunion miners from out of town to work in Coal River. Antagonism grew into a large and ultimately destructive union rally.

Union members claim that a large crowd of union men rallied at a business down the road from the mine's main entrance. The crowd, estimated by several consultants to be around 2,000 people, was incited by a fiery speech by area union leader (now UMWA president) Cecil Roberts. After the rally, the group marched to the mine entrance, stormed the two-lane bridge over the river, and destroyed a guard shack and other storage buildings. A management official from the mine corroborates the details of the mayhem, emphasizing property destruction and lost time for the mine. While locals do not seem to recall the outcome of the multimillion-dollar lawsuit that Massey filed against the union, consultants agree that the injunction against the union has been instrumental in allowing Massey to preserve its nonunion workplace in a region once known as a union stronghold.

With operations in Appalachia, Wyoming, and other western states, Arch Coal has become the second largest coal producer in the United States through acquisitions and mergers. Unions and coal opponents alike point out the strange competitive relationships between eastern and western mines. Companies like Arch threaten to close their Appalachian mines, arguing that they cannot compete with the efficient mines in Wyoming and Utah. Many locals believe these threats are designed to reinforce industry power over state and local regulators and policy makers. These two corporations serve as examples of how American coal producers have become integrated into transnational corporate structures and practices of restructuring, buying, and being bought. While mines are operated by local subsidiaries, corporate policy making is often far removed from the regions affected.

While these corporations may resemble other industries that are associated with the global economy, it is notable that the coal industry has not replaced its domestic product with coal from overseas. Geographic and logistical barriers have so far made replacing U.S.-based coal production with overseas mining unfeasible. Coal is heavy, is expensive to transport, and has to be moved in large quantities to be useful. While reduced labor costs and government regulations make mining coal in Venezuela much cheaper than in West Virginia, transporting it to American markets would be very costly. For that matter, due to differences of topography, geography, and population, producing coal in Wyoming costs only 20 to 25 percent as much as in West Virginia, but transportation costs have prevented Wyoming coal from competing in the nation's largest energy markets on the East Coast. Coal, rail, and utility companies are working to develop more efficient transportation from the Wyoming coalfields to the eastern markets using new rail lines as well as new transmission technologies to take advantage of deregulated electrical transmission lines.

Meanwhile, the coal industry has used its powerful influence over Appalachian politics and economics to create conditions in Appalachia that are more amenable to its interests. While coal has had a powerful voice in Appalachia for more than a century, efforts since the end of the last coal boom in the 1970s have attempted to circumscribe the regulations and union presence that were developed during the twentieth century. Since the early 1980s, with the help of favorable state and federal policies, coal companies have created conditions that facilitate the production and shipment of coal in ways that resemble the conditions sought by manufacturing operations overseas. Prominent among these are examples involving political appointments to regulatory agencies, law enforcement initiatives, changes in the role of the union, and environmental regulations.

Politics, the Union, and the Law

In April 2002, subsidiaries of Massey Energy were cited with two illegal water discharges in the span of one week. In the Coal River region, untainted water in an abandoned section of an underground mine blew out the side of a mountain and rushed into the river below. A mine on the border of West Virginia and Kentucky spilled tainted black slurry into a tributary of the Big Sandy River, the same river where another Massey subsidiary spilled more than 250 million gallons of black slurry in October 2000. That same week in April 2002, the Bush administration announced the selection of a Massey vice-president to sit on a federal appeals board for mine safety violations. In addition to the apparent conflict of interest, the selection of regulatory officials from Massey, a company with a litany of rules violations, is seen by many as an open declaration of the administration's allegiance to the coal industry.

Also in 2002, the West Virginia legislature considered a fiercely contested bill to enforce laws regarding weight limits for coal trucks on public roads. While the existing limits ranged from 65,000 to 80,000 pounds, trucks routinely hauled overweight loads, sometimes in excess of 180,000 pounds, fifty tons over the limit. All parties involved, including truck drivers, truck owners, coal shippers and receivers, politicians, and regulators admitted the law was broken on a daily basis. Faced with a public outcry over accidents involving overweight trucks, including eleven fatalities over a period of twenty months, a group of legislators proposed to enforce the existing limits. The coal industry responded with an aggressive public relations campaign, arguing that it could not operate profitably under the law. The industry made a counterproposal to raise the legal limit to 120,000 pounds with a 5 percent tolerance on enforcement. Though the effort to enforce the limits had popular support, the bill died in a finance committee when the chairman refused to bring it to the floor. Governor Bob Wise decided to enforce the existing laws and appointed a task force to study the question; then he called a special session of the legislature to consider the task force's recommendation to raise limits to 120,000 pounds. After the suggestion was narrowly defeated, the governor and industry supporters vowed to revisit the issue in future sessions. Such examples of selecting regulators from the industries to be regulated and extensive legislative efforts to enforce existing laws point to the coal industry's success in working with government to create a "pro-business" environment.

Adding to the industry's control over the business climate is the precipitous decline in union membership. The UMWA was once among the strongest forces in organized labor, but the union's membership and political strength have fallen dramatically in the past two decades. Part of this decline can be attributed to the number of coal jobs that disappeared during the second half of the twentieth century since the introduction of machines in the mining process.[3] Companies have further cut into union membership by offering wages higher than those required by union contracts in exchange for operating a so-called union-free workplace. To make up for the expense, companies eliminate positions (notably safety inspectors required by the union), regularly understaff shifts, reduce employee benefits, and require extensive mandatory overtime (Yarrow 1990). Such practices have made the union virtually nonexistent in many places. Although at one time thousands of Coal River miners were union members, during the summer of 2000 there were only twenty-three active union miners.[4]

The decline in union membership has not only enabled companies to operate over the objections of unions—their former political interlocutors—but also changed the dynamics between companies and the communities within which they operate. Historically, unions have represented miners with respect to community as well as workplace issues. The decline in union membership and political strength means that communities must seek new avenues for pursuing complaints against corporate practices. Emerging trends suggest that community activist organizations are emerging as a front line in a new approach to confronting corporate power.

Coal River

While the Appalachian coal industry has a product that is associated with an older industrial age and does not have highly mobile production centers associated with new economy industries, the forces shaping the coal industry over the past twenty years resemble those that continue to drive global capitalism. The collusion between government and corporations creating ineffective law enforcement illustrated by weight limits and regulatory appointments, weakened unions, and reduced environmental regulations associated with mountaintop removal have altered the experience of living in the communities of southern West Virginia. Many residents, including those who work in the mines, have come to resent what they see as the industry's power over the politics and economics of the region, as well as increasing burdens the community bears as a result of mining activity. In such contexts, the abstract policies of global capitalism become embodied in conflicts between homeowners, parents, workers, and companies.

Because of the extensive amount of land required, many people have been bought out of or forced off their land by coal companies. Entire mountain communities have disappeared in this fashion. In more established towns like Whitesville, once a thriving hub of mining and trade in the Coal River region, significant resistance to mountaintop removal has emerged. Residents complain about the explosions that rattle their homes, damaging foundations and wells, and they attribute the increasing frequency of floods to the vast tracts of treeless and geologically disturbed land in the surrounding mountains. Subtly, however, these complaints have grown to include things like ambient coal dust, road damage from overweight trucks, trains loading at all hours of the night, repeated releases of toxic black sludge into streams, and other nuisances and violations of law. These issues are more general to the mining industry and not exclusive to mountaintop removal. The way citizens include these complaints, blurring the distinction between mountaintop removal and industry practices in general, indicates that mountaintop removal has become symbolic of broader concerns in the community. Mountaintop removal has become, for many people, not just a flagrant disregard for public safety, mountain lifestyles, and landscapes, but a symbol of the industry's political power, greed, and contempt for mountain communities.

One of the organizations that promote this point of view is Coal River Mountain Watch (CRMW). Working with state and regional groups like Ohio Valley Environmental Coalition, West Virginia Highlands Conservancy, and Citizens Coal Council, CRMW raises awareness of coal issues and promotes alternatives to mountaintop removal within its local community. Founded with the help of activists and academics working in the Appalachian Mountains, the group is made up primarily of local residents who have lived in Coal River their entire lives.

Selma King is one such member.[5] Selma grew up in Old Creek Hollow. Old Creek, during Selma's childhood in the 1950s, wound more than ten miles from the main road back into the mountains to a tunnel that led through the mountain to another community on the other side of the ridge. Today, a gate blocks the road a few miles short of the old tunnel. Past the gate on company property, the tunnel sits beneath an enormous valley fill. After moving to Cleveland as a teenager, then to several southern cities after marrying, Selma returned to Old Creek to raise her family. "I just had to come home," she said watching over her toddler grandson as we spoke. Selma was at home during the first of what have become frequent incidents of flooding. One of Selma's neighbors, a woman in her late eighties, swore she had never seen the creek rise out of its banks, but on Memorial Day weekend the entire hollow was flooded with thick, muddy water, logging debris, and trash. Many homes were damaged; no lives were lost. More floods have occurred since, but after the first one, Selma prepared herself by packing all of her valuables and a suitcase of clothes in her car. "I'm ready," she said, "*if* I'm lucky enough to get out next time."

While personal experiences like Selma's are common to people in the community who actively oppose mountaintop removal, sentiment is deeply divided within the community. Many residents who are not members of CRMW are also torn between the economic impact of the coal industry and the environmental and social damage that it causes. The land where Debbie's small business sits has been in her family for seven generations. Debbie becomes visibly distraught when she speaks of the current state of the mining industry. The men in her family have worked in the mines since before she was born. "Every piece of food I've ever put in my mouth has come from the coal industry," she says, reflecting on the profound influence coal has had on her family. Nevertheless, her deep ties to the local community and the mountain landscape lead her to resent the social and environmental effects of mountaintop removal. In addition, Debbie finds herself in a strange relationship with local union miners. Locals accuse Massey of bringing in nonunion workers from other parts of the state while many local union miners are unemployed. Though her grandfather was an early union organizer and she was raised in a union household, Debbie's business is out of favor with locals because it caters largely to nonunion miners. Despite her family's long history in mining, Debbie finds herself in opposition to coal industry practices like mountaintop removal.

The economics of the coalfields, however, often prevent people like Debbie from speaking out against the industry. The only well-paying jobs in the region are those in coal or related industries such as the railroad. While most of the United States was enjoying the economic expansion of the 1990s, West Virginia was largely bypassed. West Virginia still ranks at or near the bottom of the fifty states in nearly every economic category. When the nation slipped into recession, however, the combination of Bush administration energy initiatives and the rush to build power plants after California's 2001 energy scare created a short-lived miniboom in the coal industry. While the national economy was shrinking, coal companies were, for a time, hiring workers. Lacking a clear economic alternative, West Virginia residents feel torn, forced to choose between their economy and their communities and environment.

Community-Based Opposition

Within such a divided community, organizing resistance to the industry is particularly challenging. In the Appalachian region, the UMWA is the only successful model for organizing opposition to coal industry policy. The tendency of global capitalism to undermine the power of organized labor has created a void for representing community concerns against those of industry. Groups such as CRMW attempt to fill that void. During previous decades, the opposition between industry and labor was a comparatively centralized affair in which the two sides exerted pressure on each other and government officials in an attempt to win concessions. The arrangements of global capitalism tend to diffuse these centers of power by hamstringing unions with regulations and reduced memberships while veiling company responsibility behind a corporate maze of subsidiaries and subcontractors.

CRMW and similar groups appear to be an attempt not to maintain the old union-versus-company dynamic but to construct a new form of opposition to work within the framework of globalization. The group educates residents about the adverse effects of the coal industry within the community and serves as a community resource center. People contact the group's office for emergency telephone numbers, for advice on filing legal grievances against mines and reporting violations of environmental or safety regulations, or to coordinate cleanup efforts to remove potentially damaging debris from flood-prone streams. The group also represents community concerns at public hearings and meetings with industry and regulators. Along with state and regional groups, CRMW contributes to educating policy makers, organizing demonstrations against harmful industry practices, and supporting legislative and regulatory change that will benefit the community. By working both locally and within a network of state and regional organizations, CRMW offers residents the opportunity to act directly in their community and address the systemic causes of their problems, which they believe are rooted in industry practice and government policy.

During the recent legislative debate over coal trucks, for example, CRMW was part of a coalition that advocated not just the enforcement of weight limits but also a change in the pay structure for truck drivers. Instead of being paid by the amount they haul or the number of trips they make, the coalition supported a standard hourly wage for truck drivers to reduce the economic incentive to exceed speed and weight limits. The group argued that such an arrangement would mitigate any adverse effects of the weight limits on truck drivers and create many more driving jobs at the same time. While the proposal was not included in the bill, it is an example of how these organizations are trying to create alternatives that will help preserve the fabric of the community rather than serve particular and often polarizing interests.

In addition to diffusing centers of power, globalization is profoundly influencing social and cultural life. With its emphasis on efficiency, technology, and economic logic, global capitalism is infringing on the meaningful social worlds in which people live. The conflict between the mine workers and community residents is over the character of the community. While many of the workers express resentment toward mountaintop removal and company operating practices in general, they are frustrated by their inability to affect the situation. They would rather continue mining in whatever fashion is available than lose their well-paid jobs. People like Selma do not want to have their homes and sense of security threatened by the practices of the coal industry. With fewer and fewer people receiving the benefits of mining jobs and more and more burdens being borne by the community, they argue that mining is an increasingly bad deal.

Conclusion

Within the spectrum of issues arising from globalization, the mountaintop removal case provides an example of a complex dispute over the future of a community. Politicians, company officials, and mine supporters dismiss mountaintop removal opponents as "extreme environmentalists." Most members of local organizations such as CRMW, however, do not fit the extreme environmentalist profile provided by contemporary environmental politics and direct action groups such as Greenpeace. Members are lifelong residents of the region; many are the wives or children of miners, and some are retired miners themselves. Mining opponents invoke mountaintop removal and environmental rhetoric like the Clean Water Act in much the same way that logging opponents invoked the spotted owl in Oregon. Activists in Oregon incorporated the spotted owl to attract legal and political attention into an already ongoing and deeply divided conflict between the logging industry and communities in southern Oregon (Brown 1995). The Clean Water Act and the Endangered Species Act endow nonhuman elements of the environment with legal and political power. Owls and streams have rights and legal protection that people do not enjoy. With the century-old power of the coal industry over the state government, and without significant union representation, ordinary people in West Virginia do not have any strong political representation. Drawing attention to the Clean Water Act is a way to garner political and legal support against powerful energy companies (coal and others with an interest in the outcome, notably electric utilities). Industry opponents are, in fact, concerned with their streams and are aware of environmental issues and have environmental sensibilities. For most mountaintop removal opponents, however, these issues are part of a larger social negotiation over a valued way of life, the character of their community, and confronting corporate power. The debate over mountaintop removal extends beyond common contemporary views of environmentalism to include equally important discussions of economic policy, industry regulation, and participation in democratic processes.

One of the ways groups like CRMW make their point is to examine critically the character of the community. While mining has been the dominant political and economic force in the region for more than a century, the organization and its members point out that there have always been other important aspects of mountain life. People have always hunted in the mountains, fished in the rivers, gardened on the hillsides, and eaten alongside their neighbors at seasonal ramp dinners. While there are many other examples of community practices, these all involve interaction with the mountain landscape. As companies accumulate control over, restrict access to, and physically remove more and more mountain land, the ability of residents to participate in these culturally valued activities is restricted.

While mountaintop removal makes sense in the economic logic of coal companies and politicians, it is emotionally offensive to someone whose childhood home or favorite hunting ground has been destroyed. Because culture in this sense cannot be quantified and included in cost-benefit logic, it is often excluded from consideration by decision makers. Confrontations like that over mountaintop removal and emerging organizations like CRMW are drawing attention to the need for more comprehensive negotiations over the multiple and intertwined concerns that arise when global economic forces and social values conflict. Confrontations like mountaintop removal are at the same time about the environment, economy, government regulation, and corporate policy. When the forces of globalization—forces that have heretofore been represented as unstoppable—are situated within specific communities like Coal River, people struggle to create new formats for discussing and confronting these complicated topics. It seems clear that the outcome of their efforts will influence the future of concepts like community, place, culture, and opposition, concepts that have not yet solidified in a world being reshaped by the political and economic magma of globalization.

Notes

1. The literature on globalization continues to grow. My own reading is informed by Castells 1996; Castells 1997; Dicken 1998; and Harvey 1996, to name just a few.

2. Official information on Arch Coal, Inc., and Massey Energy comes from corporate websites ⟨www.archcoal.com⟩, ⟨www.masseyenergyco.com⟩, and ⟨www.fluor.com⟩.

3. Mountaintop removal is the latest method of replacing miners with machines. Using a few enormous earthmovers, trucks, and powerful explosives, mining companies methodically remove mountain ridges to expose coal seams, dumping the removed rock and dirt into nearby valleys and hollows. The process employs few people and produces large amounts of coal. The growing incorporation of mountaintop

removal into mining activities throughout the 1990s (accounting for 35 percent of West Virginia's total production in 2000) also contributed to a large disparity between coal production and employment. In the late 1990s, the West Virginia coal industry produced more coal than at any other time in its history while employing the smallest number of people of any time for which records are available, according to data from the West Virginia Coal Association, ‹www.wvcoal.com›.

4. An accurate number of active miners employed in the region is difficult to ascertain because statistics are kept for each county. The Coal River region straddles three counties, each of which has other mining areas. An admittedly imprecise estimate based on the opinion of residents and miners suggests that local mines employed several hundred people in 2000.

5. Pseudonyms have been used for people and places to protect the identities of participants.

References

Brown, Beverly. 1995. *In Timber Country: Working People's Stories of Environmental Conflict and Urban Flight*. Philadelphia: Temple University Press.

Castells, Manuel. 1996. *The Rise of Network Society*. Malden, Mass.: Blackwell.

———. 1997. *The Power of Identity*. Malden, Mass.: Blackwell.

Dicken, Peter. 1998. *Global Shift: Transforming the World Economy*. 3d ed. New York: Guilford Press.

Dudley, Kathryn. 1994. *The End of the Line: Lost Jobs, New Lives in Postindustrial America*. Chicago: University of Chicago Press.

———. 2000. *Debt and Dispossession*. Chicago: University of Chicago Press.

Harvey, David. 1989. *The Condition of Postmodernity: An Enquiry into the Origins of Cultural Change*. Malden, Mass.: Blackwell.

———. 1996. *Justice, Nature, and the Geography of Difference*. Malden, Mass.: Blackwell.

Modell, Judith. 1998. *A Town without Steel*. Pittsburgh: University of Pittsburgh Press.

Yarrow, Mike. 1990. "Voices from the Coalfields: How Miners' Families Understand the Crisis of Coal." In John Gaventa, Barbara Ellen Smith, and Alex Willingham, eds., *Communities in Economic Crisis: Appalachia and the South*, 38–52. Philadelphia: Temple University Press.

Part Three

Globalism's Localisms

Industry and Workers

Meenu Tewari

Nonlocal Forces in the Historical Evolution and Current Transformation of North Carolina's Furniture Industry

Imports Deliver Benefits

Rise in Imports Calls for Defensive Strategies

China Imports Climbing: 46% Growth Continues Four-Year Surge

Levitz Files Amended Reorganization Plan

Exports Increase 13% in First Half; More Export Opportunities on Way, Says Fenn

—Headlines in *Furniture Today*, High Point, N.C.,
  various issues, 2000

Newly resurgent global forces are altering the structure of production across the South today—the American South as much as the global South. As neoliberal policies proliferate worldwide, and as global institutions such as the North American Free Trade Agreement (NAFTA) and the World Trade Organization (WTO) generate increased trade and intensified competition, labor-intensive industries across the world are under intense pressure to restructure. As footloose capital enters and leaves regions; as skilled and unskilled immigrants cross global and local borders in search of "good" jobs, even as the number of those jobs shrinks; and as labor markets become ever more volatile, polarized, and contingent, the policy question everywhere is, How can regions leverage advantage in the face of rising global competition?

This study focuses on the ongoing transformation of one industry in the American South, furniture in North Carolina, to explore how history may be a guide to understanding the ways in which the contradictory processes of globalization become absorbed and localized within the regions that they transform and are transformed by. A long view of this process may shed light on the conditions under which the localization of global forces may produce new institutions of resilience and advantage in the local economy and mitigate the dislocations that intensive competition can unleash.

I first ask, How new are the forces of globalism that are transforming North Carolina's furniture industry today? In tracing the origins of the industry to the construction boom of the 1870s and 1880s, and back further to the first large antebellum investments in public works (road and railroads) in the 1840s and 1850s, I show how the very origins of the industries that are being restructured today by global pressures were themselves shaped by nonlocal influences in a prior period of "globalization."

Then, as today, low wages were, on the face of it, a critical factor in the rise of the South as a prominent base for furniture production (relative to the already established sites in the Northeast and the Midwest). But, I argue, low wages by themselves were not a sufficient source of competitive advantage in the rise of the South's furniture industry. Drawing on the history of North Carolina's spectacular rise first as a regional and then as a national leader in furniture manufacturing, this study reasons that even in a labor-intensive, low-wage industry like furniture, crafting competitive advantage involved more than merely following the (cheap labor) low road. North Carolina outcompeted its southern rivals—all of whom had equally low wages and equally easy access to raw materials—by putting in place a set of institutions and organizational practices that created local and nonlocal linkages among sectors, image, and skills and helped convert the region's low wages into a source of competitive advantage.

Even as this competitive advantage has helped North Carolina remain a national leader in furniture production, embedded in this advantage were its own limitations, namely, the long legacy of insularity and segregation born out of the plantation ethos of the slave South. Even as furniture succeeded, it remained a low-wage, low-skill trap for a largely white but eventually biracial, relatively poor workforce.

Today this history is changing. Changes in product markets; surging imports from altogether new global players, such as China; the influx of a new round of immigrants, such as skilled woodworkers from Mexico; and the entry of new nonlocal (U.S.) retail interests in furniture are transforming the industry internally and externally. The industry's social and institutional history and its political past carry important insights about how these new pressures may be assimilated today. The common theme carried forward from a century of evolution in the furniture industry is the inherent limitation of low wages and low skills as a competitive—and development—strategy. Organizational practices that can ratchet up the ability of workers and firms to learn new skills, adopt new and higher social (not only productive) standards, improve technology and productivity on the shop floor, and articulate innovative social compacts between producers and workers that would improve human capital as well as wages across the industry will be critical. The call, then, according to the sector's own history, is for the adoption of an industrial adjustment process that is simultaneously a learning process.

Historical Legacies and Current Transitions

As the headlines above indicate, globalization and free trade agreements such as NAFTA and the WTO have generated considerable controversy and anxiety in the popular and trade media as the South confronts global competition and the restructuring of its industrial base. Mergers, plant closings, job losses, and the rising specter of imports and immigration have clearly shaken the industry in the past decade. Some of the best-known names in the furniture business, such as the century-old White-Rickel factory in Mebane, have shut down or have been bought out. Hundreds of workers who had long worked in the furniture business have lost their jobs. Accounts in the popular media have emphasized that an influx of Hispanic immigrants is changing the composition of the industry's workforce. Overseas imports are flooding the domestic market. For example, wooden furniture, called case goods in the trade, has long been the heart of the U.S. furniture industry. However, in 1999, more than 35 percent of all case goods sold in the United States were manufactured overseas. In 2001 this figure had risen to 42 percent, compared with less than 10 percent in the late 1980s. For many in the industry, then, this has resurrected pre-NAFTA fears of a "giant sucking sound" of jobs moving offshore.

The reality, of course, is much more complicated and mixed. Though increased international competition is clearly associated with the pain of adjustment in North Carolina's furniture industry, many of these changes were under way long before NAFTA was passed. Indeed, several of the changes that now have an international manifestation—such as the arrival of Mexican immigrants and increased imports—are as much the result (albeit indirect) of domestic shifts and policy agendas to diversify the regional economic base of states like North Carolina, away from single industries centered around traditional sectors and toward more mixed economies, as of foreign competition per se.

For example, interviews with industry officials suggest that the influx of skilled Mexican workers into High Point and Hickory that occurred over the past ten years is not merely the result of looser borders after NAFTA but a result, ironically, of a tight labor market that prevailed in North Carolina's furniture industry throughout the mid- to late 1980s and early 1990s and drove local firms to recruit abroad. This tight labor market resulted from the arrival of relatively better-paying new industries that the state of North Carolina itself had made efforts to recruit and promote throughout the 1980s: back-office work, warehousing, distribution, manufacture of auto components, and programming and other higher-tech industries. Even though many of the jobs in these new industries offered low wages, they paid better than furniture and lured many young native workers away from the region's traditional sectors. As one city manager reported to us, the furniture industry was quite aware of the effect on wages and labor supply of the state's recruitment efforts. The industry's association at first lobbied heavily against the state's promotion and development of new, nontraditional industries in the Triad (Smotherman 2001). Eventually, starting in the late 1980s and early 1990s, local furniture firms turned toward the active recruitment of skilled woodworkers from furniture-producing centers in Mexico. Immigrant workers thus began to flow into High Point and Hickory well before NAFTA was passed and at the behest of local furniture firms that recruited clusters of skilled woodworkers from Mexican villages such as Ciudad Hidalgo (Dussel, Ruiz-Duran, and Piore 1996; Epperson 2001).

Similarly, the explosion of overseas imports of furniture that is threatening the local base is not entirely the result of NAFTA. Most of the furniture imported into the United States comes from China, not Mexico, and hence has little to do with NAFTA. As I detail elsewhere, Chinese imports have grown dramatically in recent years not merely because of low wages in China but also because U.S. retailers, buyers, and furniture manufacturers have actively invested in creating an increasingly sophisticated and flexible supply base in China through extensive training, tutelage, and upgrading of local firms. This trend is associated with key changes in the product market in the global furniture industry and with the rise of new institutional actors in the U.S. furniture industry at the retail end. These buyer-driven investors are U.S. importers and manufacturers (within the South and across the country) who are doing business in a new way. They focus on managing a variety of market segments and controlling distribution and designs by consolidating around key brands. A freer flow of cost-effective imports (from China and other countries) allows these actors to compete with traditional U.S. furniture makers (who produce only two lines a year) by marketing greater product variety within shorter design cycles and mixing imports and domestic production to push novel ideas like lifestyle branding that enable them to control increasing amounts of brand rents across the furniture value chain (see Tewari 2002).

Clearly then, much more than passive free trade is at play in bringing about and shaping the changes under way in the southern—and U.S.—furniture industry today. Yet, despite the more complex and diverse forces at play, the issue of free trade and the "ills of internationalization" has captured the public imagination powerfully because the ongoing changes in the industry are colliding with three deep-rooted, long-accepted images of furniture production in the South.

In the first image, the furniture industry, along with the textile sector, has been a bastion of the southern economy for more than a century. Since the middle of the twentieth century, the South, and in particular North Carolina, has been the furniture capital of the United States, famed not just for its products but also for hosting the world's largest furniture market (or exposition) twice every year at High Point. As one furniture industry official noted, even today with all the changes in the global furniture industry, "High Point is . . . far and away the most important [furniture market] in the world" (Williams 2001).[1] High Point is North Carolina's—and America's—window on the world in the furniture sector. This has historically translated into jobs and revenues for North Carolina. The furniture industry[2] ranks second in the state in terms of manufacturing employment, constituting more than 9 percent of the state's manufacturing workforce, and ranks ninth in terms of value of shipments (Economic Policy and Research Division 2000). The current, very visible troubles of sectors like furniture and textiles clearly threaten jobs, revenues, and economic livelihoods, eroding the image of furniture making as one of the state's anchors.

The second image is that furniture was mostly a domestic business in the United States. Until less than a decade ago, much of the furniture industry in the United States was relatively isolated from international trade. The United States was never a major exporter of furniture, concentrating as it did on the massive and lucrative domestic market. Due to the large domestic market and the strong U.S. dollar, U.S. manufacturers did not find it worthwhile to ship overseas (Mendenhall 2001). Historically, the only market where U.S. exports have flourished is the high-end, high-value, handcrafted segment catering to wealthy customers in high-income countries such as Japan, Saudi Arabia, and Kuwait.[3] But even though the United States has been the third largest exporter of furniture among industrial economies since the 1970s in value terms

(Maskell 1998), the sheer size of the U.S. market has dwarfed trade as a share of total domestic production, and most sales remained local (Mendenhall 2001; Slaughter 2001). Similarly, though the United States always imported lines from Italy, Scandinavia, Southeast Asia, North Africa, and Latin America, imports were a small proportion of total output in the sector. In the late 1980s, for example, U.S. imports and exports of furniture constituted less than 10 percent of the sales revenue generated within the industry (Mann, Armistead, and Epperson 2000). The domestic U.S. market was so large, lucrative, and stable that American and North Carolinian furniture producers needed to care little about exports or about import competition from abroad.

Now, with imports exploding, this disconnection from outside markets has changed dramatically. With imports of furniture for consumption within the United States having increased more than threefold since 1992, the old assumption of unquestioned dominance by local furniture producers over the national market is being strongly challenged. Politically, in southern states such as North Carolina, this has hurt the core constituency, the largely white, low- to middle-income workforce that has long dominated the industry and that is now bearing the brunt of its restructuring. It is not surprising, then, that even while export opportunities are attracting the attention of some local firms, the most vocal political and popular reaction to the furniture sector's globalization is framed in dire terms: of dislocation, disruption, and defensiveness—with calls for increased protection.

Third, and finally, this sense of disruption of a long-standing competitive advantage of the South in furniture is exacerbated by the lore of the southern furniture industry's history as an indigenous success story. Unlike footloose industries such as textiles, North Carolina's furniture industry had a quintessentially local image. With its origins embedded in decidedly southern resources—the region's forests and its abundant labor—the industry was long seen as homegrown, locally rooted, stable, and nationally dominant. This local image was reinforced by the two institutional features of the industry's history discussed above: its virtually exclusive focus on the large domestic (U.S.) market as the place where fortunes were made or lost, and a work tradition bound up in the legacy of a low-wage but historically white foundational workforce. Today, the image of an indigenous industry being disrupted by hostile outside forces has led to an easy attribution of blame to a misleadingly simplistic characterization of globalization. This has led to equally misplaced calls for protectionism as an easy remedy (see, for example, the public debates during the senate race in North Carolina in 2002 and the antidumping ruling against China by the U.S. International Trade Commission on January 9, 2004), which obscures the lessons about successful adjustment offered by the furniture industry's own history in the South during prior periods of growth and consolidation, as we see in the next two sections.

The Origins of North Carolina's Furniture District: Immigrant Entrepreneurs and Early Links with Outside Markets

Contrary to the homegrown view of the furniture industry's origin, nonlocal forces shaped the rise and evolution of furniture production in the South in important ways. The furniture industry originated in North Carolina in the late nineteenth century with the incorporation of the first furniture factory in High Point in 1888.

The rise of furniture production in the South is often viewed as a story of endogenous industrialization—of forward linkages from the region's extensive lumber industry to furniture manufacturing, and successful import competition with the existing centers of production in the North.[4] After all, as scholars have widely noted, until the 1920s the largest manufacturing industry in the South—in terms of employment and value added—was not textiles or cotton goods but lumber and timber products (Wright 1986, 160–61; Tindall 1967). In 1910 nearly half (43.8 percent) of the U.S. employment in lumber and timber products and 38.5 percent of value added in this industry came from the South (Wright 1986, 160, table 6.2). The geography of furniture production, overlaid with the region's lumber tracts, seems to support this resource-driven view. The vast pine and hardwood forests across North Carolina, Georgia, Tennessee, Mississippi, and Missouri (eventually) coincided with towns that became famous for furniture manufacturing, such as Hickory and High Point in North Carolina and Tupelo in Mississippi.[5]

Institutionally, the endogenous growth story arguably had four key components that came together in the late nineteenth century to induce localization of furniture production in the South. The first component was the development and maturation of local woodworking skills in the nineteenth century, fueled in part by the rise of the building trades during the construction booms of the late antebellum and postbellum reconstruction periods. This produced a skilled workforce that progressively moved into value-added production, including furniture. Second, the rise of local demand for furniture, initially from institutional sources (such as the public sector's investments in railroads, roads, capitol buildings, and statehouses and private investments in churches and schools), created a growing regional market that local firms could exploit.

Eventually, as middle-class incomes gradually rose and urbanization accelerated in the South, demand for ordinary household furniture increased the size of this regional market, making successful import competition (displacement of northern furniture imports by local production) more feasible. Indeed, there is ample evidence that much of the furniture produced in the South initially consisted of cheap lines sold in the local and regional market.

Third, the availability of cheap resources, timber, and labor gave the South a decided cost advantage relative to the North by the late nineteenth century, when resource and factor costs were rising sharply across the North and East. Postbellum expansion of transportation networks (railroad and roads) accelerated regional trade. This rising local economic activity further reinforced the conditions for localizing woodworking and furniture making in the South. Finally, success in the textile and tobacco industries for several decades and the rising banking trades had created entrepreneurs who had the capital to invest in the promotion of new ventures like furniture. Indeed, there is evidence that the growth of furniture factories in the South was financed by investment from the local, white elite. For all of these reasons, one could argue that producing furniture locally in the South, for local and regional consumption, became more economically viable in the late nineteenth century than importing it from the North and provided a logical impetus for forward integration from lumber to furniture. Plausible as this account of local linkages may be, I would argue that it is incomplete. Much as local resources were important, the rise of the furniture industry in the South in the late nineteenth century was also the result of the particular way in which the larger, nonlocal forces that were reshaping the post–Civil War economy and politics in both the North and the South became localized and assimilated within the economic and social institutions of some southern regions during that historical period.

In contrast to this endogenous growth view, the most striking fact about the origin of furniture in the South from ethnographic accounts of the industry's history is that the modern furniture industry in the South was pioneered almost entirely by outsiders—nonsoutherners, transplanted post–Civil War immigrants from the North and Midwest. Its antecedents lay not only in import competition with the North but also in successful (even if short-lived) exports to northern markets. Indeed, the immediate antecedents of the furniture industry lie not so much in forward linkages from lumber to furniture, but in backward linkages from the Northeast's spinning mills to the production of wooden components by immigrant entrepreneurs in the South.

The timing of the rise of furniture manufacturing in the South is significant. Furniture production emerged there as a modern industry at a time when the established centers of furniture in the Northeast had begun to lose steam and were moving to the Midwest, toward Ohio and the Grand Rapids region in the 1870s and 1880s (Thomas 1964). As the factories of the Northeast became more troubled, skilled entrepreneurs, supervisors, and traders moved to the West and South (Klontz 1948; Thomas 1964). The changes in factor prices and labor and product markets that were driving these changes in the U.S. economy at this time were influenced not only by the end of the Civil War but also by global trade pressures during the mid-nineteenth century through World War I, a period that many have described as one of the most open in terms of transatlantic trade and migration (O'Rourke and Williamson 2000; Coclanis forthcoming).

The immigrant entrepreneurs who were coming to the South were not only leaving behind the declining textile and woodworking trades in the northern states to "bring their ideas, experience, and capital South" (Bishir 1990), to exploit cheaper local resources there; they were bringing key links to northern markets that helped them create new interregional niches for southern products. Their exposure to and knowledge of these outside networks created the conditions for the seemingly serendipitous sequence of diversifications that gave rise to modern furniture making in the South.

Consider, for example, the story of William Henry Snow, who is regarded as the "father of the furniture manufacturing business in North Carolina" and credited with starting the first furniture factory in High Point (Stockard 1902, 136, 141; cf. Thomas 1964, 49). According to one account, Snow, a member of the Massachusetts Sixth Regiment, fought the Confederacy throughout the Civil War. In the last weeks of the war, as his regiment passed through Piedmont North Carolina, he was struck by the region's natural resources and its business potential (Thomas 1964). Shortly after the war Snow moved to North Carolina with his family and set up a wooden textile supplies factory in the mid-1860s in Guilford County (Stockard 1902, 136). Snow's main market was the textile mills of Massachusetts that he had long ties with.

"Aware of the market for low-cost wooden shuttle blocks among textile plants in his native New England," which he knew were under pressure to cut costs, Snow established North Carolina's first spoke and handle factory in North Carolina to manufacture lower-cost wooden textile supplies for markets in the North. Indeed, part of the investment in the factory came from Snow's mill-owner friends in Lowell, Massachusetts, and the "first barrel of shuttle blocks" was shipped to Mr. E. A. Thissell of Lowell in 1867 (Thomas 1964, 24–25; Stockard 1902, 137).

Producing textile supplies for northern textiles mills "at much cheaper rates than were available in the North" did not mean simply using cheap labor. It involved experimentation with local inputs (timber) and an adaptive process that led Snow to produce a standard product in new ways. First, Snow introduced new technology. He is credited with bringing into North Carolina "the first Blanchard lathe and band saw operated in the state" (Stockard 1902, 136). Second, Snow experimented with new lumber inputs: "Shuttle blocks must be made of wood with a grain sufficiently fine to prevent splintering. Up until this time, most shuttle blocks were made of relatively expensive apple tree timber" (Thomas 1964, 25). "Captain Snow discovered that persimmon, dogwood and hickory timber had a commercial value. Men came from ten miles to see the man who was such a fool as to pay money for dogwood. In 1867 Captain Snow sent to Lowell a barrel of shuttle blocks made from the persimmon tree which abounded in the Piedmont forests. In 1871 the Vermonter moved to High Point where he continued the manufacture of wooden textile supplies. His shuttle block and bobbin factory in High Point became in time the . . . greatest source of those commodities" (Stockard 1902, 137; Thomas 1964, 25).

Whether Snow's reach was global or not, his effort succeeded spectacularly, and he and his business partners eventually became one of the most significant producers of wooden shuttle blocks in the country (Thomas 1964; Klontz 1948), producing more than "ninety percent" of the wooden shuttle blocks and bobbin stock used by textile industries around the world (Farriss 1896, 31; Stockard 1902, 138). The bigger point is that backward linkages with non-local markets, brought about by immigrants who were inserted into both southern and northern networks, were an important spur to the rise of the southern wood products industry.

The idea of diversifying from wood products to furniture came a few years later when Snow found a new market niche. During a visit to a furniture-producing client in Baltimore, Snow's son, a Cornell-educated mechanical engineer, was greatly impressed by the differential between the cost of components and the price of finished furniture in markets such as Baltimore and Pennsylvania. Upon his return to High Point, Snow's son organized a partnership with two others: Tate, a Canadian immigrant who had been linked to furniture making in Canada, and Wrenn, a local Englishman who traced his ancestry to the English architect Christopher Wrenn. Together they established the South's first modern furniture factory in 1888.[6] The High Point Furniture Company, as it was called, was capitalized at a little more than $9,000, and the investment was drawn mainly from the savings of the plant's three partners, who had accumulated it through their prior businesses in High Point. The factory employed about twenty-five workers at first (about fifty eventually) and became celebrated in the local and regional press as the first modern furniture factory of the South (Thomas 1964; Klontz 1948; Lounsbury 1990; Wright 1986).[7]

The company's success and the realization that there was a ready market for low-cost furniture from growing urban and institutional users in the South and industrial and residential households in the North brought a spate of new investment into southern furniture in the late nineteenth century. In 1889, for example, the Hickory Manufacturing Company, which previously produced stairs, mantels, and paneling, moved into furniture, employing "forty laborers in its factory and concentrat[ing] on church furniture" (Lounsbury 1990, 226). In 1891 a northern supervisor joined a local investor to set up the Globe Furniture Company in High Point "with the specific intention of catering to northern markets," and "the factory's first output was a line of sideboards shipped directly to New York" (Thomas 1964, 42). A third factory soon opened under the supervision of an Ohio immigrant, A. J. Rickel, associated also with the famous White-Rickel furniture factory in Mebane. By the mid-1890s there were thirteen furniture factories in High Point alone, and the High Point furniture district was born.

The growth of the South's furniture district was fueled by three sets of institutional actors, local as well as nonlocal: the local media, which gave widespread publicity to the new ventures and played the role of regional booster of southern enterprise; a large number of northern and midwestern supervisors with experience in furniture in the Northeast who became sought after by southern merchants (tobacco and textile), physicians, bankers, educators, and other investors as partners in the scores of new furniture businesses that were starting up in the South in the 1890s and early 1900s; and, finally, northern and midwestern manufacturers of furniture machinery who saw an opportunity to drum up new business for their products in the South. For example, Fay and Egan of Ohio were responsible for getting "twenty-two furniture factories started [in North Carolina], including the famous Bernhardt company in Lenoir" (Smith 1933, 45–46).

Clearly, then, more than local factors were involved in the growth and expansion of the South's furniture industry. By 1900 there were 50 furniture factories in North Carolina, and there were more than 100 a decade later. Several more furniture factories opened in Georgia, Mississippi, Virginia, and Missouri. By 1910 the furniture industry in the South had doubled in size since its inception in the late 1800s, and the South was the nation's fastest-growing furniture region (Klontz 1948). Throughout the early twentieth cen-

TABLE 1. Growth of the Southern Furniture Industry between 1919 and 1929

	Percent increase in 1929 over 1919		
	South	United States (excluding the South)	United States (all)
Number of establishments	41	18	20
Number of wage earners	83	32	40
Wages paid	100	68	72
Cost of materials	86	64	67
Value of product	84	63	66
Value added	81	66	68

Source: Klontz 1948, 34.

tury, furniture production in the South grew at a faster pace than in the rest of the country (see table 1). By 1919–20, more than 14 percent of all U.S. furniture workers were employed in the South (compared with 9.8 percent in the late nineteenth century), and the value of the product from the South rose to 10.8 percent of the nation's, relative to 8.2 percent in the late 1890s (Klontz 1948, 23, 24).

North Carolina, the South's star performer in furniture production, did even better. It accounted for 36.3 percent of all the furniture produced in the South (see table 2). As census data show (cf. Thomas 1964), capital investment in North Carolina's furniture industry escalated rapidly in the early 1900s, more than doubling between 1910 and the depression years. Annual output of furniture (in North Carolina) more than tripled between 1914 and 1919, and by the early 1920s, North Carolina ranked ninth in the United States in capital investment and eighth in annual production of furniture in the country (U.S. Bureau of the Census 1923, 195–96; cf. Thomas 1964, 394). High Point, the South's hub of furniture production, was already being called the "Grand Rapids of the South." By the early twentieth century, North Carolina's—and the South's—furniture industry "had become a factor in national markets" and a player in national furniture trade (Wright 1986, 162; Thomas 1964).

Both external and local demand was critical throughout the industry's rise. The industry grew in three cycles. The earliest demand came from outside niche markets for low-cost wooden products and furniture and from local institutions such as churches, universities, factories, and statehouses. This was

TABLE 2. Value of Furniture Produced in the Southern States, 1919

State	Value (in thousands of dollars)	Percent of All Furniture Production in the South
North Carolina	29,725.30	36.3
Missouri	16,154.87	20.0
Tennessee	9,793.22	12.0
Kentucky	5,411.67	6.6
Georgia	5,108.53	6.2
Virginia	5,042.93	6.1
Texas	4,393.91	5.4
Arkansas	3,199.54	3.9
Louisiana	1,915.90	2.3
Alabama	356.25	0.4
Mississippi	300.00	0.37
South Carolina	202.79	0.25
Oklahoma	170.40	0.21
Florida	98.29	0.12
Total	81,873.60	100.00*

Source: U.S. Bureau of the Census 1920, col. 3, 382–84; cf. Klontz 1948, 25.

*Sum of individual percentages does not equal 100 because of rounding.

followed by a period of aggressive import competition with the North when southern products almost entirely replaced northern and midwestern furniture in the South's low- and middle-market segments. Finally, by the interwar period and beyond, southern furniture was shipped throughout the country in both the price-sensitive and more competitive market segments. Between 1909 and 1919, furniture from the South was shipped in significant amounts to Chicago, St. Louis, Indianapolis, Cleveland, and other states "in competition with the cheap furniture manufactured in Pennsylvania and other Eastern States" (Klontz 1948, 23). Moreover, private demand from northern and southern markets was not the only early source of growth for the South's infant furniture industry. The contract that drew national attention most to the region's industry came from the federal government, when North Carolina's White-Rickel Company won the contract to supply furniture for housing units in the Panama Canal Zone (Thomas 1964, 398). By then, southern furniture producers were competing directly and successfully with their northern and midwestern counterparts nationwide.

Several points emerge from this account of the industry's early growth. First, more than local and indigenous factors were involved in the industry's spectacular rise. Entrepreneurs from the North, supervisors, machinery producers, and nonlocal markets for both furniture and its precursor, wooden textile products, played key roles in the emergence of the South's furniture industry. Immigrant entrepreneurs were drawn to the South's cheaper resources: the forests of the Piedmont and skilled local labor, particularly Scots-Irish craftsmen—neolocals themselves who had arrived not more than a generation earlier, drawn southward from their northern ports of entry by the antebellum building boom of the 1840s and 1850s to towns such as Raleigh, Fayetteville, Greensboro, and Charlotte.

The immigrant entrepreneurs in furniture, then, came to the South because of its abundant resources, but they also brought something important: the knowledge of and links to outside markets that made it profitable to harness these cheaper local resources for nonlocal markets when rising factor costs had created viable niches to fill. Knowledge of these opportunities made risk taking profitable. At the same time, these immigrant entrepreneurs in furniture were very different from the outsiders who invested in the South's textile and lumber industries. Unlike those upper-class corporate conglomerates that invested in textiles, immigrant entrepreneurs in furniture were much smaller players. They were a disparate group of merchants, mechanics, brokers, and former army men who drew on—and depended on—local capital for investment. In the first ten years of the founding of High Point's furniture industry, more than $200,000 was invested in furniture factories. The bulk of this capital came not from the immigrant owners who pioneered and ran the firms, but from local shareholders: merchants, bankers, and the local elite (Thomas 1964). Without the embedding of these white northern immigrants in the social networks of local southern entrepreneurs, craftsmen, farmers, and the white elite, the South's furniture industry may well not have grown so fast.

Discussions in the literature about the rise of southern industrialization are often dichotomized between the colonial narratives—of more developed but hostile northern forces colonizing the South to exploit its underdeveloped resources (Tindall 1967)—on one hand, and the celebration of local potential, such as in the growth narrative of Dalton's carpet industry, on the other. The case of the South's furniture industry, however, suggests that "globalization" is not a term that can be made meaningful in the abstract without specifying what it means in a concrete political, economic, and historical context. In the case of the southern furniture industry, globalization was not merely the outside coming in—as in advanced forces from the North coming in to colonize the South—or the inside going out, via exports and a national presence, but a process by which nonlocal forces interacted with local institutions to create something new and different. In the process, the nonlocal influences became absorbed, over time, into the indigenous and the local.

Constructing Competitive Advantages

We noted above that the low cost of resources in the South drew the first nonlocal furniture entrepreneurs to the region. The South began its furniture base by producing a cheap product: low-cost oak and pine hardwood household furniture. But did the South retain its long-term competitive advantage on the same basis? In this section, using North Carolina's emergence as a leader in furniture production among southern states, we see that while low costs were always important to the industry's rise, low costs by themselves are not enough to explain the South's dominance on the national scene for nearly half a century. I argue that the South did not passively emerge as a new center of furniture production purely because of a play of market forces—that is, lower costs relative to the existing centers of furniture making in the North and a release of entrepreneurs from the North who moved south to exploit the wage and cost differentials. Cheap labor and abundant, unexploited timber reserves in the South are important elements of the story, but much more important is what local firms, public sector agencies, and community associations did to build the institutions that turned that initial factor cost and resource advantage into a lasting, decisive competitive advantage. This involved building new identities around a craft and the rise of a new kind of organization of production.

In the late nineteenth century, when furniture firms were mushrooming across the South, there was no indication that North Carolina would emerge as a leading furniture producer not only in the South but in the nation and maintain that dominance for decades. For example, in 1890, while North Carolina had six furniture factors across the Piedmont, its neighbors were far ahead. Georgia had more furniture firms than North Carolina, more output, and six times more capital invested in furniture. Yet within a decade, North Carolina had outstripped its neighbors and had double the number of furniture factories of any other state in the South (Thomas 1964). In 1909 it produced a quarter of all southern furniture in value terms and 37 percent in terms of output, relative to 15 percent in 1899 (Klontz 1948, 23, 24). Why did North Carolina do so much better than the other southern states, all of whom had the same access to cheap labor and local timber?

Three factors were critical to shaping North Carolina's competitive advantage in ways that went beyond its cheap labor costs. These were the role of the public sector in the early years of the industry's rise, the power of image, and diverse forms of collective action, as well as very different institutional linkages between lumber and furniture manufacturing relative to other southern states.

The Public Sector

The public sector played a key role in laying the basis of growth in the region both by facilitating skill formation and by establishing the infrastructure of rail and road networks that fueled the sector's growth. The political establishment in antebellum North Carolina, like that of most southern states, was reluctant to raise taxes to invest in public services. But after a disastrous decade of outmigrations in the 1830s, the progressives (North Carolina's "internal improvement men") who came to power in the state legislature for the first time made substantial investments in the road and rail system using railroad bonds (Bishir 1990). This had three consequences. First, it converted key towns around the new transportation corridors into economically viable production sites. High Point itself was born out of the laying of the road and rail network in the Piedmont.[8] Second, these investments fueled a building boom and created a demand for woodworking skills. Large public works like the Raleigh statehouse and the university in Chapel Hill attracted skilled woodworking immigrants, especially the Scots and the Irish who settled in the Triad region and later became the backbone of the furniture industry. By the time furniture factories began to emerge in North Carolina in the post–Civil War period, a long tradition of carpentry and wood-based work had already taken root in the region. In 1860, "carpenters constituted the largest male occupational group after farmers and laborers" (Bishir 1990, 182). Finally, the state's promotion of road and rail created new markets for furniture: it fueled urban growth and linked the Piedmont to ports as well as to regional venues of demand that greatly facilitated the production and marketing of furniture across the Southeast and beyond.

Two other structural shifts in the economy helped differentiate North Carolina's furniture industry from that of its southern neighbors.

First, there was a big difference between how the backward linkages between furniture and local lumber took shape in North Carolina relative to other southern states. Unlike the large northern corporate barons who had "raided" the southern timber industry, as in Mississippi (Woodward 1971; Wright 1986), the lumber industry in North Carolina remained relatively independent and in the hands of local farmers who ran small-scale and competitive sawmills and planing operations. Until well into the early twentieth century, furniture factories in many parts of North Carolina got their timber delivered directly by local farmers at very low rates. These low transaction costs at the input level kept production costs low in North Carolina relative even to the state's southern neighbors (Klontz 1948; Thomas 1964).

Second, increased mechanization of agriculture in the Piedmont and the shift of tobacco production from the Piedmont to the bright-leaf areas of eastern North Carolina were critical factors in the furniture industry's evolution. They released larger numbers of workers in the late nineteenth century for the Piedmont's furniture industry just as its growth and production was spiking for the first time. This kept wages down throughout the boom times and though regressive for labor, further lowered the cost of production in North Carolina compared with its closest rivals, Virginia and Tennessee. At the same time the shift of tobacco to eastern North Carolina loosened the feudal and regressive labor relations that were the hallmark of segregated plantation tobacco. The legacy of this shift was mixed. On one hand, it "modernized" labor relations in these parts of the plantation South, but on the other hand, it also kept the workforce of the furniture industry, which developed mostly near the forests of the Piedmont, predominantly white (compared with the predominantly black workforce in tobacco). (See table 3.)

Image Building

Another key difference between the rise of furniture in North Carolina relative to other states was the power of image building. Local media and trade journals created a galvanized sense of entrepreneurship in places like High Point, and the buzz and image, in turn, attracted investment far beyond local expectations. In 1886, very soon after Snow and other newly arrived immigrants established factories in High Point, a new institution emerged: the weekly newspaper, the *High Point Enterprise*, which was edited by a long line of prominent industrial boosters, starting with C. F. Crutchfield. The paper did not merely report local news but served as an advocate for the region's economic possibilities, especially High Point's industrial interests. It lobbied for government support and created a crucial image of dynamism around High Point, presenting it as a place of new ideas, innovation, and growth—a town that was modernizing and where a new kind of future was being built. In 1887 the

TABLE 3. Composition of North Carolina's Manufacturing Workforce by Race and Gender, 1900

Industry	White		Black		Percent Black (% of all males and females)	
	Male	Female	Male	Female	Male	Female
Cotton Textiles	16,556	14,019	109	33	0.65	0.23
Sawing and Planing	2,598	0	1,691	0	39.4	—
Furniture	333	0	25	0	7.0	—
Tobacco	866	616	2,411	1611	73.6	72.3

Source: U.S. Bureau of the Census 1900; cf. Wright 1986, 180.

paper extolled the city's enterprise and economic climate, claiming, "Any kind of manufacturing establishment will thrive in High Point if properly managed," and "if you get the blues take a walk around amongst the factories; the hum of the wheels and rush and bustle has a wonderful cheering effect." In 1888 the paper promoted a railroad bond issue, urging that "every man boom the railroad . . . the salvation of High Point. We cannot let it slip from us" (cf. Thomas 1964, 25–28).

The image of High Point as a rapidly growing and modernizing town was so successful that by 1887 the *Charlotte Chronicle* cited High Point as "the most important manufacturing town on the North Carolina Railroad" (Thomas 1964, 26). It is not surprising, then, that the largest number of investors in furniture—whether they came from Ohio or Charlotte—chose to invest in High Point throughout the late nineteenth and early twentieth centuries, creating economies of scope and agglomeration that made a genuine industrial district out of a once-sleepy town of 300 inhabitants.

Soon after 1900 several other prominent furniture trade journals were launched: the *Southern Furniture Journal* and, later, *Furniture South* and *Furniture Today*. In 1921 the trade networks created by these journals played an important role in launching the Southern Furniture Exposition in High Point. This institution consolidated the importance of the town as a leading furniture center and helped launch a period of tremendous growth of the sector in North Carolina. As noted above, High Point's furniture market is now the largest such exposition in the world.

Collective Action

The most important difference between the evolution of North Carolina's furniture industry and that of other southern states, however, lay in the institutions of collective action that emerged at various times during the development of the state's furniture industry, and in the early rise of highly effective trade associations. These institutions were critical in helping the industry adapt and grow through a period of intense competition, mergers, failures, and fires that began in 1910, after the "easy" first couple of decades of initial growth.

In the initial years, growth came from the low costs of the simple products that southern furniture firms produced. As demand for cheap lines of oak and pine furniture stalled in the 1910s, many southern furniture firms ran into serious competition, financial problems, and takeover threats. Mergers and bankruptcies were rampant. During this period, leaders emerged who helped restructure the industry, improve production quality, and standardize the product. Some also mechanized their production lines and introduced "techniques of mass production" (Thomas 1964). William White of Mebane and Tomlinson of High Point, for example, stressed efficiency in engineering and production and gained a national reputation in implementing a set of improvements in their own plants that substantially improved the quality of their output. They promoted these techniques across North Carolina. Tomlinson was a key leader who helped to lower the collective costs of production in the region by encouraging the formation of an interlinked support and service industry and innovating with distribution mechanisms. He led the way, for example, by organizing a large sales force (within his own firm) with representatives in specific parts of the country and "inaugurated the package car express service by which dealers of a given area could realize savings on freight charges by having their orders shipped in the same boxcar" (Thomas 1964, 399).

Soon investors began to establish "supply and service" facilities, and by 1919 High Point manufacturers had "easy and inexpensive access to varnishes, stains, dyes, glue, castors, plate glass and mirrors" and other supplies that reduced the cost of production while vastly improving quality and variety (Thomas 1964). Yet others established furniture machinery plants, like Wysong's (the Ohio-trained supervisor of White and Rickel's plant) 1903 plant in Greensboro.

Most significantly, during the crisis years of the North Carolina furniture industry, some firms set an example—and made a case—for improved labor relations. Although labor improvements were not widely adopted by the industry, the firms that emerged as regional and, eventually, national leaders as they came out of the industry's first major crisis in the 1920s focused on improving labor productivity by upgrading labor standards and working conditions. One firm, for example, introduced the industry's first group life insurance plan in 1917, launched an extensive training program, and later instituted a monthly bonus plan (Thomas 1964, 399–400).

Clearly, then, while low wages were undoubtedly central to the structure of industrial production in the South, including furniture, they were not the only or even primary source of competitive advantage of North Carolina's furniture firms. The broader point that this study makes is that an advantage in wages is not by itself enough to convert a resource into a competitive strength or into a long-term competitive advantage. It is the institutional embedding of that factor within the particular economic history of a region that is critical to shaping a region's competitive advantage.

Conclusion

From this historical account of the rise of the South's furniture industry, several points can be made about the circumstances of global pressure and restructuring that the industry is facing today.

First, this history shows the highly mixed and contradictory nature of the success of the South's industry. Low wages and unexploited, cheap resources attracted outside investors into furniture—not the large lumber companies, but small merchants or managers with small capital to invest. But low wages were not the sole source of the South's, and specifically North Carolina's, dominance in furniture. Critical to the industry's enduring success were the institutions that local firms and workers built to harness its potential. These were enterprises of collective action, of image building and promotion often led by the state's various investments, and of at least two or three prior efforts at successful restructuring.

Second, global pressures are not new in the history of the furniture industry in the South. Indeed, the very origins of the industry are a product of nonlocal influences. We saw how the earliest furniture firms in North Carolina were pioneered by outsiders. The six first and largest furniture factories in North Carolina in the late nineteenth century were all owned by nonlocals—transplanted northerners and midwesterners—and worked by skilled Scotch-Irish immigrants who had been drawn to North Carolina in the late antebellum period.

Third, central to the emergence of North Carolina's and the South's furniture industry was its cheap labor and abundant local resources, which drew early entrepreneurs such as William Henry Snow from outside the region. However, though low wages are endogenous to southern industrial growth, they are not sufficient to explain the rise and sustained dominance of the South in national furniture markets for more than a century. Central to the industry's growth and evolution, I have argued, were a variety of complex institutions and instances of collective action among firms, investors local and nonlocal, distributors and technicians, the state government, and at several points in the industry's history, its workers (however short lived the compact with workers might have been). As the maturing industry passed through a variety of crises, including bankruptcies, mergers, and layoffs, that necessitated several rounds of painful restructuring just as the industry is witnessing today, the turn toward low wages was never sufficient to pull the industry out of its crisis. In each case new institutions and organizational arrangements, modernizations, and social compacts emerged and were decisive in the industry's ability to cope with and rise beyond its troubles. That North Carolina emerged as a national leader in furniture production, outstripping its southern neighbors who were equally endowed with low wages and abundant resources, illustrates this point well. It demonstrates the need to go beyond market-oriented "low-wage and natural resource abundance" factors, as Wright (2000) suggests, in explaining the rise of the kinds of distinctive institutions that the industry created that allowed it to produce the bases for more enduring competitive advantage.

The purpose of recounting the industry's global past, then, is not to set up a dichotomy between an indigenous and a more global narrative of origins. The point, rather, is to argue that the rise of the furniture industry was the result of a particular historical moment in which larger than local forces were reshaping social and political relations of production not only in the South but in the wider U.S. economy. In this wider context, a complex interaction of forces that were both intensely local (natural resources, labor, and investment capital) as well as decidedly nonlocal (immigrant entrepreneurs and links with outside markets) jointly shaped the social and economic institutions that undergirded the growth and evolution of the South's furniture industry.

These institutions, however, were unequal. There was growth, but aggregate growth masked the inequalities that underlay it (see Klontz 1948; Bishir 1990). The wages of both skilled and unskilled woodworkers remained lower than in the rest of the country, and social distance between skilled white workers and (the industry's few) black workers, and elite white entrepreneurs was great. The boom influenced only some places (Bishir 1990) and some people.

Yet the influence and the arrival of nonlocal entrepreneurs in the South's furniture industry was different both from the corporate dominance of north-ern investors in southern industries such as textiles and lumber and from the industrial boosterism that emerged in the South in the 1930s, which attracted northern industries and branch plants to locate in the South. Unlike the repa-triation of profits and the footlooseness of the industries that subsidies at-tracted, this earlier round of arrivals consisted of entrepreneurs who stayed, of links with outside markets that endured, and of modest innovation. The entrepreneurs and the immigrant workers both became absorbed in the local fabric and social structures of the region's economic life.

Today again, immigrants are putting pressure on old institutions, and change is under way. The major difference between the time when immigrants helped originate the region's furniture industry and today, when it is being restruc-tured, is a critical one: race and nationality. While earlier differences were of contention over place—North versus South—resulting, no doubt, from an indirect clash over race and social control (Peacock 2002), the immigrants themselves were white and harbingers of capital, networks, and new markets. Today's immigrants are more complex. They are workers and bring skills and labor, but in some cases they are giving rise to new, hybrid ways of organizing work—not merely as workers but also as internal contractors paid by the piece, sans benefits.

Thus, the absorption of the white immigrants from the U.S. North and Europe in the late nineteenth century—the Yankee Captain W. H. Snow was an eight-term mayor of High Point—does not foretell a similar prognosis for the immigrants migrating into the industry and the region today. Their strug-gles, as well as their institutional insertion, will be their own, and distinct. But as the industry struggles to adjust to the new local and global challenges it faces today, it would do well to recall the lesson of its own history: that in prior moments of crisis the furniture industry's resilience has come not merely from cutting costs but from the collaborative and innovative institutions that local actors jointly created, which in turn generated a more enduring compet-itive advantage.

Notes

For very helpful feedback on earlier versions of this essay, I thank Ray Burby, Gary Gereffi, Ed Feser, Ned Hill, Melissa McMahon, Carrie Matthews, James Peacock, Harry Watson, and other members of the Rockefeller Conference on the Transna-tional South at the University of North Carolina, as well as Altha Cravey, John Pick-les, and Wendy Wolford. For research funding that supported the larger project of which this paper is a part, I thank the University Research Council, the Provost's Junior Faculty Development Grant, and the Office of Economic Development at the University of North Carolina at Chapel Hill. Matthew Barnes provided excellent research assistance. All errors of fact and interpretation are my own responsibility.

1. The official continued, "Internationally Cologne is important, and to a lesser extent Tokyo[; at home] . . . regional markets in San Francisco, Minneapolis, and some temporary trade shows fill in . . . , but High Point is the most important [furniture market] in the world."

2. Classified as the Standard Industrial Classification (SIC) Code of 25—Furniture and Fixtures.

3. Clearly, the strong dollar that prevailed for much of the period since the late 1970s had a lot to do with reinforcing the industry's domestic focus and making an export strategy unsuitable for U.S. furniture manufacturers, but strong demand from the large domestic market was a key factor as well. Indeed, it was the strength of the dollar in the mid-1970s that led to a surge of European imports and the rise of European retailers in the United States such as IKEA (Mann, Armistead, and Epperson 2000, 2).

4. Surprisingly few detailed studies exist of the origin of furniture in the South, especially when compared with the vast historical and analytical literature on the textile, paper, and lumber industries (and, of course, southern agriculture).

5. Many observers have noted how North Carolina's extensive hardwood forests in counties such as Guilford, Randolph, and Chatham fueled the growth of towns in the Piedmont region and made Hickory, High Point, and Greensboro important centers of wood-based furniture and tools production by the late nineteenth century (Bishir 1990).

6. The first large-scale furniture mills in the South arose in 1888, though scattered furniture production of cheap pine and oak products with power tools existed since the 1840s.

7. A more traditional plant that made some furniture existed in Charlotte, and a few neighboring states had plants that made safes and doors and chests; but organized production of furniture began with the establishment of the High Point Furniture Company in the 1880s (Thomas 1964; Klontz 1948).

8. The construction of the "Appian Way" (the "world's largest" plank road) in 1853 and, later, the Goldsboro-Charlotte railroad created a road-and-railroad junction that became a thriving market town that was christened "High Point" by surveyors because it was "the point of the greatest altitude on the [North Carolina railroad]" (Sizemore 1947; 2. Also see Thomas 1964, 23; Bishir 1990; Klontz 1948).

References

Bishir, Catherine. 1990. "A Spirit of Improvement: Changes in Building Practice, 1830–1860." In Catherine Bishir, Charlotte V. Brown, Carl R. Lounsbury, and Ernest H. Wood III, eds., *Architects and Builders in North Carolina: A History of the Practice of Building*, 130–92. Chapel Hill: University of North Carolina Press.

Cobb, James C. 1982. *The Selling of the South: The Southern Crusade for Industrial Development, 1936–1980*. Baton Rouge: Louisiana State University Press.

Coclanis, Peter. Forthcoming. "Trade and Investment into and out of the South prior to 1950." In James C. Cobb and William Stueck, eds., *The South and Globalization.* Athens: University of Georgia Press.

Dussel, E., C. Ruiz-Duran, and M. Piore. 1996. "Adjustments in Mexican Industries to the Opening of the Economy to Trade." Massachusetts Institute of Technology, Cambridge, and the Universidad Nacional Autónoma de México, Mexico City. Mimeo.

Economic Policy and Research Division. North Carolina Department of Commerce. 2000. "The Furniture and Fixture Industry in North Carolina." Special industry study.

Epperson, Jerry. 2001. Furniture analyst with Mann, Armistead, and Epperson, Virginia. Telephone interview by research assistant Matt Barnes. March 2.

Farriss, James Joseph. 1896. *High Point, N.C.: A Brief Summary of its Manufacturing Enterprises. Together with sketches of those who have built them.* N.p.: High Point Enterprise.

Furniture Today. June 12, October 30, and December 18, 2000. Published by Cahners, High Point and Greensboro, N.C.

Kannan, Shyam. 2002. "North Carolina Knits a Network That Supports Its Hosiery Industry." *Economic Development Now* 2, no. 14 (July).

Kaplinsky, Raphael, Mike Morris, and Jeff Readman. 2002. "The Globalization of Product Markets and Immiserizing Growth: Lessons from the South African Furniture Industry." *World Development* 30, no. 7: 1159–77.

Klontz, Harold Emerson. 1948. "An Economic Study of the Southern Furniture Manufacturing Industry." Ph.D. diss., University of North Carolina at Chapel Hill.

Lounsbury, Carl R. 1990. "The Wild Melody of Steam: The Mechanization of the Manufacture of Building Materials, 1850–1890." In Catherine Bishir, Charlotte V. Brown, Carl R. Lounsbury, and Ernest H. Wood III, eds., *Architects and Builders in North Carolina: A History of the Practice of Building,* 193–239. Chapel Hill: University of North Carolina Press.

Mann, James, W. Howard Armistead, and Jerry Epperson. 2000. *Furnishing Digest* 8, no. 12 (December).

Maskell, Peter. 1998. "Successful Low-Tech Industries in High Cost Environments: The Case of the Danish Furniture Industry." *European Urban and Regional Studies* 5, no. 2: 99–118.

Mendenhall, Judy. 2001. President of the High Point Chamber of Commerce and head of High Point Partners, High Point, N.C. Telephone interview by research assistant Matt Barnes. February 16.

O'Rourke, Kevin H., and Jeffrey G. Williamson. 2000. *Globalization and History: The Evolution of a Nineteenth Century Atlantic Economy.* Cambridge, Mass.: MIT Press.

Peacock, James L. 2002. "The South in a Global World." University of North Carolina at Chapel Hill. Mimeo.

Scott, Allen J. 1986. "Economic Decline and Regeneration in a Regional Manufacturing Complex: Southern California's Household Furniture Industry." *Entrepreneurship and Regional Development* 8:75–98.

Sizemore, F. J. 1947. *The Building and the Builders of a City: High Point, North Carolina*. Compiled by the High Point Chamber of Commerce. High Point: Hall Printing Co.

Slaughter, Powell. 2001. Researcher and furniture industry analyst at *Furniture Today*. Interview. March 13.

Smith, Sarah Margaret. 1933. "A Social Study of High Point, North Carolina." Master's thesis, University of North Carolina at Chapel Hill.

Smotherman, Steve. 2001. Economic Development Council, High Point, N.C. Interview. March 13.

Stockard, Sallie W. 1902. *The History of Guilford County*. Knoxville: Gaut-Ogden.

Tewari, Meenu. 2002. "Shifting Boundaries of Control: Global Competition and the Emergence of Quasi–Buyer Driven Chains in High Point's Furniture Industry." University of North Carolina at Chapel Hill. Mimeo.

Thomas, David Nolan. 1964. "Early History of the North Carolina Furniture Industry, 1880–1921." Ph.D. diss., University of North Carolina at Chapel Hill.

Tindall, George B. 1965. "The 'Colonial Economy' and the Growth Psychology: The South in the 1930s." *South Atlantic Quarterly* 64, no. 4 (Autumn): 465–77.

———. 1967. *The Emergence of the New South, 1913–1945*. Baton Rouge: Louisiana State University Press.

U.S. Bureau of the Census. 1900. *Twelfth Census of the United States: Special Reports*. Washington, D.C.: U.S. Government Printing Office.

———. 1920. *Fourteenth Census of the United States: Manufactures, 1919*. Washington, D.C.: U.S. Government Printing Office.

———. 1923. *Fourteenth Census of the United States: Manufactures, 1920*. Washington, D.C.: U.S. Government Printing Office.

Williams, David. 2001. E-mail response to interview questions. February 27.

Woodward, C. Vann. 1971. *Origins of the New South, 1877–1913*. Baton Rouge: Louisiana State University Press.

Wright, Gavin. 1986. *Old South, New South: Revolutions in the Southern Economy since the Civil War*. Baton Rouge: Louisiana State University Press.

———. 2000. "Old South, New South, Sunbelt South." Stanford University. Mimeo.

Rachel A. Willis

Voices of Southern Mill Workers

Responses to Border Crossers in American Factories and Jobs Crossing Borders

Hla dej yuav hle khau
Tsiv tbe tsaws chaw yuav hle hau

[Cross the river, you'll take off your shoes;
Flee from your country, you'll take off your status.]
—Hmong Proverb

The Americans don't want these jobs—that is why we
(the Asians and Latinos) can get them.
—A Hispanic immigrant worker on North Carolina
   attitudes about work.

We don't seem to have any choice: they take our jobs to
Mexico—or the Mexicans take our jobs here.
—A North Carolina native on immigrants working
   in the hosiery mills

The voices of hosiery mill workers in the Carolinas have increasingly taken on accents that are foreign to the native southerners who have worked in the mills for as many as five generations. The positive roles that Hmong, Vietnamese, Hispanic, and even a few eastern European workers have played in the survival of this relatively low-wage manufacturing industry in the Catawba Valley of western North Carolina can be neither overstated nor doubted.[1] However, this does not mean that the voices of the new immigrants—who are increasingly becoming the foundation of the manufacturing labor force across the state—are in harmony with those of the native mill workers. Conflict born of difference and the sense of loss of traditional culture and community is evident in many of the Carolina communities affected by these rapid and significant labor force changes. However, along with evidence of disharmony there is also apparent a growing sense of shared purpose, respect, and a common goal.

As the areas in which mill workers live and work struggle to maintain an industry that has been critical to the economic development of the region, the strategies used for survival, as well as those for building more diverse communities by integrating the contributions of the new immigrants, have been both somewhat unusual and relatively successful within the mills and the industry. The approaches demonstrated in this industry contribute critical examples on how to deal with the domestic face of globalization at the local, regional, and state levels. They also provide guidance for national policy with respect to a complex array of issues aimed at coping with a world transformed by technology, trade, and immigration flows of historical significance.

This essay draws from an extensive archive of face-to-face interviews done over the course of more than five years as part of an ongoing study of broader labor issues in a manufacturing environment. The interviews provided an opportunity to examine the concerns of workers, supervisors, managers, and owners as they deal with border-crossing workers filling American jobs and as they watch some previously American jobs cross borders. These changes occur both as U.S. firms relocate manufacturing facilities offshore and as international competitors attract customers, forcing local firms to shut their doors. The hosiery industry offers a picture of an American industrial landscape transformed at the start of the new millennium, and of an American labor force seeking to formulate a clear sense of its identity in the changing global economic environment.

A short economic analysis of the development of the hosiery industry in North Carolina is provided. The critical role of the typically male skilled technician in the predominantly female labor force in hosiery mill manufacturing is detailed, as it is a critical link to understanding how the industry was able to develop and later implement the strategies necessary for economic survival as the world economy changed.[2] This essay continues with a discussion of the relatively recent influx of immigrant workers from Asia and Latin America into hosiery manufacturing. The three most frequently expressed themes from the interviews with both native Carolinians and immigrants are then examined. The first example of conflict within the mill comes from a lack of understanding of divergent lifestyles. The second and third examples of conflict reflect the growing sense of interdependence between the native Carolinians and the immigrant community.

An Economic Analysis of the Development of the Hosiery Industry in the Carolinas

The southeastern United States has dominated international hosiery manufacturing for nearly a century. The making of a sock seems simple: the sock is knitted as a tube, the toe is seamed, and the finished product is either bleached or dyed and then, perhaps, ironed[3] before it is packaged and sold. A knitting machine has numerous needles and yarn feeds that perform a complex pattern of movements at relatively high speeds to form a carefully sized tube of interconnected loops of yarn.[4] The success of the sock in fulfilling the demanding task of consumer wear depends on virtually every needle and yarn segment being in precisely the right position with identical tension.

The early mechanical machines stand about eight feet high, occupy about a square yard of floor space each, and are driven in a mill by a complex system of belts connecting the machines to centrally located motors. Modern electronic machines are a bit more compact, contain their own motors, and simply connect directly to an electrical source. Hosiery has few economies of scale in manufacturing, so production can and does occur at virtually any scale of operation. Individual machines of either type can easily be powered at home and produce virtually the same intermediate product: greige goods.[5] It is not unusual for a skilled employee to work in a factory with hundreds of machines and other employees and, at the same time, to run a single knitting machine at home around the clock. They then sell their relatively small—but identical—lots of greige goods to their employer.

Hosiery manufacture first came from England in the eighteenth century with "plans" smuggled into the New World in the heads of frame knitters.[6] The export of this complex technology was specifically outlawed so England could maintain its trade advantage with the colonies. Originally located mainly in New England, hosiery manufacturing moved south at the turn of the twentieth century. The low cost of energy and labor attracted many textile mills to locations along various rivers in central North Carolina. While there are virtually no economies of scale in the production of greige goods, there are positive externalities gained from spatial clustering of the mills. These externalities stem from the demand for trained workers able to make the unusually frequent and complex repairs to numerous knitting machines and from savings in transportation costs of supplies and greige goods. These location-based externalities have resulted in a concentration of mills in three geographically limited bands in western and central North Carolina, especially along the Catawba River.

The development of a self-perpetuating, skilled labor force of machine technicians in this region has been critical to the continued success of this industry in North Carolina. Known as "fixers," these men typically served apprenticeship periods of up to ten years on the mechanical machines. By the end of that time, a skilled technician could not only reset the machines for a change of style or size but, far more importantly, look at a knitted hose in production and determine precisely which needle in the small-diameter cylinder needed replacement, where an adjustment in yarn tension was required, or if something far more difficult to detect was occurring with respect to the yarn. This is critical to profitability, as undetected problems in knitting mean an enormous waste of raw materials, since the errors would later appear in either the dyeing or boarding process; then the sock could only be sold as an irregular.

Traditionally, the training for fixers was handled in-house, with the usual teacher being a male relative of the apprentice. Frequently, the complex and long-term training associated with maintenance and repair of the machines was passed from father to son on the shop floor, with a given family covering all shifts on a particular set of knitting machines. In this way, a fixer could share his dearly acquired knowledge of fixing and of a specific machine's idiosyncrasies with another technician and thus make his own shift easier.

The skills necessary to keep the machines running and the mill profitable were extremely valuable. Thus fixers attempted to pass on their knowledge only to members of their own immediate or extended family or, in more recent times, to people of their same race and nationality, as they were perceived to be less of a threat to the fixers' own future employment. Sharing valuable technical knowledge with a younger employee or a "foreigner"—who then might be willing to work for lower wages—seemed shortsighted and potentially a direct route to unemployment. Even the tools necessary to fix the machines, nearly always privately owned by each fixer, were only lent to family members. Both physical capital and human capital—the tools and the training—were not shared with those who were perceived as having different long-term interests. In economic terms, the capital assets, both physical and human, would only be distributed within a given "family."

This form of intergenerational capital transfer created a training pattern within the mills that was initially supported by the development of the mill villages. This, in turn, stimulated extensive family labor supply patterns within mills that were further augmented by the predominantly female or child labor force employed in most other parts of hosiery production. Although the skilled technician is key to the success of the production process, most of the other labor inputs in the process are unskilled. Training times for nearly every other position in a hosiery mill amount to a couple of weeks. With the exception of the dye house and the transportation of materials and finished product, nearly all other areas of hosiery manufacturing are dominated by female (and, formerly, child) employees. Paid by the piece, virtually all of the knitters, seamers, and packagers are female. While some men board socks, it is far more typical for women to fill all the unskilled and semiskilled jobs necessary to produce a finished sock.[7]

Labor unrest from 1915 through 1935 resulted in strikes, violence, and the eventual dispersion of mill village communities. Simultaneously, child labor laws were passed and, later, enforced. These changes caused the family labor patterns to change, but they persisted in an altered form, supported by the development of extensive road networks throughout North Carolina and increased employment of married women. The largely rural manufacturing labor force with a pattern of related fixers and female production workers continues to some extent to this day. The relative proximity of the mills along with the mobility afforded by car ownership, however, now means that workers are able and willing to switch employers more readily for minor differences in wage and benefit packages.

This increase in mobility coupled with increasing education and thus a decline in the supply of unskilled labor results in annual turnover in many mills of as much as 120 percent a year. This high turnover rate is precisely what initiated the employment of African Americans in what had been a nearly entirely white industry until the beginning of the 1970s. Coinciding with the decline of segregation, the troop buildup in Vietnam, and the constant need for additional workers to keep the mills in operation, the desegregation of the mills led to the first round of redefining community for the mill workers. Black men joined the mill force, typically in handling positions such as yarn, greige goods, or shipping, and worked beside white men. Segregation of women by race still occurred by shift and job, although the overall numbers show a gradual transition toward integration within the mills. This transition was marked by little turmoil or comment relative to other regions and industries. Desegregation did not occur at any measurable level within the ranks of the highly skilled technicians, so it is unclear what the training response of the fixers would have been to an "American"—though nonwhite—invasion of their employment prospects.[8]

The second wave of change in the mills, however—the entrance of non-English-speaking workers—has been met with far more concern, as it coincided with events that threatened the very survival of the mills. The two waves of immigration into North Carolina, Hmong and Hispanic, were partly the result of a series of simultaneous but unrelated political events halfway around the world, in both directions, from the North Carolina mountains. But they were also the result of an increasingly tight labor market for unskilled workers as the education levels rose among white Carolinians.

The Influx of Immigrant Workers
into the Hosiery Mills

During the Vietnam War, the Hmong people of the mountain areas of Laos
were outfitted by the U.S. military to fight against the coastal Lao people and
the Vietnamese Communists in the area referred to as the Plain of Jars. The
fall of Saigon in 1975 caused tens of thousands of Hmong to flee to refugee
camps in Thailand in the face of widespread massacres and legitimate fears of
retribution for assisting the American forces. Many refugees remained in the
camps for more than a dozen years. Eventually, however, U.S. immigration
laws and welfare support for the Vietnamese war allies, such as the Hmong,
Montagnard, Laotian, and Vietnamese, were radically modified to provide both
relatively easy entrance for U.S. allies from Southeast Asia (specifically, refugees in these groups could "sponsor themselves and their families") and generous welfare assistance (longer periods of support without employment search
requirements as well as general long-term eligibility for Social Security insurance benefits). The level of support varied substantially by state, affecting the
location of initial settlement rather significantly. Refugees had little incentive
to work in generous welfare states such as California and Minnesota, and some
of the largest Hmong populations in the world are now in Fresno and St.
Paul.

Radical changes in the support laws and removal of the refugees from the
welfare rolls, as well as the development of nonprofit resettlement activities in
the Carolinas at the beginning of the 1990s,[9] led to Hmong immigration to
the Catawba Valley beginning in 1992. The tight labor market for manufacturing workers immediately resulted in the hiring of numerous Hmong and
some Vietnamese workers in the Hickory area of the Catawba Valley. The mill
jobs offered to the immigrants, mainly seaming and boarding at first, require
few language skills, and the wages and benefits were better than those offered
in other low or unskilled jobs available to the refugees.

On the heels of the Hmong migration has come an increase in the number
of Hispanic workers in the area and in the mills. Changes in U.S. immigration
policies that accompanied North American Free Trade Agreement (NAFTA)
legislation in the early 1990s have made it easier for workers from NAFTA countries to obtain work permits. The extremely low supply of native workers for
the low-skilled jobs offered in the hosiery mills generated enormous pressures
to employ immigrant Hispanics. Originally recruited to North Carolina to
work seasonally in agriculture and related industries, the new Hispanic immigrants found that the jobs in the hosiery mills were far preferable to those in

the fields or in poultry processing plants. Attracted by better overall working environments, higher wages, and more regular hours, many of the hardest-working agricultural migrants entered hosiery.

The radical development of deskilling technologies as well as the collapse of the U.S. capital industry in textile manufacturing led many to assume that all textile manufacturing jobs would be lost to offshore operations after the passage of NAFTA. This did, in fact, occur rather rapidly in the more highly mechanized sectors of textile production, such as the manufacture of knitted fabrics, as well as in labor-intensive cut-and-sew operations that result in garment construction. However, the unusual manufacturing characteristics of hosiery, outlined above, have meant that the wholesale export of hosiery manufacturing has not happened or at least has not been possible in the same relatively short period that saw the rapid movement of machines to a number of Central American countries in other areas of textile production. The constant demands for the fixers in the hosiery mills meant consistent quality could not be guaranteed from one sock to another in these offshore operations. Fixers have not been willing to train fixers in offshore operations, holding the line on the "family" knowledge. Instead, in 2001 most socks were still made in the United States, and American companies used a variety of strategies—from increasing capitalization, investments in bilingual workplaces, a community college/industry partnership, and unusual benefit packages—to maintain a sufficient supply of production workers for the mills. Thus far, these efforts together with the concentration of experienced fixers have kept hosiery mills operating in North Carolina. But the patterns of employment in hosiery mills in North Carolina are radically different from what they were just ten years ago. The rapid influx of Hispanic workers and transplanted immigrants from Laos and Vietnam into the rural North Carolina labor force has transformed entire shifts, occupations, and in a few instances, factories into an international workforce requiring extensive accommodations for language, religious, and cultural differences.

American Jobs and the Identity of Immigrants

The transformation of the hosiery manufacturing labor force, with the introduction of the Asian immigrants, followed closely by the Hispanic immigrants, has led to conflict both within the factories and throughout the communities where the mill workers reside. The problems of assimilating immigrants into the workplace and the community are so pervasive and well known that they can be discussed in the broadest of terms for any situation, immigrant population, and time. Conflict and misunderstanding about cultural differences, religious differences, values, and language abound. Add the very real pressures associated with dramatic growth in a community, as signified in pressures in housing, schools, and employment, and the resulting crime, and there is the potential to create permanently divided communities. The challenges caused by significant immigration, the opportunities presented for building bridges between immigrants and native North Carolinians, and developing a nation-image among the old and new members of the community take on specific meanings within the context of a hosiery mill.

Using the three most common responses from the hosiery mill interviews, I will explore the difficulties in building bridges between cultures. Each issue illustrates the challenges and opportunities presented by the building of a nation through immigration. The success of this industry has been in its capacity to listen, communicate, understand, experiment, and carefully link community services and agencies wherever a need exists to support the building of better communities in the long term. It is precisely this concern for the future that marks the words of workers in the hosiery industry and has led to their integration of the immigrants into their communities.

They don't value their children—the parents are so selfish—all they care about are themselves and their own happiness, not their children's future.
—From both Americans and Laotians throughout the mills

This common theme reaches into the heart of the community to workers' views of work and family and the choices each person makes between these realms. Here the lack of understanding and quickness to assign blame are most evident. The theme is also important because one of the creative strategies used by a few firms to reduce turnover has been the provision and subsidy of on-site child care. Two of the larger hosiery mills have even been ranked in the list of top 100 corporations in *Working Mother* magazine's list of family-friendly businesses.[10] Given that this is a low-wage and low-profit industry, and one of the only industries on the list of family-friendly employers operating in a manufacturing environment, this is an even more remarkable achievement, but one necessitated by the need to maintain the overall workforce in hosiery manufacturing.

The American workers we interviewed were appalled that the new immigrants did not participate in company or community child care programs. This meant that the children might not see their mother or father for nine to eleven hours, as little housing was close enough to the mills to permit visits home during breaks or over the lunch period. Further, according to Americans, the Hmong families never "functioned" as a family—"eating dinner or going places together as a family."

Two of the mills had the highest standards for their on-site child care centers, yet the new immigrants had no interest in enrolling their children. Instead the immigrant parents would work different shifts, passing children from one to the other in the parking lot or at the time clock. Frequently grandparents shared the same home and assisted with child care as well. Americans routinely reported that these practices were due to the Hmong greediness and unwillingness to part with money for high-quality child care. This interpretation ignored the strong Hmong tradition of caring for children only with the help of family members. The sacrifice of spouses working different shifts was how the Hmong expressed their love for their children. The communal living circumstances were traditional and reinforced the role of the elders in the extended family order in Hmong culture.

Ironically, in countless interviews the Hmong routinely accused the Americans of the same lack of commitment to their children. Their "willingness to let strangers take care of their children" so that they could "selfishly have the same work schedule as their spouse" was the most common concern voiced about American parental behavior by the Hmong workers. For Americans, the financial sacrifice associated with paying out of pocket for child care was warranted by the desire to have a "normal family life." The unwillingness to ask for or accept the offer of assistance with child care responsibilities from a grandparent was a sign of their respect for their elders and their right to use their time as they wished. Even when Americans used family members for child care, they were quick to point out how they compensated the caregiver. It is clear that both cultures love their children, but they express that love in very different manifestations when it comes to child care. By "crossing so many rivers" the immigrants and the Americans alike had lost their status as "good parents" in one other's eyes. There is clearly a need to build bridges over the rivers for each group to better understand the motivations for the other's behavior.

These immigrant workers have saved our industry: they are industrious, reliable, and available. Young Americans aren't like that anymore.
—Supervisors, managers, and owners throughout the industry

Over and over we heard supervisors and managers wondering how they could fill their open slots. The limited supply of unskilled labor colors every discussion in the factory—whether to buy a new machine, to run a third shift, or to bid on that contract. Every manager we talked to knew the current unemployment rate in the Catawba Valley to the nearest decimal point; it hovers around 2 percent and has not risen above 3 percent in more than a decade. This historically low rate implies that the only unemployed people in the region "choose" to be unemployed in some sense of the word, such as through poor health circumstances or a variety of other reasons.[11] There are many industrious and reliable Americans; they are simply not available to the hosiery industry, as better job opportunities abound in the healthy economy. In particular, the entrance of electrical component manufacturing into the area (ironically attracted to the region because of the reliable and technically skilled workforce available due to the presence of hosiery manufacturing) has further tightened the market for good workers. These jobs frequently offer better benefits; thus native North Carolinians are, in fact, working hard, just in other, more lucrative industries.

Finally, the extremely low tuition rates for in-state residents throughout the North Carolina public higher education system have permitted far greater educational aspirations and access for recent generations of high school students.[12] Evidence of this is easy to see in the mill. Numerous workers have photographs of their children at work stations, in tool boxes, and in small photo albums regularly shared in company cafeterias and on loading docks during breaks. Their children are nearly always pictured in school or athletic achievement settings, wearing caps and gowns, uniforms, and other visual markers of success. American workers are proud to tell anyone of their children's accomplishments and typically end with a comment on why they encourage their children to pursue all the education they can get: "They won't have to work in a hosiery mill like me." Many of the larger companies have employee newsletters that regularly report the increasing levels of educational attainment achieved by the children of mill workers, which means this may be the last generation of "native" Americans to fill the jobs in the mills.

By contrast, the population of immigrants throughout history has been disproportionately composed of the most aggressive labor market participants. This is true for immigrant Asians as well as for immigrant Hispanics. Comparing the characteristics of the few young Americans available for hosiery mill work to those of the immigrant population gives a tremendously biased sample of the underlying labor force characteristics for each population. A strong local economy has led to better job opportunities for the Americans. The immigrants are not taking jobs but, rather, solving a difficult labor shortage problem for the industry. Without their participation, the rest of the industry would be unable to compete internationally.

This is probably the number one reason for the gradual but nearly complete willingness of the American fixers to train the immigrants in the diagnosis and repair of the knitting machines throughout the mills. This has occurred in informal settings as well as through a remarkable cooperative education program started by the Carolina Hosiery Association. The association's 1990 decision to initiate, develop, and support a Hosiery Technology Center (HC) at the Catawba Valley Community College and, later, to extend it to the Randolph County Community College (the majority of sheer hose are manufactured in Randolph County) has been critical to the transfer of technological knowledge to new labor force entrants. The more recent dramatic increase in computer use in the technology of knitting has also fueled demands for the HC training for experienced and apprentice fixers alike. In addition, the HC has underwritten the significant costs of industry-specific training in many of the female-dominated positions in hosiery manufacturing, including knitting, seaming, boarding, and packaging. Finally, the HC is taking the lead on dyeing and finishing technology training as well as in the development of industrywide quality standards for hosiery. The HC's complex and necessary alliances with the Manufacturing Extension Partnership and ESL programs, links with community partners in social services, and the regular employment of the most skilled fixers as teachers in the HC programs speaks volumes about the changes in strategy for how the mills will survive.

What is essential in building a bridge to other generations as well as to other cultures is an understanding of the dynamics of the labor markets as well as the evolution of employment prospects. This industry and state strategy to preserve hosiery manufacturing in North Carolina has been successful specifically because it looks at the data, the projections, and the long-term strategies to develop desirable industries and jobs for both native and new North Carolinians—to build communities.

We have to be willing to try the new technologies, to stay competitive, or we are going to be out of business here.—Americans and immigrants throughout the mills

The most dangerous and unpleasant part of hosiery production is boarding: pressing a sock against a hot metal form to set the dyes and retain the shape of the foot for more attractive packaging for retail sale. This job thus has the highest turnover and has, in turn, seen the greatest influx of the most recent immigrant workers, the Hispanics.

It is also the part of production with the greatest demands for technological innovation to reduce both injuries (which include both burns and significant repetitive motion disorders) and labor costs. The HC, close to the industry and its training needs, brought the technology-caused labor supply problem to the attention of key officials and faculty at North Carolina State University, the state's premiere land-grant institution of higher education. The faculty of the HC and the College of Textiles at N.C. State formed a cooperative committee that included numerous industry and trade association partners and was charged with the identification of the problem and the design of innovative solutions.

Finally, the problems with boarding were undertaken as part of a textile engineering honors seminar assignment at N.C. State with the director of undergraduate studies at the College of Textiles. Rethinking the process, teams of students were able to devise a number of prototypes for new boarding machines and then develop them for application to the boarding and, in some cases, packaging processes. One of the best of the undergraduate student designers pursued further graduate training at the College of Textiles and recently refined a design retrofit for current capital in use in boarding rooms throughout the industry. Now employed by a U.S. machine manufacturer, this graduate—who has virtually no history in the hosiery industry—is set to contribute to an innovation that will help the industry remain competitive in North Carolina.

Both national and international manufacturers of textile machinery have been frantically competing to develop the best prototype using these preliminary ideas and to win market share in a critical part of the industry ripe for capital replacement.[13] Ironically, an international beneficiary of the design ideas from the competition—a Spanish machine company—seems to be first in the race for actual design implementation. This firm recently sold a number of new machines to a major North Carolina hosiery mill. After installing the machines, assisting with some minimal training in their maintenance and repair, and returning home to Spain, they were called and asked why the Spanish-language instruction manual had been left behind. They responded that the majority of their new machine sales were to Latin American manufacturers and, thus, their priority was to complete the Spanish-language version of the repair instructions first. No English manual was available.

Thus, the willingness to try the new technology was only the first step in remaining internationally competitive. An American operations manager in this mill then realized that his Hispanic boarders, the lowest-paid workers in the mill, were fluent in Spanish, and he enlisted their help in making the repairs and adjustments to the boarding machines. Reaching out to the Spanish-speaking boarders on the shop floor to translate the repair manual and then to engage them in more technological training so that they could repair the boarding machines was the critical second step in ensuring that the mill will remain competitive, or, in the words of so many in the industry, "We are going to be out of business here." Redefining who "we" might be in the context of this example is a powerful testimony to the role of immigrants in our collective image of nation.

Over the last five years many experienced technicians have been offered astounding amounts of money to train fixers on-site in Latin American countries. Most have refused. They are far more willing to train Mexicans in North Carolina than to train Mexicans in Mexico and cause the loss of American jobs. Alternatively put, they would rather redefine "who an American is" and thus forgo the opportunity for individual profit in exchange for the transference of knowledge to their "competitors" in Mexico.

This is the true beginning of including the immigrants in the definition of nation, of building bridges between cultures, and of responding to the choice of border crossers in American factories or American jobs crossing borders. This is the voice of the mill worker.

Notes

This study would not have been possible without the scores of interviewers, translators, and industry sources, educators, owners, managers, and workers who generously gave of their time and knowledge over the past seven years. The book manuscript "Knitting the Social Fabric: The Survival of Work Family Balance in the Global Economy," by Rachel A. Willis, details the generous help of the individuals who were critical to the completion and quality of this study.

1. In 1998, hosiery manufacturing represented more than $3 billion a year in the North Carolina economy alone and more than 35,000 jobs. Down from a high of $7 billion a year nearly a quarter of a century ago, hosiery manufacturing has remained extremely labor intensive relative to other textiles and has not disappeared from the North Carolina landscape since the passage of the North American Free Trade Agreement. While some producers have experimented with offshore production facilities, there has been an equal amount of new development of physical manufacturing facilities as well as the acquisition of state-of-the-art knitting, seaming, dyeing, boarding, and packaging technology at facilities in North Carolina.

2. There were two other significant factors that permitted this industry to survive the transition period long enough to develop adequate responses: the relatively small amount of labor content in the product (ranges from 10 to 20 percent depending on product line) and the relatively large volume of product relative to value (which carries a high shipping cost).

3. This process is called boarding and refers to pressing the hose against a metal form of a foot and leg so the hose acquires the proper shape while drying.

4. With anywhere from 70 to 480 needles around the narrow cylinder, a half-hose or "coarse" good machine is defined as having fewer than 300 needles. Tights or panty-hose are referred to as "sheer goods" and are produced on machines that have more than 300 needles in the cylinder.

5. From the French word *grege*, or raw, a greige good in hosiery manufacturing refers to a sock that has been knitted and seamed and is unfinished. Greige goods are frequently bought and sold from both competitors and employees manufacturing at home, as the intermediate goods for a given style and size are completely interchangeable.

6. This brief summary of how hosiery made its way to North Carolina is taken from Milton N. Grass, *The History of Hosiery, from the Piloi of Ancient Greece to the Nylons of Modern America* (New York: Fairchild, 1956), and Brent D. Glass, *The Textile Industry in North Carolina: A History* (Raleigh: Division of Archives and History, North Carolina Department of Cultural Resources, 1992).

7. Overall, the industry employed between 75 and 80 percent women as recently as 1995. The proportion of women has declined slightly as the number of immigrant employees has increased over the past four years.

8. Interview with knitting room supervisor, Upjohn, Summer 1996.

9. Specifically, the evolving organization and support of Lutheran Family Services in Charlotte and western North Carolina to aid the resettlement of the Montagnard and then the Hmong was the critical factor in the immigration patterns at this time.

10. A family-held firm with an on-site day care facility since its opening in 1979, Neuville Industries has been on the list the longest. A second hosiery mill and nearby competitor, Ridgeview Industries, has joined the list in recent years and gone public with stock ownership. The range of policies and benefits throughout the industry is enormous.

11. Drug testing is extremely common within the industry because impaired judgment not only increases health care costs but presents immediate safety problems in the mill as well as serious quality control issues in the industry.

12. Ranked among the most affordable public schools in the nation, the University of North Carolina has an extensive system of sixteen campuses, and the separate community college system has more than thirty campuses. With the highest in-state tuition still less than $2,000 per year at the top campuses and community college rates as low as $15 per credit hour, economic access to education and training opportunities are widely available in the region and throughout the state.

13. The typical age for boarding machines in operation throughout North Carolina just three years ago was more than thirty to forty years. The machines were paid for and did the basic job, and thus owners were reluctant to replace the machines unless there would be a significant reduction in the amount of labor involved. Thus, a retrofit of the machines may be more cost effective for older companies with lots of machinery; the new technology may be more profitable for expanding companies.

Steve Striffler

We're All Mexicans Here

Poultry Processing, Latino Migration, and the Transformation of Class in the South

This is an unfashionable book. It defends an unfashionable
thesis about an unfashionable class formed in an unfashionable place. The class is the industrial proletariat. The place is
the point of production. And the thesis has two parts. First,
I shall argue that the industrial working class has made significant and self-conscious interventions in history. Second,
I argue that these interventions were and continue to be
shaped by the process of production.
—Michael Burawoy, *The Politics of Production* (1985)

I arrive at Tyson's Northwest Arkansas Job Center in Springdale at 10:00 in
the morning. At the center of the most productive poultry-producing region
in the world, Springdale is an unremarkable working-class city that is home
to the corporate headquarters of Tyson Foods. The Tyson job center itself is
a small, unimpressive building with a sparse interior that resembles a government office. Signs surrounding the secretary's desk suggest a certain seriousness. In Spanish one says, "Do not leave children unattended," and another
warns, "Thank you for your interest in our company, Tyson Foods, but please
bring your own interpreter."

The receptionist, who begins the process of turning applicants into employees, seems surprised by my presence. She apologizes: "Sorry, hon, there
are no openings for a mechanic. Fill out the application and we'll call you."
Somewhat puzzled, I assure her that I am amazingly unqualified to be a mechanic. "I'm hoping," I tell her, "to get a job on the production line" at one
of Tyson's three major processing plants in the area. With a confused look she
hands me a thick packet of forms and asks, "*You* want to work on the line?"

As I turn to take a seat, I begin to understand her confusion. The secretary
and I are the only Americans, the only white folks, and the only English speakers in the room. Spanish predominates, but is not the only foreign language.

Lao is heard from a couple in the corner, and a threesome from the Marshall Islands is speaking a Polynesian language. Within less than two decades, the poultry industry has become a key site for "workers of the world" to come together in a region of the United States—the South—that has received relatively few foreign immigrants during the twentieth century. Attracted by employment opportunities in the poultry industry, Latin Americans first began to enter northwest Arkansas in the late 1980s. Today about three-quarters of plant labor forces are Latin American, with Southeast Asians and Marshallese accounting for a large percentage of the remaining workers. U.S.-born workers are few and far between.

It is not just the workers who look different. What passes for industry and a factory job has dramatically changed in the recent past as well. In July 1974, when Burawoy began his unfashionable study of the labor process, it was no wonder that he chose the place, the job, and the corporation that he did. Working in Chicago as a machine operator in the engine division of a multinational corporation, Burawoy was situated in what many considered to be the heart of American capitalism at the time. His was a study of real men making real things in a real factory at the heart of real, that is, industrial, America.

What a difference twenty-five years make. I began factory-based fieldwork in May 2000. The location was not Chicago, however, but the semirural area of northwest Arkansas. The factory did not build engines or tractors; it processed chickens. The workers were not named Charley, Morris, or Harry, but Jesus, Miguel, Angelina, Maria, Mana, and Lem. They did not come from mid-America but from Mesoamerica, Southeast Asia, and the Marshall Islands. We were not organized; we were employed by a company that vilified labor unions with a religious fervor. Culture was not something we simply formed in the workplace—what Burawoy called workplace culture. It was a set of contradictory frameworks and prior experiences that both informed and was informed by our lives at work and home. It determined the content of our lunchboxes and shaped our diverse understandings of work, home, family, and politics. And above all, I was not a skilled machine operator, but a *harinero*, or breading operator.

This is not to argue that everything about factory work has changed or that the changes are best understood in terms of a series of oppositions: union vs. nonunion, North vs. South, engines vs. chickens, skilled vs. unskilled, Harry vs. Miguel (or Maria), and so forth. Nevertheless, southern poultry plants are perhaps at least as good a place from which to examine American industrial capitalism in 2000 as Burawoy's Chicago machine shop was in the mid-1970s. The central tensions and contradictions of American capitalism—including the combination of vertical integration and subcontracting, the decline of labor unions, the feminization of the industrial labor force, and the undeniable importance of immigration—are brought into sharp relief through an analysis of the poultry industry. The history of poultry is a tale about the southernization of American industry. As American industry transformed the South, the South transformed American industry.

Chicken itself has a peculiarly southern flavor, even if the industry's defining features are now commonplace throughout much of the global economy. The pre–World War II origins of the industry can be found in Delmarva, but the breeding, raising, and processing of chickens quickly moved (farther) south into economically depressed regions such as northern Georgia, northwest Arkansas, and western North Carolina. The rise of poultry as America's favorite meat was made possible by a rural, southern poor who—during the postwar period—would raise more chickens at a lower cost than ever before. The market for poultry exploded after World War II, and poor farmers on declining cotton farms in Georgia and devastated apple orchards in Arkansas jumped at the chance to raise chickens. A rural, underemployed, and often black population provided processing plants with cheap labor. These workers endured savage line speeds while producing cheap chicken for American consumers.

In 1950 no one corporation controlled even a single aspect of the industry (such as breeding, growing, processing, etc.). Firms specializing in a particular facet of the business were linked to independent farmers through a relatively free and competitive market. This would all change within less than a decade as the vast majority of production and processing came under the control of vertically integrated firms. By 1960 a relatively open market had given way to one characterized by binding contracts and the intense concentration of power and profit. "Independent" growers became bound to integrated firms that owned or controlled virtually every aspect of the industry.

Today a handful of extremely large corporations controls the industry from egg to market. Tyson Foods, the world's largest processor of poultry, beef, and pork, is headquartered in Arkansas; but its poultry operations are spread throughout the southern United States, and its empire is global in nature. Chicken dominates the rural South (it's bigger than cotton or tobacco), and the South dominates chicken (the major producers are all southern states). During the last fifteen years, this low-wage industry has come to depend on an increasingly foreign labor force that is largely Latin American in origin. Marginalized by nationality, language, and ethnicity, Latin Americans have been actively (and at times illegally) recruited by poultry integrators as a source of cheap and (in theory) docile labor. This Latinization of processing plants (and southern agriculture in general) has occurred unevenly across both space and time, but the shift from a U.S.-born labor force to a foreign one is unmistakable.

This study takes the reader into a Tyson processing plant. The story begins on the plant floor and provides a firsthand introduction to the conflicts and problems that contemporary workers face. As an older generation of plant workers would attest, these struggles have defined poultry processing from its inception. The second part provides a glimpse into how Latin American workers view themselves and their social location both at work and in southern communities. What does it mean to be Mexican in the New South? Together, these anecdotes tell a larger story about the social costs and benefits surrounding a universal, common, and yet peculiarly southern commodity: the chicken.

Tyson processes job applicants like it processes poultry. The emphasis is on quantity, not quality. No one at the job center spends more than a minute looking at my application, and no single person takes the time to review the whole thing. Efficiency rules. Bob begins and ends my "interview" with "What can I do for ya?" I tell him I want a job at a processing plant; he makes a quick call, and in less than five minutes I have a job on the line. My references, which someone has already called, check out, and I pass both the drug test and the physical. I am Tyson material.

I arrive at the plant the following Tuesday ready for work. It is massive, and its exterior is put together much like the job center—quickly, cheaply, and piece by piece. At 3:00 P.M. sharp, Javier, my orientation leader, gathers up the new recruits and escorts us into a small classroom that contains a prominently displayed sign: "Democracies depend on the political participation of its [*sic*] citizens, but not in the workplace." Written in both English and Spanish, the message is clear in any language.

The nine (other) people in my orientation class are representative of the plant's second shift. Eight are Latin Americans, with six coming from Mexico and two from El Salvador. Six men, two women. As younger men frequently lament, the women in the plant tend to be slightly older than the men. In this respect the two in our group, Maria (early forties) and Carmen (early fifties), are typical. The six men vary considerably in age. Juan, from El Salvador, is only twenty-three, but Don Pablo is well into his sixties. Jorge, in his mid-thirties, has lived in California for the past thirteen years, the vast majority of it working in a textile factory. Although he has only been in Arkansas for a few days, he already appreciates the region for many of the same reasons that draw other Latin Americans. Like Jorge, most of the Mexican workers come from rural areas in the state of Guanajuato. They pass through California, where they work in factories or pick fruit, and then find their way to the promised land of Arkansas. Not only is everything in Arkansas much cheaper, but Tyson Foods pays around eight dollars an hour, offers insurance, and consistently provides forty hours of work a week. Poultry processing is a tough way to achieve upward mobility, but that is precisely what these jobs represent for most immigrants.

After putting on our smocks, aprons, earplugs, hairnets, beard nets (men), and boots, we begin the tour of the plant. No one is unaccustomed to hard work, and most have killed chickens on farms in Latin America; but nobody is prepared for the overwhelming combination of sounds, sights, and smells that await us. It does not help that the tour begins in "live hanging" (*pollo vivo*). Carmen says what we all are thinking: "My God! (*¡Dios Mio!*) How can one work here?" The answer, it turns out, is quite simple. Live hanging pays a bit more, and there is actually a waiting list to spend the day attaching live chickens to the production line. Chickens are flooding into a completely dark and uncomfortably warm room at about 200 a minute. The smell is indescribable, suffocating, and absolutely unforgettable. Five or six workers grab the flailing chickens, hooking them upside-down by their feet to an overhead rail system that transports the birds throughout the plant. Blood, feces, and feathers are flying everywhere.

Fortunately, I land a job on Saw Lines 1 and 2. It's not exactly pleasant, but it's a long way from live hanging. These further processing lines are at the heart of the revolution that has transformed the poultry industry and American diets over the past twenty-five years. A quarter of a century ago, most Americans bought chicken in one form: the whole bird. Today, Tyson alone produces thousands of "further processed/value-added" poultry products, including nuggets, patties, franks, pet food, and a range of parts that come in a multiplicity of shapes, sizes, textures, and flavors. Where I work, the process is relatively simple. There are two identical lines. Each takes a whole chicken, cuts it, marinates it, and then breads it. With about twenty to twenty-five workers, Lines 1 and 2 each process about eighty birds a minute, or 40,000 pounds of chicken a day.

My coworkers on Saw Lines 1 and 2 are an interesting and diverse bunch. Of the twenty or so workers who keep the lines running, two (excluding myself) are white Americans. Most white workers left area poultry plants during the region's economic boom of the 1990s, and those who remain tend to fall into two categories. An older group has been working at Tyson for more than twenty years; they have found a niche and hang on to the benefits that seniority bestows. The few white workers who started at Tyson more recently did so because poultry is one of their only options. Jane, for example, is well into her sixties and worked at the plant during the 1960s before Tyson bought it. She subsequently moved out of the area and spent most of her life working in a factory that produced surgical equipment. After her husband died, she returned to northwest Arkansas. Every day she walks to the plant from her small apartment. Factory work is all she knows.

Most of those who work directly on the line are women, often "older" women in their forties and fifties. Jane usually sorts chicken on Line 2 along with Alma, Gabriela, and Blanca. Alma and Gabriela are Mexican sisters in their forties. Blanca, also from Mexico, has a husband and four children working at Tyson, including Maria, who checks the marinade. Their counterparts on Line 1, Li and Lem, are both from Laos, in their fifties, and could not be more different. Lem is friendly, always willing to help out coworkers. Li has two personalities. On the plant floor, she barks out orders like a drill sergeant, seemingly oblivious to the fact that no one can understand her. In the break room, she is one of the sweetest people, sharing her culinary delights with Laotians, Mexicans, Salvadorans, and hungry anthropologists alike.

The fact that most on-line workers are women is neither coincidence nor insignificant in a plant where about two-thirds of the workers are male. On-line jobs are the worst in the plant. They are not only monotonously repetitive; they are dangerously so. When the line is working properly, on-line workers can hang chickens at a pace of forty birds a minute for much of the day. They stand in the same place and make the exact same set of motions for an entire shift. In contrast, although auxiliary workers tend to do the same tasks all day long, they are not doing the exact same set of movements with nearly the intensity as on-line workers. Women are concentrated in on-line jobs because they are effectively excluded from all jobs that involve heavy lifting or the operation of machinery. Mario, Alejandro, Roberto, Juan, Jeff, Carlo, and I come from all over the world, but in the plant we are "young" men who clean up waste, bring supplies, lift heavy objects, and operate handcarts and forklifts. As auxiliary workers, we do on-line work, but only intermittently.

I am to be the *harinero* (breading operator), or as my twenty-two-year-old supervisor Michael likes to call me, the little flour boy. Michael cannot do the job himself, and his instructions are simple: "Do what Roberto does." Roberto provides little formal training, a fact that makes learning my new task a bit tricky. Roberto has five years on the job, and everything is natural to him. He is an experienced worker and can do every job on the line, fix the machines, and carry on a conversation all at the same time. He is neither friendly nor cool when we first meet, and unlike virtually everyone else in the plant, Roberto is thoroughly unimpressed by the fact that I speak Spanish. We would eventually talk about everything, including his wife's struggles at a nearby turkey plant, his kids' achievements in local schools, and our own problems at the plant. I would even visit his parents in Mexico. In the beginning, however, I just watch, hoping to gain his respect and learn anything that will allow me to survive the first week.

I learn quickly that "unskilled" labor requires an immense amount of skill. The job of *harinero* is extremely complicated. In a simple sense, the *harinero* empties fifty-pound bags of flour all day long. The work is backbreaking, but it requires less physical dexterity than many of the jobs on the line. At the same time, the job is multifaceted and cannot be learned in a single day. Controls on the breader and rebreader need to be continually checked and adjusted, the marinade needs to be monitored, the power needs to be shut on and off, and old flour needs to be replaced with fresh flour. All of this would be relatively manageable if the lines functioned properly. They never do.

The rebreader is the source of more than 75 percent of all the lines' problems, particularly snags that force a shutdown. It is here, with Roberto, that my education both as *harinero* and worker begins. One of the first things I learn is that I will be doing the job of two people. There have always been two *harineros*, one for each line. However, Michael recently decided to operate both lines with only one *harinero*. He is essentially doing what he has done, or will do, with virtually all of the jobs on the Saw Line. Where there used to be three workers hanging chicken, there are now two; where there used to be three or even four workers arranging parts, there are now two; where two people used to check the level of marinade, there is only one. Nor is this limited to our section of the plant. About six months prior to my arrival, an older generation of supervisors, most of whom had come up through the production lines, were essentially forced from their jobs when new plant managers took over. The new managers made the older supervisors push the workers harder and harder. The supervisors, who knew what it was like to work on the line, eventually refused by simply leaving the plant. As a result, a younger generation of college-educated supervisors, personified by Michael, was brought in.

Michael is a working-class kid clawing his way into the middle class. One of the first in his family to attend college, he just graduated from the University of Arkansas with a degree in poultry science. Although he "never imagined" that he would earn so much in his first year out of college, the trade-off was considerable. He had no life outside the plant. Supervisors start at less than $30,000 a year. Michael arrived every day at 12:30 in the afternoon and never left the plant before 3:30 in the morning. Unlike line workers, of course, he enjoyed a job with some variety, almost never got his hands dirty, and could hope to move up the corporate ladder. At least in the short term, however, he was consumed by the plant just like the rest of us.

Nevertheless, it was Michael who was the focus of our anger and Michael (guided by his bosses) who was implementing the latest round of Taylorization. Part of the reason why all this was possible—besides the fact that there was no labor union or binding job descriptions—was that reducing the number of on-line workers does not necessarily prevent the line from running. The remaining workers simply have to work faster to keep pace with the line. As Roberto was quick to point out, the position of the breading operator is somewhat different. When the breading operator does not keep up, the entire line comes to a standstill. And Michael was replacing two experienced *harineros*, Roberto and Alejandro, with a single trainee—me. As Roberto explained, "When Michael told us he was going to only have one *harinero* we were not totally surprised. I told him I was quitting as *harinero* and would work on the line. Alejandro left [as *harinero*] in less than a week. Michael couldn't find anyone to take the job. He posted the job announcement, but everyone in the plant quickly learned what was going on and wouldn't do it. It was too much work. So he had to get a new guy who couldn't say no—someone like you. Alejandro and I have seniority, so it is easy for us to switch jobs."

Roberto's understanding of the situation was absolutely correct, but he was being less than honest. It *did* matter to him. Alejandro, however, was more forthcoming about his feelings: "I had eight years as *harinero*. I like the job. It's like family here. It doesn't mean anything to Michael. For him it's just a job and we're just Mexicans. He doesn't know anything anyway. I wanted to stay, but why? Fuck that! Twice as much work for the same salary. I did my job well. I have nothing to be ashamed of."

During my first weeks on the job, the line is continually shut down for one reason or another. Few of the problems have anything to do with me, but the entire process is slowed by the fact that there is only one real *harinero*—Roberto. The *harinero* has to fix just about everything, but the central problem is that the rebreader simply does not have sufficient power to circulate the flour through the apparatus while pushing the chicken along the conveyor belt. In short, when one opens the valves and allows enough flour to flow through the machine in order to bread the chicken, the machine bogs down, the chicken piles up, and the parts begin to fall on the floor. This results in loud shrieks from just about everyone on the line. The breading operator, in this case Roberto, has to shut down the entire line and figure out exactly which part of the rebreader is malfunctioning.

There are several solutions to the general problem, the exact nature of which provides the contours for an ongoing struggle between Michael, Roberto, and (now) me. First and most obviously, the mechanics could feed more power to the machine, thus giving it the capacity to handle the weight of the chicken and flour. This is clearly what Michael wants. Second, we could run less chicken, which, by reducing the weight on the conveyor belts, would allow the rebreader to operate properly with the existing amount of power. From Michael's perspective this is simply unthinkable. Our guiding principle is to keep the line running at all times, at maximum speed, and at full capacity.

Consequently, Roberto and I adopt two strategies in order to keep the rebreader working properly and the lines running smoothly. First, we change the flour frequently. Fresh flour that has not yet clumped and been weighed down from the wetness of the chicken is necessarily lighter and therefore circulates more smoothly through the entire apparatus. Michael, however, does not like this option because it is more expensive. Second, we use only as much flour as the rebreader can support. But again Michael insists both that the rebreader can handle more (old) flour and that the levels we run it at are inadequate to bread the chicken sufficiently.

The difficulty for Roberto and me is that Michael is simply wrong. He passes by every hour, sees there is not enough flour on the conveyor belt, and tells us to increase the flow. Confident that he has set us straight, he then leaves, and with remarkable precision the machine bogs down. Roberto and I have to stop the production line, clean up the mess, and readjust the flow of the flour so the machine can run without stopping. Michael then returns, wonders why there is not more flour on the conveyor belt, and the process begins again.

This uneasy and somewhat absurd tension characterizes the workday from beginning to end. Only occasionally would Michael be present when the rebreader bogged down as a result of his own miscalculations. These were the moments Roberto and I relished. Roberto would suddenly forget how to fix the machine. He would simply watch Michael try to correct the impending disaster by frantically calling a mechanic on his walkie-talkie. The mechanic would eventually arrive, talk to Michael, stare at the machine for ten minutes, and then swallow his pride and ask Roberto what the problem was. Roberto would then look at Michael, smile at me, and fix it in a matter of seconds.

Looking back, I find it hard to explain why this petty struggle seemed so damned important at the time. The irony, of course, is that in a very real sense it was in our interests to follow Michael's (uninformed) directions and let the rebreader bog down and the production line stop. It was a pain to continually fix the machine, but we got paid the same amount regardless of whether we were emptying bags of flour, fixing the rebreader, or standing around talking.

Moreover, a shutdown generally proved that Michael was wrong—something that Roberto and I took great satisfaction in even as we were simultaneously annoyed that the lines were not running. Finally, it was obviously in the interests of *every other* worker to have the Saw Lines shut down; it gave them a break.

Why, then, did Roberto and I, as well as the on-line workers, become profoundly irritated when one or both of the Saw Lines shut down? Several factors seem to be at work. First, there was the general context of Michael's attempt to reduce not only the number of *harineros* but the number of workers in general. This Taylorization angered everyone and confirmed our collective perception: Michael's lack of experience led to decisions that made our lives intolerable and were economically unsound. We believed we could run the lines better than Michael. Second, and perhaps most important, by concentrating decision making in his own hands, Michael was degrading the work of the *harinero*. He was removing the very thing—control over the labor process—that gave the job meaning to Roberto, Alejandro, and myself.

Finally, the fact was that virtually all of the workers took great pride in jobs that had, for the most part, been thoroughly degraded. To be sure, there were times when we enjoyed a shutdown. The more frantic Michael got, the more we celebrated. Most of the time, however, we workers relished the agony that a stoppage would inevitably cause the supervisor while simultaneously being frustrated by the fact that we were having a "bad" day. We took great pride in doing our jobs well.

Despite our protests, Michael forges ahead with his plan, and on the Monday of my fourth week I begin running both lines by myself. What Michael does not tell us, however, is that he has finally gotten the mechanics to boost the power going into the production lines. On that fateful Monday, when Roberto and I arrive, we know Michael has won. With increased power, the rebreader runs smoothly and almost never bogs down. This has the effect of deskilling the job of the *harinero*. Running the lines no longer requires the expertise of someone like Roberto. There are almost no problems to correct. Now the lines not only run with fewer problems; they run faster and can handle more chicken. From my perspective, it means that the job involves less skill but much more work. I fill the flour not only for two lines, but for two lines running faster and more consistently. With the sometimes entertaining struggle between Michael, Roberto, and myself now resolved, I become the *harinero*, and the intensity and monotony of the job is almost unbearable. For the rest of the workers, particularly those on-line, it is devastating. The lines shut down less, there are fewer breaks, and the pace is quicker. By the end of the week, Blanca, who is in her fifties, is simply overwhelmed. She has been hanging chickens for too many years, and her body simply cannot withstand the faster pace of the production line. She had been hoping to stay at Tyson until she could retire to Mexico, but Blanca is forced to quit within the week.

Forms of worker expression are necessarily muted on the plant floor by the intensity of the work, the noise, and the supervision. Knowing glances, practical jokes, cooperation, and shared pain bind workers in ways that require little acknowledgment or expression. In the cafeteria or break room, however, the situation is quite different. What the plant floor suppresses, the break room embraces. Twice a shift, for thirty minutes, workers watch Spanish-language TV, eat and exchange food, complain about supervisors, and relax their bodies. More often than not I was the only American in the main break room. The few American workers on the second shift were almost always congregated in a smaller break room where smoking is permitted and the TV programs are in English. Supervisors almost never enter the break room, and when they do, they are noticeably uncomfortable. At least here, the inmates are in charge.

The following conversation took place in the main break room after I had been working at the plant for only three weeks. However else I was seen by my new friends—as a strange gringo who spoke Spanish, as a *blanco* who was too stupid to get a good job, or as an inept breading operator—I was not seen as an anthropologist or a professor at this time, although I would eventually tell everyone at the table who I was.

One other thing is important. On this particular day, Michael had pushed us hard and brought free boxes of fried chicken to thank us. It was a gesture that he would make half a dozen more times while I was working in the plant. It always produced roughly the same reaction from the workers. We would look at the chicken, then stare at each other; someone would say some version of the following in Spanish: "Pure asshole. I am not going to eat this shit." Then there would be an awkward moment when we would quickly look at each other, look away, and pretend to not know what was going on. Then someone would say, "We can't throw away good food and we're all hungry. Let's eat this shit." More pissed off than when we came on break, we would grab the chicken and eat most of it or carefully pack it away to take home to family.

Michael's gesture was insulting for many reasons. First, he wasn't just giving us food; he was giving us chicken. Second, the gesture did not come close to making up for what the workers had just left on the plant floor. As paternalism, it was so pathetic and transparent that it was nothing less than insulting. (Why Michael did not understand this is a different issue.) Finally, it was insulting because we knew, even as we hesitated, that we were going to eat the chicken. We would process our chicken and eat it too.

Here, then, is the conversation that ensued at the table where I sat as we chewed the chicken. It is interesting to note that no one ever directly talked about Michael's gesture or our acceptance of it. There seemed to be a collective agreement not to relive the humiliation.

Roberto welcomes me into the group: "Ai, Steve, you are almost Mexican. All you need is a Mexican wife to cook you some decent lunch and you would be Mexican."

Alejandro, also from Mexico, chimes in: "Yes, Steve is a Mexican. He speaks Spanish, eats with Mexicans, and he works like a Mexican. It's pure Mexicans here. We all eat chicken."

Elisa, three years on the job, kindly protests: "Ai . . . I'm not Mexican. I'm Salvadoran."

Alejandro gently explains: "Look, we're all Mexicans here [in the plant]. Screwed-over Mexicans." Pointing to Li, an older woman on our line who is from Laos, he continues: "Look, even she is a Mexican. Pure."

We laugh as Li, who can't hear us, quietly devours a chicken wing.

Elisa, catching on to what Alejandro is suggesting, finally agrees: "Yes, it's the truth. We are Mexicans here in the plant, especially inside [on the floor] when we are working."

I ask, somewhat interested, "And outside the plant, in Fayetteville, Springdale, and Rogers? Are we all Mexicans outside?"

Roberto quickly responds: "Outside, we are all fucked. We're in Arkansas." Everyone laughs.

Alejandro, more seriously, says, "Outside, you're a gringo [talking to me]. You are from here. Outside, we are Mexicans, but it is different. We're still screwed, but in a different way. We are foreigners. We don't belong. At least here in the plant we belong even if we are exploited. Outside, we live better than in Mexico, but we do not belong, we are not from here and keep to ourselves."

I then ask, "And in Mexico? Who are we in Mexico?"

Roberto says, "In Mexico, you [referring to me] are a gringo. You are a foreigner, but not like we are here in Arkansas. You are more like a tourist; treated well. We are not tourists here. We are treated more like outsiders. In Mexico, we are normal people, just like everyone else. Because it's all Mexicans. But in Mexico there is no future. My children were all born here, they are Americans. They have a future. Now, when I return to Mexico I feel like a tourist. I have money, travel, visit people. Our future is here now."

Alejandro ends on a light note: "At least in Mexico the chicken has some fucking taste."

When Alejandro looks around a cafeteria filled with people from Mexico, El Salvador, Honduras, Vietnam, Laos, and the Marshall Islands and says that we are all Mexicans, he is making a statement about class. He is not confused by the bright lights of the postmodern world or unclear where he is located, socially, racially, and geographically. Rather, he is consciously playing with the word "Mexican," using it almost as a synonym for "worker." "Yes, we are all Mexicans here" is almost the same as saying "Yes, we are all workers here." It is not exactly the same, of course. "Mexican" does not simply mean "worker" —any kind of worker—but one who is doing what is socially defined as the worst kind of work. Shit work. In this respect, Li from Laos is not singled out by accident. She is Mexican, one of us, because she does the same crap as everyone in the room, because she eats Michael's chicken, and because she is Mexican to Tyson's all-white management.

This conversation suggests that we should at least consider the possibility that transnational migration and the resulting experiences may make people question the very categories that borders support. Both immigrants and the native born may develop notions of affiliation, identity, and loyalty that run counter to established ideologies of citizenship and national allegiance—and some of these identities may, however vaguely, be grounded in class. We must consider, or pose as a problem, that globalization can lead not only to the internationalization of capital but to the internationalization of workers. Poultry plants are, after all, one of the places where workers of the world come together. This does not mean that such sites will be similarly experienced or understood, or that they will automatically unite this diverse working class any more than factories did in nineteenth-century England. What it does mean is that if we are going to understand transnationalism in a more profound way, then we need to see culture not just in terms of cultural difference (where culture is a set of ethnic-national primordial rituals and customs) but also in terms of class formation. The Mexicans, Salvadorans, Vietnamese, and Americans I worked with experienced cultural difference every day in the form of exchanging tortillas, tacos, rice, beans, and turkey sandwiches while on break. But they also shared—in different ways—the cultured class experience of eating chicken that is as painful to swallow as it is to process. Exactly how these contradictory sets of experiences will translate politically, and what they will mean in terms of alliances between foreign and American workers, is one of the urgent questions facing the transnational South today.

Note

A slightly different version of this chapter was published in *Labor History* 43, no. 3 (2002): 305–13. Thanks to the journal (‹http://www.tandf.co.uk›) for the kind permission to reprint. I would also like to thank the University Center for International Studies (University of North Carolina, Chapel Hill) for providing me with a Rockefeller postdoctoral fellowship and a wonderful place to think and write.

References

Burawoy, Michael. 1979. *Manufacturing Consent: Changes in the Labor Process under Monopoly Capitalism.* University of Chicago Press.
———. 1985. *The Politics of Production.* New York: Verso.

James L. Peacock, Carla Jones, and Catherine Brooks

Gatokaca Drive

Global Relations between Souths in Mobile, Alabama

Since the Civil War, economic development in the American South has been depicted—somewhat accurately—as colonization by the North. Quite similarly, but on a global scale, economic development is often depicted as a colonization of the world's Souths by the world's Norths; in fact, "South" and "North" often replace "third world" and "first world" or similar terminologies. Whether in the American or global context, Souths are the site of cheap labor, once exploited agriculturally and then industrially for the profit of the colonizing and industrialized and technologically advanced Norths.

In this framework, our case is particularly suggestive, for it treats a partnership of two Souths: Mobile, Alabama, of the American Deep South, and Indonesia, the third largest of the global Souths—in short, two Souths uniting in a venture of engineering and manufacturing for a market in the North.

For Indonesia, this effort was resonant with meaning because it turned colonialism on its back in a daring experiment to produce a high-tech product in and for North America and thus reverse the pattern of the past 400 years, which is that Indonesia was a colonized area for exploitation by industrialized nations. For Mobile, the effort was also significant, as it was part of a creative endeavor to connect with another South as part of globalizing entrepreneurial initiatives in the American South. Both Souths, then, bid to move forward through a fertile and suggestive, if unexpected, partnership. Even though the initiative has been stifled by the Asian crash of 1997, it is not dead, and efforts to date are instructive.

This essay will discuss the implications of establishing business relations between the Indonesian company PT Industri Dirgantara, known as Industri Pesawat Terbang Nusantaras (IPTN), or Aircraft Industry of Indonesia, and the American city of Mobile, Alabama, prior to September 2000.[1] Business relations between these two entities depended to a large extent on symbols and ceremony. This story began as a fierce bidding competition among U.S. cities, apparently culminating in Mobile as victor, but then ended without a reward for Mobile. However, despite IPTN's failure to establish its aircraft factory, business relations between Indonesia and the United States remain symbolically significant.

In February 1994, city officials from Mobile attended the Singapore air show for the purpose of making contacts with the aerospace industry. Those attending the show included members of the Mobile Area Chamber of Commerce, Alabama Power, the Mobile Regional Airport Authority, and the Alabama Economic Development Partnership. While at the show, they learned that a company called Industri Pesawat Terbang Nusantaras was looking for a site in the United States at which to build a factory to manufacture twin-engine turboprop aircraft for commercial use. At the time, IPTN was involved in building parts for Boeing and was working on helicopters in Europe. It hoped to establish a factory in the United States so that the Federal Aviation Administration (FAA) would eventually certify the company. "Like the spark that starts any new relationship, being at the right place at the right time was a crucial part of landing IPTN," said Sara Lamb (1995), a columnist for the *Business Reporter*. The representatives from Alabama met with the company during the show to discuss constructing the plant at Brookley Field in Mobile. According to Gay Haas, director of the airport authority, one of the main reasons IPTN agreed to meet with them on such short notice was that many of the important figures from Alabama attended the air show. Their presence was a sign of their regard for the aerospace industry and their seriousness about establishing relations with them. Another factor that aided the Mobile representatives was their five-year relationship with Singapore Aerospace's subsidiary, Mobile Aerospace Engineering.

Perhaps important also was a friendship that Michael Dow perceived between himself and B. J. Habibie, Indonesia's minister of research and technology and overseer of IPTN. The two personalities are alike in being energetic, aggressive, and willing to experiment (Peacock 1996). While the asymmetry between leading the fourth largest nation in the world and leading a city (albeit one in the third largest nation) is salient, visiting Mayor Dow in his top-floor office in the new civic building of Mobile is enough to affirm his presence and strength of personality; he has plenty of what Indonesians term *wahju* (charisma). As for Habibie, his chutzpah is well known (and can be observed today by viewing his personal website).

City officials fought hard to have Mobile added to the list of prospective sites for the factory, which included twenty-seven other cities. The plant would employ up to 1,000 workers to build N-250 twin-engine turboprop airplanes from Indonesian-made parts. In March 1994, Mobile officials traveled to Seattle, Washington, to provide more research and information to IPTN's North American office, in hopes of becoming one of the sites under consideration. During the same month, Gay Haas and Jay Garner, the economic developer at Mobile's chamber of commerce, went to Washington, D.C., to meet with Indonesia's ambassador and U.S. representative Sonny Callahan.

Once Mobile was added to the list in April 1994, city officials made it their goal to distinguish Mobile from the other cities. They did this by presenting unexpected "gifts" at each meeting to draw IPTN's attention. "What we called them were our little surprises," said Haas. For example, the chamber of commerce translated all their brochures and a short video about Mobile into Indonesian. They also renamed a street Gatokaca Drive. Another surprise was a computer-animated program showing the entire site at Brookley field and IPTN's airplanes at different stages of construction. These surprises were presented in May to Habibie during his tour of possible sites in the United States.

To continue their lobbying efforts, Alabama officials traveled in late June 1994 to Jakarta and Bandung, home of IPTN's main plant in West Java. As a sign of respect for Indonesia's culture, the officials wore traditional batik shirts while there. During their trip, they made their presentation of Mobile and met with both Habibie and the president at the time, Suharto. They returned to Indonesia again in November of that year for the ceremonial unveiling of the commuter plane IPTN planned to construct in the United States. According to the *Business Reporter*, this ceremony was "steeped with honor and splendor."

During the May visit, Habibie was received with less ceremony than on later visits because the meeting was relocated from Mobile to Montgomery at the last minute, and it was all officials could do to scramble to the new location. However, when Habibie returned to Alabama in October, he was presented with a very elaborate welcome ceremony attended by more than 400 guests. This included a twenty-one-gun salute from the Alabama National Guard, a jet fly-by, the playing of the Indonesian national anthem, and a large sign stating, "Selamat datang ke kota Mobile" (Welcome to Mobile). When Habibie came to the podium to make his speech, he announced, "I did not expect this honor." He stood sideways as a sign of respect for the important state officials behind him and told them, "I cannot give you my back."

Habibie announced at this time that General Electric would join IPTN as business partner in the project and that discussions of partnership were also under way with Boeing. While the participation of General Electric and the possible collaboration of Boeing made the proposal even more attractive to Mobile officials, the involvement of these outside parties also raised the interests of other cities, increasing the competition for the factory. However, a decision by the FAA inadvertently improved Mobile's chances: the FAA gave the Mobile Airport Authority $2.6 million to repave Brookley Field's longest runway (Casey 1994).

By October 1994, Mobile had made the short list of cities still being considered by IPTN. These included Portland, Oregon; Phoenix, Arizona; and two last-minute additional sites, Macon, Georgia, and Long Island, New York. By early 1995, IPTN had announced that they had narrowed their search to just Mobile and Macon. Finally, in May 1995, officials from IPTN traveled to Alabama to announce Mobile as their preferred site, a decision that was later made official at the Paris air show (Lamb 1995). While at the show, Habibie said, "Upon the prestigious occasion of the Paris air show, we declare our intention to shape the future relationship of the state of Alabama and the Republic of Indonesia by signing our historical declaration of intent." In October of the same year, Habibie and the IPTN once again visited Mobile to commemorate the site with a plaque and a live oak tree, both symbols of the commencing business relations. Despite the fact that the competition was finally over, officials in Mobile did not lose focus on the project but continued their work to ensure a good relationship with IPTN. As Haas stated, "We're not going to be successful with the project until they're making and selling airplanes."

Mobile's success in luring IPTN to the city depended on symbols and attention to intercultural communication. Although Macon, Georgia, made a more economically lucrative offer to IPTN, the Indonesian company selected Mobile in part due to "a solid impression that they [Mobile officials] had done their homework about Indonesia" (Jones 1996). According to one IPTN marketing representative, "Mobile offered unified community support, from the Mayor to the Chamber of Commerce to citizens" and "communicated more welcoming and support to attract the project than any other site" (Jones 1996). This support extended beyond symbols (such as the street sign) and ceremony (such as Mobile schoolchildren singing a song in Indonesian). Mobile also solicited testimony from Singaporeans associated with the Singapore Airlines project living in Mobile. The testimony of Asian neighbors who claimed to be happy living in Mobile indicated both a concern on the part of Mobilians for Asian businesspeople in their community and a potential for Indonesians themselves to successfully integrate into the community.

From the beginning, Mobile officials devised tactics to draw the attention of the company and convince them that Mobile was the preferred location. As mentioned above, at the Singapore air show in 1994 the IPTN was impressed by the attendance of very important Alabama officials. This was a sign of their seriousness about beginning business relations with the aerospace industry.

City officials of Mobile also went through a great deal of planning to welcome the Indonesians to their city. The red carpet was rolled out, and many important people were in attendance when officials from IPTN visited. It must have caused Americans quite a bit of concern to ensure that none of their customs offended their visitors, whose traditions are quite different from those in the United States. Mobile's attention to the customs and culture of this largely Muslim Southeast Asian nation contrasted flatteringly to the faux pas other cities made in ignoring them. For example, Salt Lake City officials, overlooking the fact that Indonesia is the most populous nation of Muslims in the world, offered IPTN representatives pork barbecue (pigs are considered unclean by Muslims) when they visited the proposed Utah site (Jones 2001).

Although Mobile bested competing U.S. cities to lure IPTN to Alabama, Mobilians have yet to see this international venture realized. By January 1996, the ground still had not been broken, and Mobile officials were still waiting for IPTN to announce official plans for the aircraft factory. Bishop State Community College and Alabama Industrial College in Ozark were prepared to begin training programs for the workers who would eventually be employed by the factory; however, training would not begin until officials received word from IPTN. An entire year went by while the company waited for the N-250 aircraft to be certified for manufacture in the United States by the FAA. Meanwhile, IPTN continued trade of aircraft and other products with Thailand and South Korea. The N-250 flew for the first time in front of an international audience at the Paris air show in June 1997, but the company was still waiting to receive word from the FAA. According to Green B. Suttles III, project manager of business development, the market eventually shifted from turboprop to jet design, which caused the project to be delayed as IPTN constructed a regional jet model (Jones 2001). Unfortunately, during the time it took them to develop the new model, the political and economic situation in Indonesia collapsed, and the factory was never established.

Yet symbols of the business plans between the two countries endure. For example, the street sign reading "Gatokaca Drive" presented to the IPTN has more meaning than just the fact that it was an Indonesian word. Gatokaca is a legendary figure known as the "flying hero." This symbol reflects Indonesians' desire to create and market their own aircraft. The tree and plaque that were dedicated at the site are symbols of the relations established between the two countries. The act of planting the tree proclaimed, in essence, that as long as the tree survives, the interactions between the two areas will continue. To this day, Mobile officials and IPTN continue to exchange holiday greetings (Jones 2001). Despite the fact that the plans for the factory collapsed, Suttles says, "we [still] have a street with a strange name and a lovely industrial site with a healthy tree growing on it to represent the longevity of the relationship."

Although it is unfortunate that the plans for the N-250 aircraft factory fell through, the established relations between Indonesia and Mobile are very significant. Whereas international corporations traditionally established factories in Indonesia, in this case Indonesia created plans to build a plant in another country. This is symbolic of the increasing globalism and development of the two Souths.

Note

1. This brief report is based on interviews by Carla Jones with the Indonesian head of IPTN; by James Peacock with Michael Dow, mayor of Mobile; and by documents and conversations research by Cathy Brooks. Peacock also visited the Brookley field site at Mobile, which is the location of Gatokaca Drive.

PT Industri Dirgantara is a client of Global Visions, an air industry liaison/public relations marketing firm.

References

Casey, Dave. 1994. "Plane Plant Competition Gets Tougher: Indonesian Officials Visiting Mobile Reveal Two More Locations Added to List of Possible Production Sites." *Mobile Register*, December 7.

Jones, Carla. 1996. Interview with Satya, IPTN marketing representative. January.

———. 2001. Interview with Jean-Marc Iloy of Global Visions. February 20.

Lamb, Sarah. 1995. "Airplane Maker Plans Paris Announcement: City to Be Represented at Air Show when Mobile Officially Named as Factory Site." *Mobile Register*, May 25.

Peacock, James. 1996. Interview with Michael Dow. February.

Part Four

Flexible Citizenship

Transnational Professionals

Sawa Kurotani

The South Meets the East

Japanese Professionals in North Carolina's Research Triangle

> Imagine a state where one can have a comfortable and ful-
> filling life. In that state, workers are productive and they
> would not start a strike. From the president to the new em-
> ployee, everyone is enjoying the mild climate and rich
> living environment.
> —North Carolina Executive Summary, Japanese version;
>   translation my own

The South and Japan had little to do with each other historically and have oc-
cupied very different places in the world system, but they have one thing in
common. Both have managed through their modern and contemporary transformations to hang on to their essentialized identities, which are understood
to be deeply rooted in the respective region's/nation's past and critical for its
future, and the enduring sense of unique local identity continues to weigh
heavily in the consciousness of people who identify themselves with these
places. In fact, the American South and Japan both entered the modern world
as latecomers who had to take extraordinary means to catch up and compete
against their more industrialized powerful others—the North and the West,
respectively. In this catch-up game, both the South and Japan chose to play
the regional card, so to speak, or to capitalize on their unique economic, social, and cultural attributes that made them attractively different. At the same
time, these place-based identities proved flexible and adaptive enough at crucial times—the Civil War and Reconstruction for the South, and Meiji Res-
toration and World War II for Japan, for instance—through which these regions remade themselves while simultaneously retaining their regional specificity
(see, for example, Woodward 1971 on southern industrialization and Harootunian 1993 on Japan).

Why contemplate "the South meets the East" at this moment of history, in
the so-called age of globalization? Because the degree to which spaces are re-

organized by flexible capitalism in the last three decades puts the question in our face, as we look at places like North Carolina's Research Triangle, where new and unexpected crossroads are emerging. The advent of globalization and the secondary role of nation-states have transformed the process through which particular locations become the loci of new economic development and cultural production. While places far from the center of international commerce have been incorporated into the global assembly line (Freeman 2000; Ong 1987), second-tier cities, which previously served as the social, economic, and cultural hubs of the region, have become new loci of global economic activities (Markusen, Lee, and DiGiovanna 1999). Metropolis no longer enjoys the monopoly of cosmopolitanism and hybridity, as global influences seep out to its adjoining areas (Marcuse and van Kempen 2000; Soja 2000).

My research in the Research Triangle area of North Carolina, one of those second-tier cities that grew rapidly over three decades, between 1999 and 2000 specifically focused on Japanese transnational capitalism and the expatriate Japanese families who are stationed there by Japanese corporations. One of the few non-Western players in the global economy dominated by the West, Japan oscillates between the conflicting demands of going global and remaining Japanese. North Carolina is a relative newcomer to the globalization bandwagon and is eager to project a newly cosmopolitan image of the American South to (prospective) foreign investors. In this scene of transregional engagement, many—and often contradictory—global aspirations and imagined regionalities intersect and collide with one another.

Intersection 1

The opening statement of the North Carolina Executive Summary prepared by the Business/Industry Development Division of the North Carolina Department of Commerce pitches North Carolina to potential Japanese investors as an internationalized, business-friendly state full of happy, productive workers enjoying a comfortable lifestyle. In this succinct statement, the past and the future of the South come together—of the region that is defined by its economic "backwardness." This backwardness is at least in part a self-selected label that traveling representatives from the southern states found necessary for regional economic development. Lacking sufficient investment capital within the region, they often emphasized docile (nonunionized) labor, the tradition of hospitality, mild climate, business-friendly government, and tax incentives to attract investors from the North during Reconstruction as well as through the post–World War II push for industrialization (Boles 1999;

Kim 1995). In the late twentieth century, the same appeal was used again, but this time for Japanese and other foreign investors in the high-tech industries, such as microelectronics and biotechnology, instead of textile and other labor-intensive industries. In this statewide initiative to increase foreign direct investment, the Research Triangle between Raleigh, Durham, and Chapel Hill is of extreme importance. Research Triangle Park, or RTP, and its adjoining areas are an example of successful planned economic development that has attracted industrial ventures in microelectronics and biotechnology. Unlike the traditional manufacturing sector, these post-Fordist manufacturing industries are environmentally clean and are expected to create well-paying jobs for highly trained and educated workers. While the conceptualization and building of RTP began much earlier, 1980 was a benchmark year in its global aspiration, when the state of North Carolina, in cooperation with the Research Triangle Foundation and local chambers of commerce, began an aggressive campaign to invite foreign investment in the Research Triangle.

If the South sold itself to the outside for economic development in its post-bellum history (Kim 1995; Woodward 1971), the transnational marketing of the South creates a new challenge for regional players. North Carolina (as a state within the nation-state) and the Research Triangle (as a region within that state) collaborate in this scale-jumping project of circumventing the national and appealing directly to foreign investors.

Japan was one of the countries that North Carolina's political and economic leaders targeted as a potential source of foreign capital. Japanese direct investment was relatively small in the United States and virtually nonexistent in North Carolina in previous decades, and in the 1980s Japan's economy was in an unprecedented boom. These statewide efforts resulted in the increased Japanese direct investment in the state of North Carolina throughout the 1980s, from practically zero prior to 1980 to $353 million in 1990 (Kuroda n.d.). Major investors included Mitsubishi Semiconductor (1983), Sumitomo Electric Lightwave (1983), Konica Manufacturing (1986), and Matsushita Compressor (1989), of which Mitsubishi and Sumitomo Electric chose the Research Triangle as the location of their manufacturing facilities.

For several reasons, Japan presented a particularly complicated case for North Carolina's political and economic leaders who wanted to make North Carolina an attractive relocation site. Since the end of the energy crisis in the late 1970s, Japan's economic fortunes had been on a rapid rise, and superfluous investment capital was increasingly finding its destination in the United States. While a Japanese "buying frenzy" caused alarm in the American public throughout the 1980s, that also made Japan the most desirable client for the southern states that sought foreign investment. However, Japan was, in contrast to Europe and its investors, considered culturally different and required special accommodation. North Carolina offered an attractive package to potential Japanese investors, combining tangible economic benefits, cultural programs, and symbolic gestures. Translating the business executive summary and other introductory brochures into Japanese was one of the steps to this end, as well as hiring Japanese-speaking staff at the state Department of Commerce to help Japanese corporate leaders learn about the advantages of North Carolina without having to speak fluent English. The state also established the North Carolina Japan Center at North Carolina State University in Raleigh, to act as a mechanism for cultural and academic exchange through which the information about North Carolina is disseminated to the Japanese, and vice versa. Japanese corporate representatives are treated deferentially throughout the relocation process, from their initial site visit to well after the opening of their facilities in North Carolina.

The state's public relations campaign seemed largely successful among expatriate Japanese in the Research Triangle. Most of the Japanese business managers whom I interviewed in the Research Triangle praised the cooperative state and local government agencies, friendly local populations, and the convenient, comfortable, and affordable lifestyle. Many of my expatriate Japanese informants knew of the older, backward image of the South and, prior to their arrival in North Carolina, were somewhat concerned and uncomfortable with the idea of potential racial discrimination. When they arrived, they were pleasantly surprised by how few signs of racism they encountered in their daily life and were quickly enamored by the friendliness and politeness of local residents and the comfortable lifestyle that was available to them in upscale suburban communities. However, expatriate Japanese whom I interviewed quickly pointed out that this was not necessarily the typical situation in the South, and they largely attributed their positive impressions to the hybridity of the particular location of their residence: Cary and other fast-growing suburban communities that house many of the RTP workers and their families from around the world. "There are no southerners in my neighborhood," one of my informants in Cary quipped. "The family next door is from California, and the one across the street is from Germany. The retired couple two doors down lived all over the world, including Japan, because of the husband's job (with a major U.S. computer manufacturer). Come to think of it, I don't really know anybody from the South."

The close relationship between local business leaders and the state legislature is another important aspect of transnational development in North Carolina; in fact, it is a typical setup in the American South (Kim 1995). While this blurriness between the public government sector and private business interests may raise the question of accountability (see Guldbrandsen in this volume), the close cooperation between governmental and corporate entities is more familiar and comforting to Japanese investors than laissez-faire capitalism, which made North Carolina (and the South) a highly desirable relocation site for Japanese corporations. In addition, educational and research institutions play critical roles in this government-business connection, as they have cultivated close relationships and resource sharing with RTP and are also the source of highly educated labor for transnational corporations that relocate in the area. In addition, the state offers specialized industrial training programs through local community colleges, free of charge to new incoming corporate investors. North Carolina State University has also played a major role in the recruitment of Japanese corporations, particularly through its North Carolina Japan Center, which combines academic research, cultural exchange, and social services for expatriate corporate Japanese and their family members.

This intersection tells us two stories about the transnational engagement between the South and the East. First, there is an uncanny resemblance in business practices and social networks that North Carolinian and Japanese actors find in their direct dealings with one another. While the North Carolina government tries to capitalize on the recognition of such similarity in its transnational marketing of the region, it is also aware that such symbolic familiarity itself is not sufficient to sell North Carolina, hence the commingling of the naturalized regional character (docility and hospitality) with tangible economic advantages becomes the key. Second, while the majority of expatriate Japanese are pleasantly surprised by the friendliness of local residents and government agencies toward foreign newcomers, they are also aware of the peculiarity of the hybrid space that they occupy within the region. As if to confirm this point, my informants who had regular exposure to local residents and government agencies outside that hybrid space reported incidents of overt and covert racism. Then it was not just the official discourse of the region that led to the successful transnationalization in and around RTP, but the material transformation of—as well as the will to transform—the community that convinced Japanese corporations and their expatriate workers of the value of North Carolina as a location of their transnational operation. Such self-reorganization of the local, then, is driven by the needs of the global, as North Carolina attempts to remake and present itself as the appealing location for transnational investors (see Dirlik 1999).

Intersection 2

I arrived at the office of Metal Technologies, Inc., in RTP a few minutes earlier than the time of my appointment with Mr. Saito, the president of this U.S. subsidiary of a large Japanese manufacturer. There was no one around the entrance area, but through the partitions I could hear the voices of a few men speaking in English; I was struck by the familiar and informal tone of their exchange. Then an Asian man in his forties emerged from behind the partition; he saw me standing at the reception desk and quickly bowed. That was Mr. Saito.

Mr. Saito seemed to me a very serious-minded and intelligent man who spoke English quite well and was an effective manager of both American and Japanese workers. His background and work history seemed to confirm this impression. He originally came from the northeastern region of Japan (which is known for its hardworking, single-minded ethos), studied science at a highly regarded university there, and after he graduated in the mid-1970s, entered a large company with strong ties to the steel industry. In his late thirties he was sent to the company's New York branch as a midlevel manager; five years later, in 1995, the company opened a new venture in North Carolina, and he was reassigned there as president. In response to my question regarding the nature and scope of his subsidiary's operation, Mr. Saito stated that it was a very important project for his company despite its relatively small scale. The Japanese as well as the U.S. steel industry had been in decline for some time, and his company, which manufactured materials for steel production, had been looking to diversify. This North Carolina venture represented his company's serious attempt for diversification and thus was key to its future in a global economy. Mr. Saito felt both a heavy responsibility and a sense of excitement at being put in charge of such a critical operation, and he found the opportunity to manage a U.S. subsidiary an invaluable experience that he would have never had if he had stayed in Japan.

Metal Technologies, however, had difficulty becoming profitable, and Mr. Saito, at the helm of this struggling venture, seemed to be deeply concerned. Japanese corporate management was not prepared for the degree of customization required by high-tech industry clients, and recouping its rather sizable initial investment would take many years to come. Moreover, Mr. Saito himself had to face a major adjustment due to the shift from one industrial culture to another. Steel was considered the critical basis of Japan's postwar industrial development, and government-protected giant corporations operated less like a profit-motivated capitalist organization but more like a government agency. When Mr. Saito dealt with clients in the Japanese steel industry, relationship building was of utmost importance, and price negotiation, product specification, and other relevant issues were handled in the context of a stable, long-term association that everyone was in together. Coming into the world of high-tech industry with this work history, Mr. Saito was astonished by the lack of client-vendor loyalty and the utter competitiveness that places tremendous pressure on vendors to continuously improve their products, to meet a tight delivery time frame, and to be light-footed enough to keep up with the ever-changing climate of a consumer-driven industry.

Throughout the 1980s and early 1990s, Japanese direct investment in the United States shifted from the large-scale manufacturing of the earlier decade and toward technology-intensive, post-Fordist ventures, particularly in microelectronics and biotechnology. Even corporations in conventional manufacturing sectors began to move their research-and-development functions to the United States and/or start exploratory enterprises in these fast-growing industries. RTP is one of the popular destinations for Japanese corporations that aimed to take full advantage of innovative technologies and the proximity to a large consumer market. This trend was greatly facilitated by the rising value of the yen against the U.S. dollar, the availability of superfluous capital, and the optimistic mood of the late 1980s, which loosened the purse strings of otherwise fiscally conservative Japanese corporations.

There were miscalculations and unforeseen changes, however. For one thing, Japan's economic "bubble" collapsed in 1991. Investment money from Japan instantly dried up, and Japanese direct investment in North Carolina quickly dropped after it had peaked in 1989. Some of the established Japanese subsidiaries also divested from North Carolina in the mid-1990s. The close correlation between the patterns of Japanese direct investment in the United States and that in North Carolina suggests that the state of Japan's national economy and the foreign investment trend among Japanese corporations are the primary determinants of Japanese direct investment in North Carolina, and that other more regionally specific incentives and advantages are, after all, insufficient to overcome macroeconomics.

Second, some of the Japanese-owned subsidiaries appeared to be ill conceived from the beginning. By the mid-1980s, the Research Triangle was recognized among Japanese corporate planners as the new Mecca of the high-tech industry and a prime site for relocation. This knowledge resulted in two types of Japanese direct investment. The first type is made by Japanese corporations with a long-standing and substantial history in microelectronics who sought to establish manufacturing sites in the United States. The other type is made by those who saw a new business opportunity in supplying materials and components for major microelectronics manufacturers in the area, of which Metal Technologies is one. It appears that the latter type of Japanese-owned ventures in and around RTP had experienced difficulty for two main reasons. First, neither the local managers who are in charge of these subsidiaries nor the corporate managers in Tokyo were prepared for the competitiveness, the high degree of customization, and the short product cycle that characterize the high-tech industry. Particularly those corporations that previously operated in the economy of scale—the steel industry being a prominent example—appeared to experience much difficulty as they struggled to shift to highly customized, small-batch production in this competitive environment. Many Japanese managers also began to realize that production costs around RTP were too high to remain competitive against products made in offshore locations, while physical proximity to microelectronics giants, including IBM, did not give them much advantage. Mr. Numata, another expatriate Japanese manager of a small manufacturing subsidiary that produces accessories for lap-top computers, explained: "To make these simple [parts and accessories], RTP is much too expensive, where both land prices and labor costs have been rising very fast. If I am to plan another manufacturing plant like this, I will take it to somewhere cheaper, let's say, Mexico or China."

Intersection 3

When I walked into the hotel in the heart of RTP, the site of the conference "North Carolina and Japan: Trade and Investment," on a bright fall day in 1999, I guessed that the crowd was about 60 percent American, 40 percent Japanese, 80 percent male, and 20 percent female. The conference was geared toward "senior North Carolina business and community leaders," and most of the participants appeared to represent businesses—local companies that sought to initiate or increase business with Japan and Japanese-owned companies located in North Carolina. Mixed in were a handful of North Carolina government officials and legislators as well as a few students and academics from the universities in the local area. It appeared that all the major Japanese-owned businesses had sent at least one of their managers to the event, and the Japan External Trade Organization representative was seen speaking with North Carolina State Department employees. During the break, I ran into Mr. Saito from Metal Technologies and we exchanged the usual greetings. Then I was cornered by two state legislators who were, once they found out that I was Japanese and a visiting researcher at the University of North Carolina, eager to know my opinion as to whether the state was doing a good job making Japanese businesses feel welcome.

When we moved to a banquet room for lunch, I joined Mr. Saito and another Japanese businessman, Mr. Tanaka, who was visiting from New York in preparation for the new North Carolina office of his company, a well-known general contractor. Upon hearing about Mr. Tanaka's situation, Mr. Saito offered that he, too, had been stationed in New York and was transferred to North Carolina several years ago. After reminiscing about his days at the busy subsidiary in the bustling city, Mr. Saito said, in an ironic tone, "*Yah, miyako-ochi desuyo* (Oh, it was the removal from the Capitol)." In Japan's earlier history, one of the most feared consequences to a nobleman who fell from grace with the Emperor or others in power was *miyako-ochi*, or the banishment from Kyoto, on an indefinite appointment to a remote location far from the political and cultural center. In today's corporate world of work, too, the transfer from the center to the periphery implies a downward mobility in professional and social terms. Mr. Tanaka chuckled nervously and explained on my behalf that many Japanese companies were moving their U.S. subsidiaries away from costly metropolitan cities and that his company also found it more advantageous to move its U.S. base to the South, where their (Japanese corporate) clients were building more and more manufacturing plants.

This conference scene illuminates, on one hand, the close connection between industry, government, and academia that I discussed above and the ongoing effort of the local governmental and semigovernmental entities to maintain, nurture, and articulate the cooperative nature of transnational economic development in the state. In this sense, the conference was a show, a display, as much as an actual scene of information dissemination and exchange, about the successful transnational relationship between North Carolina and Japan —North Carolina as a state that is eager to cultivate international business and Japan as its important client/investor. Even the visiting academic whose Japaneseness in this milieu is marginal at best is expected to play the role of a gracious guest by engaging in a polite conversation with state lawmakers.

On the other hand, my main aim here is to shift our perspective for the moment away from the construction of regionality and focus on the subjective experience of transnational mobility among expatriate Japanese workers. We may be inclined to categorize them as part of that highly successful new global elite class, the worldwide managerial and entrepreneurial class (Hannerz 1996, 129), or highly educated salaried professionals, technical specialists, managers, and administrators who assume powerful positions in the running and servicing of large corporations and state agencies (Pinches 1999, 25). Yet the narratives of Japanese corporate workers indicate that their immediate experience of the global is contingent on their corporation's—and their own—positioning within the ever-changing conditions of late capitalism.[1]

Many of the expatriate Japanese workers and spouses whom I met in the Research Triangle were affiliated with Japanese corporations in the communications, microelectronics, and pharmaceutical industries and were involved in research and development in and/or the management of highly specialized, small-scale production sites. After several interviews with male Japanese workers who worked in this technologically driven corporate environment, I was struck by a matter-of-fact, almost nonchalant attitude common among them about their U.S. assignment. They presented themselves in our conversations as already globalized. Even before they arrived at their foreign posts, their work activities (in Japan or elsewhere) routinely crossed geographical and national boundaries. I also detected that corporation-employee relationships in high-tech companies were much less paternalistic than those in conventional manufacturing sectors, and as a result, workers had a greater sense of control over their professional development in general, and their foreign assignment in particular.

At the same time, not all expatriate Japanese workers are in these globalized high-tech workplaces, and some are struggling with a sense of disempowerment and loss in their careers as a member of a corporate collective. Japanese companies often appropriate the ideology of *uchi*/in-group to encourage their workers to recognize the collective goals as their own (Kondo 1990; Rohlen 1974), while belonging to the tight-knit corporate community affirms the masculinity of their male core workers (Allison 1994). This corporate solidarity is, then, implicitly understood as the source of productivity as well as a uniquely Japanese advantage in the world of late capitalism. Whether an objectively valid argument or not, both outside scholars and Japanese corporate insiders alike see an intrinsic connection between Japaneseness and productivity and cite cultural attributes based on the ideology of *uchi*—group solidarity, loyalty, modesty, and self-sacrifice—as the key to Japan's capitalist success story (Harootunian 1993; Vogel 1979).

Mr. Saito's experience of two U.S. assignments suggests that this work-centered identity of Japanese corporate workers may be severely and quickly disrupted by the global ambitions and shifting priorities of their employers. He has a good educational pedigree and began a promising career in a top-ranking manufacturing company. He had became socialized during the period of high economic growth, as an elite as *sarariiman*, or white-collar core corporate worker, who worked in and around the *kikan sangyo* (foundational industry) that led Japan's postwar prosperity at least until the mid-1970s. The downward shift in this industry is directly connected with the different tones with which Mr. Saito spoke of his two U.S. assignments: the New York assignment at the height of his career and the North Carolina assignment as the often difficult readjustment to a different industrial climate and the removal from the mainstream of the corporate agenda. At what is considered *hataraki-zakari*, or the prime of his work life, he cannot conceal the overwhelming sense of ambivalence about his professional present and future.

Mr. Saito's is just one of the many narratives of disjuncture that I encountered in RTP. Another example is Mr. Numata, who was mentioned above in Intersection 2. Now in his early fifties, he has been with Kansai Denki for more than thirty years, and although his firm is internationally known for its consumer products, he spent most of his career in the division of the company that designed and built power plant turbines. Working on large projects in and outside Japan, he developed a strong sense of purpose through his work and learned the importance of an informal network of relationships in gathering information, garnering support, and harnessing resources across the formal boundaries of the company to get the job done. In the meantime, Kansai Denki, seeing the decline of heavy industry, was quickly divesting from this less-profitable territory and focusing on consumer products, most importantly, microelectronics. After a long assignment in Houston, Texas, in the 1980s, Mr. Numata returned to Tokyo to find that the priorities in his corporation had shifted from heavy industry to microelectronics, and as a result, he was squeezed out of an upper management position for which he should have otherwise been a candidate. Furthermore, during his long absence from Tokyo, many of his key connections within the corporate ranks had retired or been transferred away, making it difficult for him to get back into the tight-knit and complex network of managers and specialists of which he was once part.

A year after he returned from Houston, Mr. Numata was reassigned to the United States to utilize his international management experience at a new plant in North Carolina for highly specialized computer hardware parts. His narrative of North Carolina assignment had an uncanny resemblance to that of Mr. Saito. This important new venture was part of Kansai Denki's strategy to diversify their microelectronics division, which was, in fact, the only segment of the company that remained profitable after the collapse of the economic boom in 1991. However, this venture was plagued by miscalculations and misconceptions. To start with, the U.S. market for microelectronics hardware was already highly competitive and less profitable than the software business. While Mr. Numata's discussion of his subsidiary was presented as his views as a representative of a corporate organization and an internationalized business manager, I could not help but think of the implications of these management difficulties to Mr. Numata as an individual worker. His disparaging tone as he spoke of a total lack of loyalty between vendor and client suggested that he personally found this industrial environment less desirable than his earlier experience in heavy industry, and that he resented the sudden change in his career forced on him by his corporate employer. Noticing my sensitivity to his predicament, he quickly changed the tone of his voice, cheerfully assuring me that he thought absolutely nothing of his reassignment and ensuing adjustment. After all, this was his *shigoto* (work, responsibility), and he gave his best in doing whatever the company required of him.

Mr. Numata's and Mr. Saito's narratives of corporate work and transnational migration have many similarities. Both men completed college at prestigious universities and became elite workers in first-tier companies, which only a small fraction of the highly stratified Japanese workforce manages to do (Kondo 1990). Their first U.S. assignments occurred in the context of their upwardly mobile career trajectories, and their critical importance to the earlier globalization effort of their respective employers validated their sense of self-worth as successful professionals. Their fortunes were quickly and unceremoniously reversed, however, as they faced their second U.S. assignments in a much changed economic and social climate in the mid-1990s, as they were sent on risky and difficult assignments in highly competitive microelectronics on the periphery of their corporate visions.

The fate of corporate solidarity at the post-Fordist transnational turn in Japan's economy is less than desirable to these corporate workers. While Mr. Saito had worked in an international milieu and experienced his first U.S. assignment at the height of his career, his recent transfer to North Carolina represented a professional downturn, as he was sent away from the center to manage a high-risk venture in an unknown territory, dealing with unfamiliar clients in a location that is still considered the periphery in the Japanese business world. Despite the officially stated importance of the subsidiary in his charge, he, in fact, felt a serious disruption in his professional identity and sense of accomplishment, closely connected with his initial experience in a specific industrial niche. Expectations of job continuity—of tasks, structure, and even position—seem tragically outdated in the world of late capitalism, and men like Mr. Saito and Mr. Numata are forced, midway through their professional careers, to adapt to the new flexible labor regime required by transnational capitalism (Martin 1997).

Intersection 4

I knew that I had taken a wrong turn at the crossroads.

I arrived in RTP too early for my appointment with a Japanese executive and decided to look around a bit to get a sense of the place. Wide, straight streets marked with large, easy-to-read signs, glassy brand-new buildings surrounded by manicured lawns and leafy trees, and fast luxury cars—these were the signs of prosperity that the occupants of this industrial park enjoyed. I drove through well-maintained streets, turning randomly at intersections, only to see more of the same. Then I must have inadvertently strayed out of the boundary around this well-groomed industrial park. Suddenly the signs of rural poverty replaced the glitter and abandon of RTP. Deteriorating narrow roads, rusted tin roofs, and front yards with overgrown tall weeds, junked cars, and overflowing garbage cans existed only one quarter-mile from the scene of state-sponsored transnational capitalism.

Expatriate Japanese families who work and live in the Research Triangle are, by and large, unaware of and unconcerned with the regional economic disparity that I found at the edge of RTP. They only see the urban, internationalized, middle-class part of today's American South as extended visitors, and although they live in North Carolina, they too often remain strangers to the region. Middle-class Japanese corporate workers who arrive in the Research Triangle as managers, engineers, and specialists essential to transnational capitalism have relationships to global processes that are very different from the relationships of the unseen owners of the rundown wooden shacks that stand precariously outside the glitter of globalization. The fact that these subjects live only a few miles apart does not seem to affect their differences in terms of race, class, and region. Yet all of their lives are equally vulnerable to the changing priorities of transnational corporate management, the ups and downs of the Japanese national economy, and the whims of global forces that sent these expatriate Japanese workers to North Carolina yesterday but tomorrow may take them back to Japan—or elsewhere in the world, for that matter.

The overwhelming concern for the majority of expatriate corporate Japanese is in their "real" home, Japan. Their consciousness is always based in Japan, and the anxiety of transiency too often overrides any possibility of true and sustained connection to the place in which they live during their foreign assignment. Between living and traveling, the experience of corporate-driven transnational migration poses a serious conundrum to their sense of home. If they live in the United States, does it mean that this foreign place has become their home? If so, what is Japan to them? Can they possibly call both places home? As some of my exceptionally articulate informants put it, every expatriate corporate Japanese—with perhaps the exception of those globalized high-tech specialists—lives in a double bind: while the concrete demands of their lives abroad fill their everyday life, they are, in their minds, "always facing toward Japan" (*itsumo Nihon wo muiteiru*). As the globalization of Japanese capitalism makes foreign job assignments more frequent and prolonged, expatriate Japanese families wonder whether they can ever go home, or if they will become a modern version of Urashima Taro, a tragic hero in a Japanese folktale who, after a prolonged visit to the kingdom under the sea, found himself a stranger in his own village.

In this location of transnational capital, in fact, just about everyone is a stranger in his own village: transnational professionals from around the world who do not belong to North Carolina but to its globalized, hybrid space; expatriate Japanese who are always worrying about their homecoming to Japan; the local economic and political leaders who are busy packaging the region for sale; transnational corporations to which North Carolina simply offers a convenient location for the moment; and ordinary North Carolinians who benefit little from economic development quite literally in their backyard.

Global capital constantly reorganizes itself, reterritorializes the local in which it operates, and redirects the lives of those who find themselves along its tracks. With the reconstituting of the local in the globalization process, new class lines are also forming as a result of transnational economic development. There is no doubt that the Research Triangle area as a whole has benefited from state appropriations and the injection of transnational capital. However, many residents who have their origins in this geographical area have not had much to do with RTP and its wealth, while geographically mobile, skilled workers are recruited from outside the region. In turn, with an increasing number of transplants from all over the world, local communities are being transformed and the image of the region is being renegotiated. At the same time, the division among Japanese core corporate workers suggests that, even within an occupational class, the outcome of globalization may vary greatly, and many live their transient lives in a foreign place with the anxiety of placelessness. In other words, class divisions are made much more complex, fluid, and deterritorialized in the transnational South as the crossroads of global capitalism. Therefore, it is imperative that we think ever more flexibly of places, be critical of overgeneralizing class analysis, and resist easy dichotomy of the global versus the local. Otherwise, we risk becoming trapped in the imagined regionalities that global capitalism has long appropriated to its own end.

Notes

This essay is largely based on the field research that I conducted as a Rockefeller post-doctoral fellow at the University Center for International Studies (UCIS), University of North Carolina, Chapel Hill, during the academic year 1999–2000. I would like also to acknowledge the support from the National Science Foundation for my dissertation research, of which my postdoctoral work at UCIS is an extension, and to thank Wendy Wolford for her comments on the earlier version of this paper presented during the conference "Creating the Transnational South," organized by the University Center for International Studies, University of North Carolina, Chapel Hill, April 11–13, 2002. In particular, her questions regarding the different scales in which globalization takes place helped me clarify and articulate the implicit thought that runs through this essay regarding the multiplicity of global processes and their outcomes.

1. The anxiety of placelessness is not a unique phenomenon among expatriate Japanese but, instead, a thread running through the experience of transnational migrants in many different circumstances (e.g., Bammer 1994; Clifford 1997; Levitt 2001). Class and professional standing appear to be one of the differentiating criteria. For example, there is much in common in the discourses of the home among the Japanese and the Indian professionals in the Research Triangle (see Ajantha Subramanian's essay in this volume).

References

Allison, Anne. 1994. *Nightwork: Sexuality, Pleasure, and Corporate Masculinity in a Tokyo Hostess Club*. Chicago: University of Chicago Press.

Bammer, Angelika. 1994. *Displacements*. Bloomington: Indiana University Press.

Barlow, Tani, ed. 1997. *Formations of Colonial Modernity in East Asia*. Durham, N.C.: Duke University Press.

Beck, John, and Martha Beck. 1994. *The Change of a Lifetime: Employment Patterns among Japan's Managerial Elite*. Honolulu: University of Hawai'i Press.

Boles, John. 1999. *The South through Time: A History of an American Region*. Vol. 2. Upper Saddle River, N.J.: Prentice Hall.

Clifford, James. 1997. *Routes: Travel and Translation in the Late Twentieth Century*. Cambridge, Mass.: Harvard University Press.

Cole, Robert. 1977. *Japanese Blue Collar: The Changing Tradition*. Berkeley: University of California Press.

Comaroff, Jean, and John Comaroff. 1991. *Of Revelation and Revolution*. Vol. 1, *Christianity, Colonialism, and Consciousness in South Africa*. Chicago: University of Chicago Press.

Dirlik, Arif. 1992. "The Asia-Pacific Idea: Reality and Representation in the Invention of a Regional Structure." *Journal of World History* 3, no. 1: 55–79.

———. 1999. "Globalism and the Politics of Place." In Kris Olds, Peter Dicken, Philip Kelly, Lily Kong, and Henry Wai-chung Yeung, eds., *Globalisation and the Asia-Pacific*, 39–56. London: Routledge.

Freeman, Carla. 2000. *High Tech and High Heels.* Durham, N.C.: Duke University Press.

Goodman, Roger. 1990. *Japan's "International Youth": The Emergence of a New Class of Schoolchildren.* Oxford: Clarendon Press.

Hannerz, Ulf. 1996. *Transnational Connections.* New York: Routledge.

———. 1998 "Reporting from Jerusalem." *Cultural Anthropology* 13, no. 4: 548–74.

Harootunian, H. D. 1993. "America's Japan/Japan's Japan." In Masao Miyoshi and H. D. Harootunian, eds., *Japan in the World,* 192–221. Durham, N.C.: Duke University Press.

Jessop, Bob. 1999. "Reflections on Globalisation and Its (Il)logic(s)." In Kris Olds, Peter Dicken, Philip Kelly, Lily Kong, and Henry Wai-chung Yeung, eds., *Globalisation and the Asia-Pacific,* 19–38. London: Routledge.

Kim, Choong Soon. 1995. *Japanese Industry in the American South.* New York: Routledge.

Kondo, Dorinne. 1990. *Crafting Selves.* Chicago: University of Chicago Press.

Korhonen, Pekka. 1998. *Japan and Asia Pacific Integration: Pacific Romances, 1968–1996.* New York: Routledge.

Kuroda, Junichiro. N.d. "North Carolina's Recruitment Policy of Japanese Companies: A Report to Steve Brantley, International Development Representative." Manuscript. North Carolina Department of Commerce, Business and Industry Development Division.

Lancaster, Roger. 1992. *Life Is Hard.* Berkeley: University of California Press.

Levitt, Peggy. 2001. *Transnational Villagers.* Berkeley: University of California Press.

Mannari, Hiroshi, and Harumi Befu, eds. 1983. *Challenge of Japan's Internationalization: Organization and Culture.* Tokyo: Kodansha International.

Marcuse, Peter, and Ronald van Kempen, eds. 2000. *Globalizing Cities: A New Spatial Order?* Oxford: Blackwell.

Marcusen, Ann, Yong-Sook Lee, and Sean DiGiovanna, eds. 1999. *Second Tier Cities: Rapid Growth beyond the Metropolis.* Minneapolis: University of Minnesota Press.

Martin, Emily. 1997. "The End of the Body?" In Roger N. Lancaster and Micaela di Leonardo, eds., *The Gender/Sexuality Reader: Culture, History, Political Economy,* 543–58. New York: Routledge.

Ong, Aihwa. 1987. *Spirit of Resistance and Capitalist Discipline.* New York: State University of New York Press.

Pinches, Michael, ed. 1999. *Culture and Privilege in Capitalist Asia.* London: Routledge.

Rohlen, Thomas. 1974. *For Harmony and Strength: Japanese White-Collar Organization in Anthropological Perspective.* Berkeley: University of California Press.

Said, Edward. 1978. *Orientalism.* New York: Vintage.

Sassen, Saskia. 1998. *Globalization and Its Discontent.* New York: New Press.

Soja, Edward. 2000. *Postmetropolis: Critical Studies of Cities and Regions.* Oxford: Blackwell.

Stephens, H. Morse, and Herbert Bolton, eds. 1917. *The Pacific Ocean in History.* New York: Macmillan.

Vogel, Ezra. 1979. *Japan as Number One.* New York: Harper.

White, Merry. 1992. *The Japanese Overseas: Can They Go Home Again?* Princeton: Princeton University Press.

Wolf, Eric. 1982. *Europe and the People without History.* Berkeley: University of California Press.

Woodward, C. Vann. 1971. *Origins of the New South, 1877–1913.* Baton Rouge: Louisiana State University Press.

Yoshino, Kosaku. 1992. *Cultural Nationalism in Contemporary Japan.* London: Routledge.

Ajantha Subramanian

North Carolina's Indians

Erasing Race to Make the Citizen

In April 2001, former Democratic governor Jim Hunt of North Carolina delivered a keynote address to the Cary, North Carolina, branch of the Indus Entrepreneurs, a professional networking organization of South Asian Americans started in the Silicon Valley. "You are a true asset to our state," he lauded the sizable audience. "With your technical and intellectual contribution, you have helped to usher North Carolina into the twenty-first century." Hunt then proceeded to note the cultural similarities between South Asians and North Carolinians. "We are all people of the South," he quipped, "and we share so much. A belief in the sanctity of the family, of religion, of education, and of hard work. For us, our entrepreneurial values are rooted in our cultural values."

Governor Hunt's creative invocation of a new South-South solidarity encapsulates the logic of American multiculturalism, the basic premise of which is the understanding of group identity as essentially cultural and of cultures as the basic units of American society. Culture has emerged as a key political trope of globalization and has been put to multiple uses by states, corporations, and transnational subjects. Its ubiquitous presence in immigrant Indian discourses of self and community forces an examination of the implications of culture's elevation to global prominence for the politics of transnationality, and for the politics of race and class in the United States. My research suggests that the key to the puzzle of culture's ubiquity lies in the very nature of the term. Culture appears to be atomistic and power-neutral. Cultures can be pluralized without suggesting inequity and accommodated without contradictions within a single global or national framework. In the case of the United States, culture has emerged as a form of collectivity that fits neatly into the logic of corporate capitalism, and Indian professionals have been extremely adept at navigating the terrain of this corporate multiculturalism.

Indians are currently one of the most affluent U.S. minority populations (Hing 1993; Leonard-Spark and Saran 1980; Liu 1992; Prashad 2000). They have all the characteristics of a model minority: they are hardworking, they have their community institutions and practices, and they subscribe to a political conservatism that supports their material interests. Most importantly, they have attempted to define themselves in cultural terms that avoid any obvious racial referent. The coincidence of Indian professional migration to the United States and civil rights legislation that instituted a formal, race-neutral equality has allowed for a superseding of race by culture as the definitive characteristic of Indian immigrant identity.

But Indian professionals in America did not always stake claims to citizenship in terms of culture. As Sucheta Mazumdar has argued, in the past, elite Indians responded to American racial hierarchies by adopting strategies such as claiming Aryan, or white, identity (Mazumdar 1991). Today, with the post–civil rights celebration of multiculturalism, the early Indian claim to whiteness might sound both unnecessary and absurd. But we must ask to what extent the racial hierarchies of the early twentieth century have been dismantled or whether they continue to structure American society and Indian American politics.

Legal theorist Cheryl Harris has questioned the retreat from racial thinking that has marked post–civil rights cultural politics. She points to the landmark judgment in *Brown v. Board of Education* as a turning point for American racial politics, not only because it marked the end of legal segregation, but because it permitted the reemergence of white privilege in a more subtle form. "White privilege accorded as a legal right was rejected," she argues, "but de facto white privilege not mandated by law remained unaddressed. In failing to clearly expose the real inequities produced by segregation, the status quo of substantive disadvantage was ratified as an accepted and acceptable base line —a neutral state operating to the disadvantage of Blacks long after *de jure* segregation had ceased to do so" (Harris 1993).

How does the liberal base line apply to professional Indians? And how, in particular, does it apply to them in the U.S. South? North Carolina has had its own share of Indian immigration. South Asians are currently the fourth largest group after whites, African Americans, and Latinos. The number of South Asians who entered North Carolina increased rapidly in the 1970s. The largest wave, however, came in the 1980s. This group, especially the Indian majority within it, consisted overwhelmingly of educated professionals, namely doctors, engineers, academics, and scientists.[1]

The affluence of Indian professionals has ensured their segregation from other nonwhite populations and their entry into previously white-dominated social spaces of the university, the corporation, the research institution, and the gated community. John Cherian, an early migrant to North Carolina, remembered how rapidly his neighborhood of Cary changed and how it dove-tailed with the Indian influx. "When I first moved to Cary in the 1970s, there were three or four others who worked at [North Carolina State University], people who worked at IBM, public school teachers, insurance salesmen. It was not an elite community. But when the RTP [Research Triangle Park] started to grow, houses went from being modest homes to much bigger ones. And at the same time that it became more prosperous, it also became more diverse. Soon we had an incredible number of Indian neighbors!" (Cherian 2001).

In both North Carolina state government and Indian American cultural discourses, the transformation of North Carolina into a favored destination for corporations and professionals is the flip side of its resurrection as part of the New South, a space of multiculturalism where the racism of the Old South has been eclipsed. Sita Sharma, who has lived in Cary since the late 1960s, pointed to the creation of the corporate RTP, the developmental linchpin of this new South, as the salvation of the state. "The image of the South when I moved here wasn't good," she recollected, "and the biggest thing that happened in North Carolina to change the image and reality of the South was opening the RTP. Now, the South is so nice to live in, it's so cosmopolitan. It used to be so difficult to get Indian spices and videos, and now there are so many groceries and restaurants to choose from!" (Sharma 2001). Like Sharma, Ravi Srinivas, a south Indian professor of psychiatry at Duke who arrived in the state in 1986, also attributed North Carolina's acceptance of foreigners to the economic boom: "We moved into a predominantly white neighborhood," he told me, "but felt no racism at all. I thought the South would have been more hostile to foreign-ers but it was not so because the growth of the RTP has changed peoples' atti-tudes, made them more open" (Srinivas 2000). A number of local Indians spoke of the ease of living in the post-RTP South without mentioning the in-sularity of their social worlds or the growing disparities of wealth that have pushed North Carolina's poor white, black, and Latino residents to the mar-gins. Rather, they referred to their comfortable relationships with white col-leagues in professional settings as a sign of the spread of liberal values in the South, and an end to racism.

Significantly, the black South was a marked absence in Indian American professional narratives of self and community. Very few Indians addressed their relationship to *black* southerners as a way of situating themselves in North Carolina. Sanjay Wadhwani, the CEO of an Internet technology firm in Cary, was one exception. Interestingly, Wadhwani was also the only person who ex-plicitly addressed Indian American class privilege: "Indians have enjoyed eco-nomic independence here. We are not even considered minorities, because we're economically well off. By extension, we don't think of ourselves as minorities. Let me be frank: most Indians here cross the street when they see a black person. We tend to associate more with successful people because they are our colleagues and neighbors" (Wadhwani 2000). Wadhwani's sense of how Indians identify along class lines is very relevant. This class-based identification has meant an equation of southern society with white society, and an erasure of the presence of black North Carolinians.

These narratives of migration and acceptance claim a shift in the structural position of Indians in U.S. racial hierarchies from the first to the second half of the twentieth century. Other experiences, however, betray this narrative of an accommodative society and show that Indian American claims to equal citizenship on the basis of class and culture have not exempted them from the U.S. racial order. Even those Indians who lauded the transformation of North Carolina into a multicultural haven expressed their frustration over a permanent sense of not belonging. Srikanth, a mechanical engineer and resident of Cary recollected an incident that made him feel unsafe for the first time: "We do have experiences. There was an Indian cultural program in N.C. State that we went to with friends. After the program, we were walking to our cars when two carloads of white boys drove by and started yelling, 'You Indians, why don't you go home?' They were just kids, but they were drunk and seemed violent" (Srikanth 2000). Being from upper-caste or affluent backgrounds, many local Indians are incensed when they do experience discrimination, especially when it blurs the boundaries between themselves and other, less prosperous or "respectable" minorities. Speaking resentfully of white North Carolinians' confusion between Latinos and Indians, Kumar Luthra, a staff person at Duke University, confessed his outrage at being mistreated at a local bank: "It has never happened to me before. I went into the bank and tried to cash my check and they asked me for two forms of I.D. Two! So I challenged them and said, 'I've never shown more than one so why are you asking for this?' When the clerk said it was bank policy, I said, 'I have been coming here for the last thirty years and it has never been policy before!' She saw that I was getting angry, so she called the manager, who came out, saw who I was, and apologized. He said the clerk had mistaken me for a Mexican" (Luthra 2000).

Other Indian Americans express this experience of discrimination in terms of differentiated citizenship. Lalit Patel, an executive at Hewlett Packard, pointed to an America with degrees of citizenship where "ethnics" were permanent foreigners. "After twenty-six years," he said with regret and not a little anger, "many people still ask me when I came here. I've been a citizen for twenty years, but that's the perception, the stereotype." When I asked who was assumed to be American, he stated strongly, "In America, whites are American. Even Irish and Germans who have just arrived here, the first instinct is that they're American." When I followed with "What about black Americans?" he hesitated, then replied, "Well . . . yes, they are considered to be American . . . up to a point" (Patel 2001). Although Patel did eventually include African Americans in his characterization of who is "automatically" American, the total absence of black America in his initial consideration of U.S. society, and his subsequent hesitation over the status of African Americans, speaks volumes. For him and other Indian American professionals, U.S. national identity is structured by a racial hierarchy in which "whiteness" is the mark of privilege and first-class citizenship and "blackness" is the "internal Other." Black America represents the negative side of belonging, a racialized citizenship that is at a permanent disadvantage (Gregory and Sanjek 1994; Haney López 1996; Lipsitz 1988).

North Carolina's Indians have attempted to negotiate the tension between class privilege and racial difference by embracing the model of multicultural America espoused by Governor Hunt that equates a particular kind of cultural rootedness with capitalist success. I would add that the overcoming of racial difference is another, less explicit goal of Indian American cultural politics. Culture has served North Carolina's Indian Americans as leverage to gain the right kind of citizenship while avoiding the wrong kind.

Consider this quote from Sanjay Basu (2001), a member of the executive body of the Indian American Forum for Political Education, a lobby group operating both nationally and locally:

> In this country you protect your interests, your visibility, your long-term survival only by showing your involvement as a cultural community. If you isolate yourself, nobody will recognize your interests. Jewish people are the shining example of solidarity and success: they have a strong community, they have a lobby. The global environment, it used to be more a melting pot, but nowadays the situation has changed. Now, your identity as a community has to be cultivated. You have to show that your community is involved in mainstream America. Nowadays, people are looking at what the Indian community is doing locally, statewide, or nationally. . . . Without that community-based unity, you can't speak to the American political leadership.

Basu presents a picture of the American political system as a balancing act of different cultural groupings, each with its own interests and demands. He equates community with interest group and represents American society as the sum of its constituent cultural communities.

Jaideep Subramaniam, an engineer and board member of the Indus Entrepreneurs, offered his take on the economic dimension of American communitarian politics:

> If you're white, you're automatically identified as American. I don't resent
> it. It's the way the system works. But we don't use our economic clout to fight
> anti-immigrant sentiment. After all, we're less than a hundredth of 1 per-
> cent but control 5 percent of wealth. We need to educate politicians and in-
> dustry leaders about how we're contributing to this society. Indians own 30
> percent of hotels in America, we're giving 10,000 jobs to Americans. Same
> way with stores and the construction businesses. We need community sol-
> idarity and philanthropy in business. Nobody is going to give you a loan for
> your idea because we're ethnic. We have to give ourselves loans. (Subrama-
> niam 2001)

The importance of wealth for the consolidation and protection of immigrant
culture is a theme that cuts across lines of age, gender, and religion. Gautam,
a student at Duke who grew up in Durham, commented on the rules of acceptance in his high school: "If you have money, you can buy your kids acceptance. But if your kid wears K-Mart and not Abercrombie, *and* he's doing
cultural stuff, he'll definitely be ridiculed" (Gautam 2000). Rather than identifying with other nonwhites against white privilege then, these local Indians
pit the positive associations of class privilege coded as cultural difference against
the negative associations of racial difference to secure a niche for themselves
in the United States.

How do Indian Americans define culture? For most, culture is biological
and national; it is an expression of ethnicity, and it is derived from an original homeland. The link between immigrant cultural identity and an original
homeland is a formulation shared by most minority populations in the United
States. Deriving a sense of cultural selfhood from an original homeland is an
understandable way for minorities to seek validation in a country where whiteness is the only sign of unquestioned citizenship. However, the original homeland that minorities turn to is often imagined in unitary terms in order to un-
derscore its difference from Anglo America. In the case of many local Hindus,
who constitute the majority of North Carolinian Indians, "India" has been dis-
tilled to the West's Oriental Other, an ancient Hindu land whose mother tongue
is Sanskrit. Even while many of the Hindu residents I spoke with recognized
the cultural complexities that have always characterized the subcontinent,
they nevertheless identified an underlying essence, an original Hinduness to
which other qualities were added in increments. Ironically, the affirmation of
minority cultural identity in the United States translates into support for a

version of India that is majoritarian—a version that privileges the identity and interests of upper-caste Hindus.

In part, this reduction of India to a Hindu land comes out of the privileging of religious identity within American multiculturalist notions of cultural difference. I would argue that for North Carolina's Indian Americans, the importance of religiosity in the South is an added factor. North Carolina's social landscape is quite clearly also a religious geography dotted with innumerable churches and mosques, and religious institutions play a central role in consolidating community identity. Many Indian Americans I spoke to remarked that their interest in religious ritual practice as central to cultural preservation was a postmigration phenomenon. For instance, a number of Hindu residents of Cary and Raleigh remarked that they were not regular temple-goers before they migrated to the United States. As one of them put it, "Doing *pujas* (prayers), being with other Hindus, these things weren't as important to me in India. But here, it gives us a feeling of community. And when our kids come to the temple, they can understand and experience their culture. This is why we regularly visit the temple on Sundays, just like Christians go to church" (Srinivas 2000). Indeed, most Hindus in the area socialize exclusively with one another in venues like the Hindu Society or the Sri Venkateswara Temple. That these religious spaces double as Indian community spaces makes the reduction of India to a Hindu land that much easier for these immigrants.

This redefinition of India as Hindu is also facilitated by the work of Hindu nationalist organizations in the United States. Hindu Americans' yearning for an authentic and ancient cultural identity that can be wielded with pride and used to claim equal citizenship in the United States dovetails neatly with the cultural package provided by groups such as the Vishwa Hindu Parishad (VHP) or World Hindu Organization.[2] The package that the VHP offers reduces India to a few central symbols: Sanskrit as its ancient language, Hinduism as its national culture, and the Gita as its core religious text. Even when the equation of Hindu with India is not explicit, the process of selecting common symbols for culture and nation makes this equation more than apparent. The VHP's work in the United States has reaped significant successes. A number of Indian American professionals, including some in North Carolina, send their children to VHP summer camps, conduct Gita readings in their homes and at the temples, and contribute financially to "Hindu" causes such as temple construction.

The emphasis on culture and community and their definition in terms of an original homeland has also grounded ongoing efforts by Indian American professionals to invest financially in India. A board member of the Indus Entrepreneurs explained to me that this was a process by which the "brain drain" of Indian professionals migrating to the United States was being reversed: "India is now at an advantage because of Non-Resident Indian investment. We NRIs are the cultural offspring of India and we have not forgotten that. We have been economically successful here in the U.S. and now we're giving back to our homeland. We're going from brain drain to reinvestment. I guess you could call it 'trickle back!'" (Patel 2001). The past decade has witnessed a sharp increase in NRI funding, both for economic development projects and for the political project of Hindu nationalism. A number of North Carolina's Indian professionals have sent money to fill the coffers of the VHP and financially support causes such as the construction of the Ramjanmabhoomi temple in Ayodhya. They have also been at the forefront of efforts to push through a policy of dual citizenship for India so that they can participate in Indian elections and ensure expatriate Hindu support for the Hindu nationalist Bharatiya Janata Party, the political party that they feel best supports their interests as members of a global Hindu community and a global capitalist class.[3] I would argue that this drive for dual citizenship reflects not just support for Hindus' majoritarianism but a persistent insecurity over their status as unequal, racialized citizens of the United States. These investment strategies extend the logic of corporate multiculturalism to a global scale. The NRI, armed with cultural links to the homeland and business acumen, is to usher India into the twenty-first century and secure its place as a proud Hindu nation in the global order of nation-states. The process by which Indian Americans as members of a global capitalist class will develop India economically is folded into a cultural narrative of the reunion of distant offspring with their mother, a reunion that will compensate for their racial inferiority in the United States.[4]

In concluding, I would like to make three observations about the dynamics of late capitalism, the politics of multiculturalism, and the U.S. immigrant experience. First, the universalizing logic of capitalist expansion does not mean an erasure of particularity. Indeed, in this latest era of globalizing capital, Indian Americans are only one group among many that have come to articulate their own brand of "vernacular capitalism" based on community solidarity and cultural identity as a response to Anglo-American hegemony. Second, national citizenship is yet another arena defined by the tension between universalism and particularism. The U.S. civil rights movement both ushered in equality of a civic variety—a civic universalism—and set the stage for a rapidly proliferating politics of cultural particularism. In the case of Indian American professionals in the U.S. South, the claim to cultural difference has obscured the persistence of substantive inequality structured by race and class beneath the liberal base line of a multicultural democracy. Third, I would argue that, far from being class-neutral, multiculturalism is a hegemonic discourse through which Indian Americans have rearticulated their racial minority status in cultural terms that secure class privilege. In the case of many Hindu Americans, their participation in minority cultural politics in the United States has produced not greater empathy for Muslim, Christian, and Sikh minorities in India but support for Hindu majoritarianism.

Notes

This article is a revised version of "Indians in North Carolina: Race, Class, and Culture in the Making of Immigrant Identity," *Comparative Studies of South Asia, Africa, and the Middle East* 20, nos. 1 and 2 (2000).

1. See 2000 census results for the state of North Carolina.

2. For an elaboration of this point, see Prashad 2000, chap. 8, and Rajagopal 2001, chap. 6.

3. On January 9, 2004, the Indian government announced its decision to facilitate legislation permitting dual citizenship for People of Indian Origin (POI). Significantly, the government has limited eligibility to POIs living in affluent areas—the United States, Canada, England, the European Union, Australia, New Zealand, and Singapore—a restriction that reveals the importance of class privilege in the government's conception of the diaspora. The benefits made available through the new legislation include travel to India on a free visa, permission to stay longer than currently allowed, and eligibility to purchase agricultural land and to have access to housing schemes of the state-run Life Insurance Corporation. However, dual citizenship does not include the right to contest or vote in Indian elections.

4. I would like to note that this essay is by no means an exhaustive treatment of Indian American cultural politics, either in North Carolina or in other parts of the United States. There are innumerable examples of Indian Americans who have rejected the terms of corporate multiculturalism and instead chose a variety of other political trajectories in negotiating identity, community, and citizenship in the United States. For a sense of some of these other trajectories, see Srikanth and Maira 1996; Srikanth and Shankar 1998; Prashad 2000; Dasgupta 1998; Khandelwal 2002; and Maira 2002.

References

Basu, Sanjay. 2001. Interview with author, Cary, N.C., March 13.

Cherian, John. 2001. Interview with author, Raleigh, N.C., March 15.

Dasgupta, Shamita, ed. 1998. *A Patchwork Shawl: Chronicles of South Asian Women in America*. New Brunswick, N.J.: Rutgers University Press.

Gautam. 2000. Interview with author, Durham, N.C., August 30.

Gregory, Steven, and Roger Sanjek, eds. 1994. *Race*. New Brunswick, N.J.: Rutgers University Press.

Haney López, Ian F. 1996. "The Legal Construction of Race." In Haney López, *White by Law: The Legal Construction of Race*, 111–55. New York: New York University Press.

Harris, Cheryl I. 1993. "Whiteness as Property." *Harvard Law Review* 106:1707.

Hing, Bill Ong. 1993. *Making and Remaking Asian America through Immigration Policy, 1850–1990*. Stanford: Stanford University Press.

Khandelwal, Madhulika S. 2002. *Becoming American, Being Indian: An Immigrant Community in New York City*. Ithaca, N.Y.: Cornell University Press.

Leonard-Spark, Philip, and Paramatma Saran. 1980. "The Indian Immigrant in America: A Demographic Profile." In P. Saran and E. Eames, eds., *The New Ethnics: Asian Indians in the United States*, 136–62. New York: Praeger.

Lipsitz, George. 1988. *The Possessive Investment in Whiteness: How White People Profit from Identity Politics*. Philadelphia: Temple University Press.

Liu, John M. 1992. "The Contours of Asian Professional, Technical, and Kindred Work Immigration, 1965–1988." *Sociological Perspectives* 35, no. 4: 673–704.

Luthra, Kumar. 2000. Interview with author, Durham, N.C., August 10.

Maira, Sunaina. 2002. *Desis in the House: Indian American Youth Culture in New York City*. Philadelphia: Temple University Press.

Mazumdar, Sucheta. 1991. "Racist Responses to Racism: The Aryan Myth and South Asians in the United States." *South Asia Bulletin* 9, no. 1: 47–55.

Patel, Lalit. 2001. Interview with author, Durham, N.C., February 12.

Prashad, Vijay. 2000. *Karma of Brown Folk*. Minneapolis: University of Minnesota Press.

Rajagopal, Arvind. 2001. *Politics after Television: Hindu Nationalism and the Reshaping of the Public in India*. Cambridge: Cambridge University Press.

Sharma, Sita. 2001. Interview with author, Cary, N.C., April 10, 2001.

Srikanth. 2000. Interview with author, Durham, N.C., November 2.

Srikanth, Rajni, and Sunaina Maira, eds. 1996. *Contours of the Heart: South Asians Map North America*. New Brunswick, N.J.: Rutgers University Press.

Srikanth, Rajni, and Lavina Shankar eds. 1998. *A Part Yet Apart: South Asians in North America*. Philadelphia: Temple University Press.

Srinivas, Ravi. 2000. Interview with author, Durham, N.C., September 17.

Subramaniam, Jaideep. 2001. Interview with author, Cary, N.C., April 4.

Wadhwani, Sanjay. 2000. Interview with author, Cary, N.C., October 10.

Part Five

Application
Activist Approaches to the Transnational South

Gregory Stephens

Monolingualism and Racialism as Curable Diseases

Nuestra América in the Transnational South

As a southwesterner, when I first relocated to North Carolina, I was impressed by the fact that my colleagues thought of the border as being the Mason-Dixon line—that would be the North as the Other of southern oppositional identity. This was a long way, further in cultural and psychological terms than in geographic distance, from the border I grew up facing, which was with Mexico. It is impossible for most people in the Southwest to think of the United States and Mexico as completely separate cultures. For most residents of that region, Mexico is not an Other against which they are opposed.

My worldview has been indelibly shaped by having worked in border cities such as Laredo, Texas, and San Diego, and having been an undergraduate in Tucson, in southern Arizona. In the Southwest it is normative to think of the border as a region that extends in both directions, rather than a line. (I am thinking of Carlos Fuentes's novel *Old Gringo*, for instance.) Where is the border drawn between Spanish-speaking and English-speaking peoples? This is something we are being forced to reexamine. From my perspective, the orientation of many southerners toward an often racialized North-South border of memory has left them ill prepared to deal with a new demographic coming from the South.

Demographic changes in the transnational South challenge us to develop new paradigms of intercultural and international relations. A working assumption of mine has been that a bilingual or multilingual workforce must be one component of a transnational South that is prepared for the economic, political, and cultural exchanges of a global market. Furthermore, moving toward a bilingual, transnational South will also involve a reorientation of what it means to be a southerner, as well as what it means to be an American. In particular, putting into practice more inclusive and more productive forms of politics, education, and socioeconomic exchange will require southerners to develop alternatives to two forms of myopia that are endemic to the region: monolingualism and racialism.

My research took three forms. I did ethnographic research among Spanish-speaking immigrants in Oklahoma and North Carolina in which I sought their perspective about their transition between two nations, cultures, and languages. I did a comparative study of dual language programs in those two states, with classroom observation at Shidler Elementary in Oklahoma City.[1] And I interviewed many educators and opinion leaders about the place of bilingualism in the globalized South and about the difficulties that the black-white worldview presented for individuals trying to come to terms with new demographics such as Latinos.

The Bilingual Crisis in Living Color

By early 2002, the number of foreign-born U.S. residents and children of immigrants had reached the highest level in history, 56 million. Mexico alone accounted for more than a quarter of all foreign-born residents. Only 34 percent of residents older than twenty-five years and born in Mexico had completed high school, while 95 percent of those born in Africa had. The median household income for those born in Latin America was $29,338, but $51,353 for those from Asia. Such economic and educational disparities are reflected in a persistent "achievement gap."

The number of North Carolina Latinos increased by 394 percent between 1990 and 2000. The increase in the number of Mexicans in North Carolina was almost 600 percent. During the last decade of the twentieth century, North Carolina had the highest proportion of low-English-proficiency immigrants in the nation. The proportion of increase in the number of monolingual Spanish immigrants is higher in North Carolina than in any other state.[2]

The North Carolina Commission on Raising Achievement and Closing Gaps spent more than a year studying why 80 percent of the state's Anglo and Asian students score at grade level, compared with 60 percent of Latino and American Indian children and only 52 percent of African Americans. In February 2002 administrators were mandated to come up with a time line within a month for implementing a state plan to close the achievement gap in North Carolina schools. In a ruling on April 4, 2002, North Carolina Superior Court Judge Howard Manning of Wake County wrote, "The state must step in with an iron hand and get the mess straight." Schools are under pressure because they face loss of federal dollars if they do not close this gap quickly, under the "No Child Left Behind" law passed in January 2002.[3]

A dramatic variant of the challenge faced by districts in southern states can be glimpsed in Oklahoma City, where massive Latino immigration began several years earlier than in North Carolina. The percentage of Latinos in Oklahoma City Public Schools has doubled in less than four years, to 27 percent as of January 2002. This proportion is expected to pass 50 percent within this decade. As of the fall of 2003, there were no Latino administrators in Oklahoma certified in secondary education (Font 2002).[4] When I was hired in August 2002 at Shields Heights Elementary, a school that is 47 percent Mexican, I was the only certified teacher that spoke Spanish. This was also the case when I began work in September 2003 at Capitol Hill Elementary, which was 60 percent Latino.

The Shortage of Bilingual Professionals

In early 2002 federal civil rights enforcers told North Carolina's Department of Health and Human Services that the state's shortage of interpreters violates the Civil Rights Act of 1964. Health care and social service agencies in North Carolina were told that they must employ more interpreters or risk losing federal money (North Carolina funnels $4.5 billion annually from the federal government to these agencies). Agencies also may face discrimination lawsuits if they do not comply, as the lack of interpreters impedes delivery of constitutionally guaranteed services.

The scope of this crisis can only be sketched in broad form here. It is not possible to offer one-size-fits-all solutions that educators and policy makers could apply. My focus is on a change in orientation—a different worldview, really—that will be necessary in order to begin recognizing that the people of the demographic discussed here are not just a "problem" but bring valuable resources. The questions we should be asking, I believe, would require us to reexamine our must fundamental preconceptions. How do we begin seeing this new demographic as they are, and as they describe themselves, rather than how we think they are, or wish they would be?

Greater Mexico and *Nuestra América* in the Transnational South

I use the terms "*nuestra América*" and "greater Mexico" as framing devices to help visualize or conceptualize our interconnectedness within the region in which Spanish- and English-speaking communities are intersecting. José Limón coined the term "greater Mexico" to describe a region with a long history of interpenetration between peoples of the United States and Mexico (Limón 1998). He sketches several parallels in histories and cultures of the

American South and northern Mexico, which suggest that our differences are not nearly so great as language might make it seem. For instance, plantations and haciendas play somewhat parallel roles in southern and Mexican history and memory. I might add that African Americans and indigenous peoples play a similar role in both regions: they are both a despised Other for some and yet also an idealized embodiment of our democratic aspirations. Without their inclusion in the political process, the humanistic potential of the South or the promises of the Mexican Revolution will remain deferred dreams.[5]

This greater Mexico is now among us. It is here to stay. What will be our relationship with its people? How can we teach them our language and our culture? Just as important, to what degree are we willing to reeducate ourselves about theirs? How do we come to terms with these other Americans, now an exploding presence in our America? How do we conceptualize and communicate with them?

A transnational view requires us to realize that North Americans cannot continue to consider ourselves as co-extensive with "America." America is a continent and, indeed, a hemisphere, not just a nation, the United States. Within what José Martí called *nuestra América*, or "our America," a majority are Latinos, speaking Spanish or Portuguese.[6] Spanish is the dominant language within the hemisphere. In 2000, the population of Latin America was double that of the United States.

It is now, of course, impossible to draw a clear distinction between these Americas, since so much of "our America" resides within the borders of the United States. So we are now being called upon to undergo a paradigm shift in which we learn to listen to our other America, what North Americans used to refer to as our backyard. We do not have a very good track record at this. Nobel Laureate Octavio Paz referred to the United States as an "Imperial Democracy." "North Americans are outstanding in the art of monologue," he wrote, "but conversation is not their forte; they do not know how to listen or to reply."[7] Yet self and Other always have a relationship: "El otro define nuestro yo," as the Mexican novelist and essayist Carlos Fuentes writes. The other defines our I, both with and against.[8] In simplest terms, we must start recognizing that we have a relationship, a developing intersubjectivity, with our America. And what does this other America say to us?

Monolingualism Is a Curable Disease

Carlos Fuentes once told a North American audience that "monolingualism is a curable disease" (Saffa 1989). Fuentes made this tongue-in-cheek comment by way of explaining why he was going to read from his works in Spanish, even though he is fluent in English. The United States has traditionally perceived "foreign languages" and, indeed, often bilingualism as a problem. When people come to the United States, we have traditionally expected "English Only." When North Americans travel abroad, too often they expect that people will speak to them in English. Fuentes is suggesting that monolingualism is really the problem, in a hemispheric and global context.

In an effort to describe in living color (rather than black and white) what *nuestra América* means for the transnational South, by default I must sketch in very broad strokes here. What I have in mind is a sort of "Latin America 101" for southerners who have been caught unaware while still gazing northward toward the Mason-Dixon line. The key term I have adapted to describe that America, from south of the other border, is "multicentric." Guillermo Gómez-Peña, a Mexican-born "border artist," argues that we need to adopt a "multicentric perspective" in order to understand the interpenetrations of two or more cultures. He suggests that living in more than one culture or nation or being a by-product of more than one "race," is actually normative in "our America," despite binary racial mythologies. Speaking from the borderlands, Gómez-Peña insists that "the dominant culture is no longer dominant," and that if there is a dominant culture, it is border culture—people with their feet in more than one culture or nation (1993, 46).

In a similar way, Fuentes (2000, 25) writes that after the Cold War, we entered an era in which "se encuentra con muchos centros, no sólo dos; muchas culturas, no sólo una." We have many centers and many cultures now, not just one or two. "Sólo las culturas que se comunican viven y florecen." Only cultures that communicate with different cultures can survive and flourish in our era.

One finds a multicentric perspective voiced most eloquently, perhaps, by Latin Americans such as Fuentes or Martí who have spent a great deal of time in the United States. From within the "belly of the beast," as Martí once said, spokespersons from *nuestra América* have been able to see more clearly how different is the embrace of a multicentric mixture of cultures that they grew up with from the us-versus-them worldview that has often been dominant in the Unites States. The opposite of multicentrism is monocentrism or a unicentric worldview. Carole Boyce Davies (1999, 96) uses these terms to critique a variety of one-sided worldviews, and the resulting "isms and schisms" they engender, such as Eurocentrism, Afrocentrism, and unilateralism.[9] One can make a case for a unicentric worldview such as Afrocentrism or Zionism as a historically necessary corrective, or a form of psychosocial self-healing, occasioned by previous oppression and exclusion. Yet such isms, defined so much by opposition to their Other, inevitably generate an action-reaction cycle. As Clarence Walker (2001, 133) writes, "I do not think anything calling itself 'centrism' is critical." Gayatri Spivak (1990) points out that merely opposing Eurocentrism, for instance, reifies that center. Such critiques presume that forms of unicentrism, be they Eurocentrism, monolingualism, or unilateralism, are myopic and in need of a corrective, a multicentered perspective.

As a variant of monocentrism, monolingualism becomes a form of "linguicism" when it has institutional backing—that is, the domination of one language at the expense of another, along with a devaluation of the linguistic resources and cultural capital of the excluded language (Skutnabbs-Kangas and Cummins 1988, 13). Monolingualism in the South is currently having negative consequences of several sorts: limited economic development, a failure to provide constitutionally guaranteed public services, and a flawed public education system that tends to reinforce class and ethnic divisions.

The Philosophy and Practice of
Dual Language Programs

I will now focus on the educational side of the bilingual crisis and look toward a working solution. The number of language-minority students is increasing more quickly than that of any other "special group." The proportion is expected to double from 20 percent of the school-age population (as of 1997) to 40 percent by as soon as 2020. This increase is causing a nationwide drop in school district test scores. It threatens national productivity as underprepared language-minority students replace baby boomers in the workforce (Thomas and Collier 2000). Everyone agrees with the goal of teaching these students to be fluent in English. The degree to which English Language Learners (ELL) will be transitioned to fluency in English by using content instruction in their native language is what makes this a political issue.

Dual Language Program (DLP) advocates argue (backed by cognitive psychologists and linguists) that children learn a second language more easily and more fluently when they retain fluency in their native language (Hoch 2002).[10] Skills such as decoding and sound blending, which are taught more effectively in a child's first language, are "clearly transferable among languages that use phonetic orthographies, such as Spanish, French, and English" (Slavin and Cheung 2003; August 2002). Furthermore, "research has shown that postponing or interrupting academic development while students learn a second language is likely to promote long-term academic failure," Wayne Thomas and Virginia Collier (1997) emphasize.

Research about native language instruction has been politicized. Rossell and Baker (1996) argued that research does not support bilingual education. However, a "meta-analysis" by Greene (1997) concluded that the "methodologically adequate" studies surveyed by Rossell and Baker did favor bilingual over English-only approaches. There is a growing consensus about the value of native language instruction in teaching transferable literacy skills. In 2001 the U.S. Department of Education and two other federal agencies funded a comprehensive review on this subject by the National Literacy Panel on the Development of Literacy Among Language Minority Children and Youth. Robert Slavin, a member of this panel, published his findings in a rigorous study released in December 2003 (Slavin and Cheung 2003). "None of the studies that met the inclusion standards found bilingual education to be . . . worse than (English) immersion," concluded Slavin and Cheung, while most studies show that students are testing higher with dual language than with any other approach currently available for ELL students.

As of 2001 there were 260 DLPs in twenty-three states. Many more are in development. DLPs are becoming popular with middle-class parents because research shows that children raised bilingually have a higher level of cognitive development than their monolingual peers and, more importantly, because bilingual students entering the job market have more choices and greater earning power. But there are institutional and ideological forces aligned against adopting innovative educational strategies such as DLPs. The political backlash against bilingualism is so charged in many parts of the South, in particular, that Raul Font (2002) told me that the very words "bilingual" or "multicultural" "make people sweat" in Oklahoma, where he was in charge of ESL programs for Oklahoma City Public Schools. Similarly, Ryuko Kubota, who trains ESL teachers at the University of North Carolina in Chapel Hill, alludes to "the B-word."[11]

Such tensions reflect wider cultural misconceptions, as when Newt Gingrich (1995, 162) wrote, "Bilingualism keeps people actively tied to their old language and habits and maximizes the cost of the transition to becoming American." In the 2004 election cycle, opposition to bilingualism has reached hysterical and, indeed, racist proportions, as Carlos Fuentes and others have pointed out. In a *Foreign Policy* essay, Samuel Huntington (2004, 45) decries the "dual loyalties" of bilingual Americans and concludes, "There is no Americano dream. There is only the American dream created by an Anglo-Protestant society. Mexican Americans will share in that dream and in that society only if they dream in English." Former Colorado governor Richard Lamm (2002) is even more explicit: "It is a curse for a society to be bilingual."

I wonder what a polyglot like Thomas Jefferson, who had side careers as a diplomat in France and was a practitioner of miscegenation, would have thought of the notion that Anglo-Protestant culture and monolingualism are synonymous. One might also rhetorically ask how many languages the writers and subjects of the New Testament spoke. The notion that citizens in a multinational nation-state of nearly 300 million people should not have dual allegiances or speak more than one language is clearly a racialized form of nativism. The idea that bilingualism is a curse is, of course, contradicted by abundant evidence of the economic benefits of bilingualism.

Especially in the South, one is forced to return to the racialized foundations of the insistence on monolingualism as an American virtue. At the University of North Carolina, Kubota emphasized that creative solutions to language learning and, more broadly, to a multiethnic curriculum reform were hampered by a black-and-white worldview. ESL programs in North Carolina were very Anglocentric, she said. By "Anglocentric" she meant not only Eurocentric, but that most people in higher education that she worked with thought of cultural diversity almost exclusively in terms of African Americans. Kubota pointed out that of more than fifty full-time professors in the School of Education, there were no Latinos and only two Asians.

In terms of institutional resistance, most schools are heavily invested in ESL programs, even though research shows that this is the least effective strategy for ELL. Another major impediment is that students are not being tested on language learning because of a narrowly defined reemphasis on "fundamentals." Until statewide testing policy is changed, teachers and administrators will have little incentive to emphasize language learning, since they are under pressure to raise test scores, especially to close the so-called achievement gap.[12] In fact, DLP can be an important component of closing that gap, and not only for Latinos. African American children at the Jones Elementary program in Greensboro, North Carolina, and at Shidler Elementary in Oklahoma City, the school I have been studying in depth, are among those scoring higher than their monolingual peers.

DLPs can help to ameliorate some negative aspects of class and racial divisions. Well-implemented DLPs or enrichment programs help level the playing field for students of low socioeconomic status (they score much closer to their more privileged peers). More specifically, DLPs problematize racial language and the way that schools have traditionally followed racial categorization.[13] DLP students are divided into two groups: native English speakers and nonnative English speakers. In a Spanish/English program, the English speakers can include Mexican American students as well as African Americans, Anglos, and Asians, since many Mexican American families in fact use English as a first language. Conversely, Spanish speakers can also be of any ethnicity. As our own census forms tell us, Hispanics can be of any race, which points to the decentering of race in *nuestra América*. For instance, most people of African descent in the Americas speak Spanish or Portuguese, not English. Students in DLP classes often socialize according to language more than ethnicity or race; at the same time, the structure of the program facilitates a great deal of interchange between language groups.

Thinking in Black and White: A Myopic Schema

There is one more term in my title that needs to be defined: racialism. Racialism is "the insidious confusion of race with culture which haunts our society," as Ralph Ellison (1995, 606) said, the belief that phenotype or outward appearance is a meaningful way to determine someone's culture, intelligence, or aptitudes. The social science consensus now, to the contrary, is that "race has no biological justification." No matter whom we blame for the origins of racial mythologies, racialism is a problem perpetuated by people of all colors, as Frederick Douglass had the courage to say long ago. Douglass called racialism a "diseased imagination."[14] It is also a curable disease. If we cannot completely cure the disease, we can at least contain it by articulating a more attractive alternative. To even conceive of an alternative, however, we first have to agree that racialism is a concept with insidious consequences.

We are still having a hard time putting into practice a more attractive alternative to racialism, in part, because racialism is a mostly unconscious way of thinking, an "imaginative pattern," as Mary Midgley says in *The Myths We Live By* (2003). It is what Freud called a "schema" and what Jung termed a "category of the imagination" (Jung 1958, 518). In other words, it is a blueprint or a script. When people follow a schema or a script, they are usually unconscious of its origin. They think that this is "their" thought, while typically they are following a script whose structure and broad outlines were crafted by forces and generations unseen. Racialism, in the form of a "one drop" ideology that our institutions still largely enforce, was articulated by white supremacists, a link that many who advocate racial solidarity today seem unaware of or untroubled by.

Freud once wrote, "We are often able to see the schema triumphing over the experiences of the individual" (qtd. in Adams 1996, 45). We project unconscious thought patterns, such as racialism, onto the world and then we reject or tune out experiences that do not fit this pattern. North Americans still tend to project a racialized black-and-white schema onto a full-color, multi-centered social world. Nowhere is this tendency more ingrained than in the South.

As Latinos became the largest minority in the United States, many African Americans expressed resentment or the perception that Latinos were "trying to be white."[15] This seems to be a case of a schema being projected onto a demographic that does not fit into this racial binary and does not see the world in that way. Yet this point of view also clearly expresses a psychological reality. However understandable this may be in psychological or historical terms, racialized perceptions of competition can lead to support for monolingualism, which is what happened when African Americans led opposition to bilingual education in Houston.[16]

Monolingualism often reinforces racialism. Anglos who speak Spanish are going to be less likely to perceive Latino immigrants as "wetbacks" who need to "swim back." They will probably feel some sort of kinship with Spanish-speaking peoples. African Americans who know Spanish will be less likely to try to project a black/white binary and its racialist assumptions onto Latinos. They, too, are likely to develop a sense of kinship, to understand that millions of people from *nuestra América* are, in fact, of African descent, although a concept of blackness and an opposition to whiteness may not be central to their identity and sense of community.[17]

"The presence of large proportions of Asians, Hispanics and black immigrants are changing Americans' notions of race," notes Nancy Foner (2000). I would argue that this can only be a healthy thing for all of us. Latinos are going to play the key role in this process for the foreseeable future. We should not condescend and imagine that they need to learn our truth about race. Our racial definitions continually reproduce a cultural and political myopia toward people that do not fit into North America's binary black-white racial divide. Racialism also contributes to a concept of patriotism that conflates the United States with America and does not allow for the increasingly normative experience of people who retain allegiances to more than one nation, culture, and language.

Reorienting Ourselves toward
Nuestra América

A multicentered model of intergroup relations in the South would undertake what I see as a fundamental challenge of inclusive democracy: building institutions and social spaces in which commonality and difference can coexist. If commonality and difference are to coexist, we cannot avoid debate about racism and racialism, yet we must decenter the privileged place of race in our imagination. And we must come to understand that we are situated within a region in which English must be decentered to some degree. We will have to question some of the universalist assumptions of English monolingualism.

In the final analysis, practicing a multicentered and multilingual model of intergroup relations in which commonality and difference can coexist means that we have to develop some sense of kinship with people that do not look like us or speak our language.

Jim Peacock suggests that the model the South is following is in transition from its former stance of opposition within the nation (opposing the North, its Other) to integration within the world. But even that oppositional mentality can have some benefits, he believes, structuring how the South integrates globally. Because of its history of opposition to military intervention and northern materialism, the South may be more inclined to oppose North America's role as transnational bully, Peacock believes. It is more apt to be sympathetic to other nations that have also suffered occupation and defeat. (See Peacock 2002.) The notion that the South will offer a critique of the worst aspects of Americanism, such as materialism and military adventurism, is hard to square with the conservatism and deep-seated patriotism of the region. However, I do believe that the South could develop such a critical consciousness if it undertakes a more successful internal integration. One route would be to discover our kinship with *nuestra América* and to recover the political implications of that concept.

José Martí has iconic status throughout Latin America and, interestingly, is embraced both by those in Cuba who remain committed to communism and by right-wing Cubans in Miami who want to overthrow Castro. I want to make three observations about the context in which Martí developed his notion of *nuestra América*. First, he did most of his writing during a two-decade "exile" in New York, from where he was in a unique position both to celebrate North America's strengths and to criticize its myopia and adventurism. Second, antiracism is a foundational element of Martí's thought—not only antiracism but antiracialism, I should say, an embrace of a *mestizo* identity. Third, the very concept of *nuestra América* was an explicit critique of North American imperialism and ethnocentrism. By distinguishing *nuestra América* from imperial America, Martí wanted to give voice to previously excluded/silenced peoples, the true majority in the Americas, people of African and native descent and, more broadly, all people whose language and culture give them a critical perspective on North American monocentrism. By integrating *nuestra América* into the transnational South, along with all its cultural, ideological, ethnic, and linguistic diversity, we can incorporate both Martí's critique and his celebration of the best of North America's cultural and political traditions.

Civil rights leaders are among those helping to develop a multicentered notion of kinship across the lines of difference. During a conference on coalition building between African Americans and Latinos in Musgrove, on Sam Simon's Island in Georgia (sponsored by the Southern Regional Council), Latino immigrants began explaining to their African American peers some of the specifics of immigration policy, such as the way it sometimes tied them without choice to one employer. "My God, that's slavery," the African Americans responded. "You don't need to approach us on the basis of our self-interest. This is a question of justice." Understanding the ways in which Latino immigrants had been denied justice evoked a feeling of kinship among African Americans who heard this humanizing story.

That awakening sense of kinship across the lines of ethnicity or language, however, is still all too rare. Teodoro Maus, former Mexican counsel in Atlanta, speaks about the African American perception that Latinos, as immigrants, "lack a root in America." Lacking that root, they will therefore not fight for its betterment, some think.[18]

One must insist again on asking, Which America? Immigrants from Latin America have roots in more than one America and are struggling for betterment on more than one side of it. They are remitting huge amounts of money back to their home communities outside the United States, but they are also becoming involved in the education of their children and other activities that demonstrate their increasingly strong roots in North America.

In the spring of 2002 I interviewed Barbara Smith and Marcela Mendoza of the "Race and Nation in the Global South" project in Memphis.[19] The heart of their project centered on tensions between Latino immigrants and African Americans. As a sociologist and a North American, Smith was inclined to argue that racial formations justified African American resentment and would prevent Latinos from inhabiting a third space between racial binaries. As an anthropologist from Argentina, Mendoza resisted racial binaries. She was impatient with what she saw as a paternalistic attitude among some African American leaders who took the attitude that Latinos were "not ready" for coalition building until they can be educated about the endurance of American racism. In a sense, the attitudes of Smith and Mendoza represent the different worldviews of North America and "our America." They had to agree to disagree on some issues, but they were still working together on shared interests.

The capacity of Latin Americans to maintain allegiance to more than more one nation, language, culture, and race is a fundamental challenge to many of our prior assumptions about identity and community. Meeting this challenge requires us to evolve beyond a binary worldview and to embrace multicenteredness as a more attractive alternative to racialism and monolingualism. As Marcela Mendoza said to me over lunch, after we concluded our formal interview, "Bienvenida la mezcla."

Conclusion: Reimagined Communities

The biggest obstacle to integration of *nuestra América* in the transnational South is cultural myopia, which renders "our America" invisible. But this myopia is curable if we recognize that integration is an intersubjective process. We southerners are also being integrated into *nuestra América*. I think of a story told by my officemate David Camp about his first trip to Texas. He was sitting in a mall in San Antonio, and he was stunned by the sea of colors he saw moving through that mall. He tells how it was a treat to his eyes, and he just feasted on that range of colors. It was so very different from what he was accustomed to seeing, he recounted, and perhaps more to the point, from what he had been acculturated to see in the South, which is black and white. To understand both our similarities to and differences from our neighbors from our other America, we have to see them with new eyes, in living color, rather than in black and white.

Notes

1. Because of a dual-state residence necessitated by having two children in Oklahoma City, I was "pushed into taking one site as [a] primary perspective" (Burawoy et al. 2000, vii), i.e., Oklahoma City, where my daughter was a student in a Spanish/English double immersion program.

2. Interview with Nolo Martinez, North Carolina governor's liaison for Hispanic and Latino affairs. See also Stephens 2002.

3. See "North Carolina Faces Lawsuits" 2002; "Achievement Gap" 2002; and "Ruling Should Light Fire" 2002. See also the Chapel Hill/Carrboro School District's Minority Student Achievement Plan at ⟨http://www.chccs.k12.nc.us/minoritystudent-achievement.htm⟩.

4. Interview with Raul Font, then-director of external funding, Oklahoma City Public Schools.

5. Regarding parallels in representations of African Americans in North America and native people in Mexico as the true embodiment of their respective nations' democratic aspirations, see Gregory Stephens, "Frederick Douglass' Biracial Abolitionism: 'Antagonistic Cooperation' and 'Redeemable Ideals' in the July 5 Speech," *Com-*

munication Studies (Fall 1997), and writings by Subcomandante Marcos, collected in *Our Word Is Our Weapon* (Seven Stories Press, 2001).

6. For writings about Martí's concept of *nuestra América*, see Belknap and Fernandez 1998; Abel and Torrents 1986; and Saldivar 1991, chap. 1. See also Stephens 2004.

7. "Imperial Democracy": I have adapted this from Paz 1985, 375. Quote from p. 219.

8. See Fuentes 2000, 25. What is a Mexican, after all? A *mestizo*, a mixture of European and native peoples, traditions, and languages. The discourse on *mestizaje*, in much of Latin America, is about a three-way mixture: African, European, and native (Esteva-Fabregat 1995). There is also a large body of scholarship that is critical of romanticized notions of *mestizaje*, of Brazil's myth of itself as a mixed-race utopia, etc. See Rudin 1996, 112–29. For an example of a growing chorus critiquing Brazilian racialism, see Twine 1997.

9. Thanks to my student Sekou Clancy at the University of Oklahoma for pointing me to this piece. "Isms and schisms" is a reference to a line from Bob Marley's song "Ride Natty Ride," from *Survival* (Island/Tuff Gong, 1979). The notion of "One Blood" or "One Love" as a diversity-in-unity consciousness that is an antidote to schizmatic monocentrisms is a central tenet of Rastafarian thought.

10. Interview with Fran Hoch, section chief for second languages, ESL, information and computer skills, arts education, and healthful living, North Carolina Department of Public Instruction. For a brief overview of Dual Language Education, see ‹http://www.unc.edu/courses/hnrs030/alderson.htm›. Proposition 227 was a response to public perception that bilingual education is often "equated with remedial education," Ruth Sadelle Alderson notes. Dual language education manages to escape this perception because it is popular with middle-class English-speaking parents.

11. Interviews with Ryuko Kubota of the education department at the University of North Carolina at Chapel Hill, and Raul Font.

12. Interviews with Kathy Hodges, director of Alliance for Language Learning, North Carolina, and Fran Hoch.

13. Interview with Patrick Marc-Charles, codirector of Oklahoma Title 7 Dual Language Grant, Hennessey Elementary. A good overview of political debates about bilingualism is Galindo 1997.

14. Frederick Douglass wrote of a "diseased imagination" in "The Races," *Douglass Monthly* (August 1859), quoted in Blight 1994.

15. On accusations of "trying to be white," see Darrity 2002; interviews in Shipler 1997, 492, 461; and Stephens 2003.

16. See Paul Levengood's essay in this volume.

17. The John Sayles film *Lone Star* is an excellent dramatic illustration of the coexistence of conflict and the development of a sense of kinship in a border culture setting where Mexican Americans, Anglos, African Americans, and Native Americans coexist. See also José Limón's commentary on this film (Limón 1998, 149–60).

18. Teodoro Maus is interviewed in *Dialogue for Inclusive Democracy* 2002.

19. Interview with Barbara Smith and Marcela Mendoza, "Race and Nation in the Global South," University of Memphis. The Southern Regional Council's Inter-

Group Project "attempts to shift the existing paradigm in Atlanta from a black-white paradigm to one that involves leadership from growing populations of Latinos and Asian Americans in the metropolitan area" (Southern Regional Council website at ⟨http://www.src.w1.com/partner/index.html⟩). Many working-class African Americans perceive that Latinos are taking their jobs, although studies have shown little basis for this sort of direct economic competition. See Morris and Rubin 2000; Hamermesh and Bean 1998; Cornelius 1998, 11–155; Hing 2000.

References

Abel, Christopher, and Nissa Torrents. 1986. *José Martí: Revolutionary Democrat.* Durham: Duke University Press.

"The Achievement Gap." 2002. *Raleigh-Durham News and Observer*, February 8.

Adams, Michael Vannoy. 1996. *The Multicultural Imagination: "Race," Color, and the Unconscious.* London: Routledge.

Alanis, Iliana. 2000. "A Texas Two-way Bilingual Program: Its Effects on Linguistic and Academic Achievement." *Bilingual Research Journal* 24, no. 3 (Summer). Retrieved from ⟨http://brj.asu.edu/v243/articles/art2.html⟩.

Amaral, Olga Maia. 2001. "Parents' Decisions about Bilingual Program Models." *Bilingual Research Journal* 25, no. 1–2. Retrieved from ⟨http://brj.asu.edu/v2512/articles/art11.html⟩.

Anderson, Benedict. 1991. *Imagined Communities.* Rev. ed. London: Verso.

Appiah, Anthony. 1992. "Illusions of Race." In Appiah, *In My Father's House: Africa in the Philosophy of Culture*, 28–46. New York: Oxford University Press.

August, D. 2002. *English as a Second Language Instruction: Best Practices to Support the Development of Literacy for English Language Learners.* Baltimore: Johns Hopkins University, Center for Research on the Education of Students Placed at Risk.

Belknap, Jeffrey, and Raul Fernandez, eds. 1998. *José Martí's "Our America": From National to Hemispheric Studies.* Durham: Duke University Press.

Blight, David. 1994. "W. E. B. Du Bois and the Struggle for American Historical Memory." In Genevieve Fabre and Robert O'Meally, eds., *History and Memory in African-American Culture*, 45–71. New York: Oxford University Press.

Burawoy, Michael, et al. 2000. *Global Ethnography: Forces, Connections, and Imaginations in a Postmodern World.* Berkeley: University of California Press.

Cornelius, Wayne. 1998. "The Structural Embeddedness of Demand for Mexican Immigrant Labor: New Evidence from California." In Marcelo M. Suárez-Orozco, ed., *Crossings: Mexican Immigration in Interdisciplinary Perspectives*, 115–55. Cambridge, Mass.: Harvard University Press.

Darrity, William, Jr. 2002. "Racial and Ethnic Economic Inequality: Why Culture Is Irrelevant." Race, Ethnicity, and Culture in Research and Service, lecture cosponsored by the School of Social Work, University of North Carolina at Chapel Hill, January 14.

David, F. James. 1991. *Who Is Black? One Nation's Definition.* University Park: Pennsylvania State University Press.

Davies, Carole Boyce. 1999. "Beyond Unicentricity: Transcultural Black Presences."
Research in African Literatures 30, no. 2 (Summer 1999): 96–108.

Davis, Darién. 1999. "Pan-Africanism and Afro-Latin Americans." In Kwame Anthony Appiah and Henry Louis Gates Jr., eds., *Africana: The Encyclopedia of the African and African American Experience*, 1487–90. New York: Basic/Civitas.

Dialogue for Inclusive Democracy. 2002. Video produced by George King for the Southern Regional Council's Partnership for Racial Unity.

Ellison, Ralph. 1995. "Going to the Territory." In *The Collected Essays of Ralph Ellison*. New York: Modern Library.

Esteva-Fabregat, Claudio. 1995. *Mestizaje in Ibero-America*. Tucson: University of Arizona Press.

Foner, Nancy. 2000. *From Ellis Island to JFK: New York's Two Great Waves of Immigration*. New Haven: Yale University Press. Quoted in *Hispanic News*, May 29, 2004. Retrieved from ‹http://www.hispanic.cc/foreign_born_in_us_at_record_high.htm›.

Font, Raul. 2002. Interview with author, February 7.

Fuentes, Carlos. 2000. *Los cinco soles de México: Memoria de un Milenio*. Barcelona: Seix Barrall.

———. 2004. "Looking for Enemies in the Wrong Places." *Miami Herald*, March 21. Retrieved from ‹http://www.commondreams.org/views04/0321-04.htm›.

Galindo, René. 1997. "Language Wars: The Ideological Dimensions of the Debates on Bilingual Education." *Bilingual Research Journal* 21, no. 2/3 (Spring/Summer). Retrieved from ‹http://brj.asu.edu/articlesv2/galindo.html›.

Gingrich, Newt. 1995. *To Renew America*. New York: Harper-Collins.

Gómez-Peña, Guillermo. 1993. "The Multicultural Paradigm." In Gómez-Peña, *Warrior for Gringostroika: Essays, Performance Texts, and Poetry*, 45–54. St. Paul, Minn.: Graywolf Press.

Greene, Jay P. 1997. "A Meta-Analysis of the Rossell and Baker Review of Bilingual Education Research." *Bilingual Research Journal* 21, no. 2/3 (Spring/Summer). Retrieved from ‹http://brj.asu.edu/articlesv2/green.html›.

Hamermesh, Daniel, and Frank Bean, eds. 1998. *Help or Hindrance? The Economic Implications of Immigration for African Americans*. New York: Russell Sage.

Hing, Bill Ong. 2000. *To Be an American: Cultural Pluralism and the Rhetoric of Assimilation*. New York: New York University Press.

Hoch, Fran. 2002. Interview with author, January 22.

Hodges, Kathy. 2002. Interview with author, February 26.

Huntington, Samuel. 2004. "The Hispanic Challenge." *Foreign Policy*, no. 141 (March–April): 30–45.

Jung, C. G. 1958. *Psychology and Religion*. Princeton: Princeton University Press.

Kubota, Ryuko. 2002. Interview with author, February 22.

Lamm, Richard. 2002. "It Is a Blessing for an Individual to Be Bilingual; It Is a Curse for a Society to Be Bilingual." Adapted from "One Nation, One Tongue," *Rocky Mountain News*, August 8. Retrieved from ‹http://www.cairco.org/language/language.html›.

Limón, José. 1998. *American Encounters: Greater Mexico, the United States, and the Erotics of Culture*. Boston: Beacon Press.

Marc-Charles, Patrick. 2001. Interview with author, October 15.

Martinez, Nolo. 2002. Interview with author, February 6.

Mendoza, Marcela. 2002. Interview with author. University of Memphis, March 13.

Midgley, Mary. 2003. *The Myths We Live By*. New York: Routledge.

Morris, Milton, and Gary Rubin, eds. 2000. *Immigrants and African Americans: Research Findings and Policy Responses*. New York: New York Association for New Americans.

"North Carolina Faces Lawsuits Re: Shortage of Interpreters." 2002. *Charlotte Observer*, January 12.

Paz, Octavio. 1985. "Mexico and the United States." In Paz, *The Labyrinth of Solitude and Other Writings*, 357–76. New York: Grove Press.

———. 2000. *El Laberinto de Soledad*. Madrid: Catedra.

Peacock, James L. 2002. "The South in a Global World." Keynote address of "Creating the Transnational South" conference, University of North Carolina, April 11.

Rossell, C., and K. Baker. 1996. "The Educational Effectiveness of Bilingual Education." *Research in the Teaching of English* 30, no. 1: 7–69.

Rudin, Ernst. 1996. "New Mestizos: Traces of a Quincentenary Miracle in Old World Spanish and New World English Texts." In Winfried Siemerling and Katrin Schwenk, eds., *Cultural Difference and the Literary Text: Pluralism and the Limits of Authenticity in North American Literatures*, 112–29. Iowa City: University of Iowa Press.

"Ruling Should Light Fire under the State." 2002. *Greensboro News and Record*, April 8.

Saffa, Joan, dir. 1989. *Crossing Borders: The Journey of Carlos Fuentes*. Profile of a Writer series.

Saldivar, José David. 1991. *The Dialectics of Our America*. Durham, N.C.: Duke University Press.

Shipler, David. 1997. *A Country of Strangers: Blacks and Whites in America*. New York: Random House.

Skutnabbs-Kangas, Tove, and J. Cummins, eds. 1988. *Minority Education: From Shame to Struggle*. Philadelphia: Multilingual Matters.

Slavin, Robert, and Alan Cheung. 2003. *Effective Reading Programs for English Language Learners: A Best-Evidence Synthesis*. Baltimore: Johns Hopkins University, Center for Research on the Education of Students Placed at Risk. Retrieved from ⟨http://www.csos.jhu.edu⟩.

Smith, Barbara. 2002. Interview with author. University of Memphis, March 13.

Spivak, Gayatri. 1990. *Post-Colonial Critic*. London: Routledge.

Stephens, Gregory. 1999. *On Racial Frontiers: The New Culture of Frederick Douglass, Ralph Ellison, and Bob Marley*. Cambridge: Cambridge University Press.

———. 2002. "Nuestra América in the Transnational South: The Bilingual Crisis in Living Color." *Global View*, Spring, 15–17. Newsletter of the University Center for International Studies, University of North Carolina at Chapel Hill.

————. 2003. "The Strangest of Kin: *Blacks and Whites in America* as Viewed from the Borderlands." In Terry White, ed., *Blacks and Whites Meeting in America: Eighteen Essays on Race*, 175–84. Jefferson, N.C.: McFarland Press.

————. 2004. "Letting Go of America." *Dissident Voice*, May 16. Retrieved from ‹http://www.dissidentvoice.org/May2004/stephens0516.htm›.

Thomas, Wayne, and Virginia Collier. 1997. "School Effectiveness for Language Minority Students." George Washington University, NCELA Resource Collection Series, no. 9, December. Retrieved from ‹http://www.ncela.gwu.edu/pubs/resource/effectiveness/›.

————. 2000. "Making U.S. Schools Effective for English Language Learners." *TESOL Matters* 9, nos. 4–6 (August 1999–January 2000). Retrieved from ‹http://www.tesol.org/pubs/articles/1999/tm9908-01.html›.

————. 2002. *A National Study of School Effectiveness for Language Minority Students' Long-Term Academic Achievement.* Santa Cruz, Calif.: Center for Research on Education, Diversity and Excellence. Retrieved from ‹http://www.crede.ucsc.edu/research/llaa/1.1_es.html›.

Twine, Frances Winddance. 1997. *Racism in a Racial Democracy: The Maintenance of White Supremacy in Brazil.* New Brunswick, N.J.: Rutgers University Press.

Walker, Clarence E. 2001. *We Can't Go Home Again: An Argument about Afrocentrism.* New York: Oxford University Press.

Jennie M. Smith

The Latinization of Rome, Georgia

Undergraduate Research and
Community Activism

In this study I discuss my experiences teaching a course in Applying Anthropology at Berry College, a small, private college in Rome, Georgia. I highlight the benefits that lie in teaching undergraduate students to conduct research on demographic changes taking place in the contemporary South. I first offered the Applying Anthropology course at Berry in the fall of 1999 and again in the fall of 2001. In the course we concentrate on Latino immigration to the United States, the Southeast, the state of Georgia, and finally, the city of Rome and Floyd County, where Berry College is located. Throughout the semester, students carry out an application-oriented research project on Latino immigration to Rome and Floyd County. They include in their research reactions to this immigration by longtime residents. Some background information on what has been happening in northwest Georgia during the past several years will reveal why I selected this particular research topic for this course.

Rome and Floyd County, Georgia

With a population of approximately 40,000, Rome is the largest town in northwest Georgia. Rome is also the economic and political center of Floyd County, which has a population of close to 90,000. Many of Rome and Floyd County's families have lived in the area for several generations and are proud of the strong, deeply rooted sense of community that has come to characterize the place they call home. It is the sort of place where high school football games draw large, enthusiastically loyal crowds; where the downtown Christmas parade is packed with Boy Scout troops, church choirs, and lovingly adorned pickup trucks—all cheered on by the masses of participants' relatives and friends who line the streets; and where American flags and "God Bless the U.S.A." signs decorate many a yard and car bumper. It is, locals like to think, small-town America at its best.

But like many other southerners, the citizens of Rome and Floyd County have seen dramatic changes taking place in their communities during the past decade. Among the most noticeable has been the arrival of thousands of new residents, many of whom are blue-collar workers from Mexico, Guatemala, and other Latin American countries. No longer can Romans think of their hometown as structured around the sometimes uncomfortable but fairly stable and clear-cut black-and-white divide (also see Duchon and Murphy 2001).

According to recent census data, more than 35.3 million Latinos now reside in the United States, comprising nearly 13 percent of the population (U.S. Census Bureau 2000b). In 1990, around 90 percent of Latinos in the United States lived in large cities. In fact, nearly half lived in one of only six cities: Los Angeles, New York, Miami, San Francisco, Chicago, and Houston (del Pinal and Singer 1997). This pattern of settlement has changed dramatically during the past decade, as Latinos increasingly have moved into rural and suburban areas (del Pinal and Singer 1997; Martin and Midgley 2003, 23–24; Cornelius 2002, 168). Many of the new "magnet" areas are located in the South, and more than a few of them are in Georgia (Duchon and Murphy 2001; Guzmán 2001; Klein 1999; Martin and Midgley 2003; Population Reference Bureau [PRB] 2002). In fact, between 1990 and 2000, Georgia experienced a 300 percent increase in the Latino population, which now constitutes more than 5 percent of the state's total population (PRB 2002).

Although the metro Atlanta area has seen the highest Latino growth rates, many small towns and rural counties have experienced dramatic changes as well. Whereas the 1990 U.S. Census found only 831 Latinos living in Floyd County, 2000 census takers recorded nearly 5,000 Latino residents (Millman and Pinkston 2001). Many experts have suggested that the actual number is probably closer to 8,000 to 10,000—perhaps more than 10 percent of the population.

Contrary to stereotypes developed during previous migrations, many of the Latinos who have migrated recently to Georgia and other areas of the South are not temporary migrants coming directly from their countries of origin and planning to return after they accumulate a few years' worth of wages. Rather, they have been in the United States for a while, often in traditional Latino enclaves in California, Texas, or Florida (Zúñiga and Hernández-León 2001). They (and those they attract from their home communities in Latin America) come to places like Floyd County looking for better wages and, increasingly, for safer, more tranquil places to raise their children. They are here, in other words, to stay.[1]

The influx of Latinos to northwest Georgia has been critical to the region's economy (Murphy, Blanchard, and Hill 2001). Nowhere is this clearer than a few miles up the road from Floyd County, in Dalton. Nestled in the folds of the Appalachian mountains just south of the Tennessee border, Dalton is widely known as the Carpet Capital of the World. In fact, the town produces more than half of the carpets manufactured in the United States. Large numbers of Latinos began immigrating here in the late 1980s to fill positions being abandoned by native Georgians. Today, more than one-third of the infants born in Dalton's Hamilton Medical Center are Latino, as are the majority of incoming kindergartners in Dalton City Schools (Millman and Pinkston 2001). The owners of Dalton's carpet mills, and the many businesses that depend on those mills, are quick to recognize the economic benefits brought by these new residents. They explain that if it had not been for the increased immigration of Latinos to their town during the 1980s and 1990s, many of them would have been forced to close their doors (see Engstrom 2001; Kirp 2000; Klein 1999; Murphy, Blanchard, and Hill 2001; Zúñiga and Hernández-León 2001). The economic benefits of Latino immigration can also be seen on the state level. As the University System of Regents reported in 1999, "The buying power of Georgia's Latino population is among the fastest-growing in the nation, currently accounting for more than $3 billion annually" (Georgia Board of Regents 1999, 3).

In Rome and Floyd County, it is estimated that Latinos make up around 10 percent of the carpet industry workforce (Willis 2001). They also fill important places in the work crews of poultry processing factories, construction companies, assembly plants, and many other large and small businesses. Yet while the "Latinization" of communities like Dalton and Rome/Floyd County has bolstered their economies, this migration also has posed "significant challenges to these regions' social service systems" (Bixler 2002). Unfortunately, to most longtime area residents such challenges tend to be much more visible than the advantages these new immigrants have brought.

Negative attitudes toward Latino immigrants are common and have been exacerbated by the fact that local government officials and business owners often have been slow to respond to the demographic changes described here.[2] According to University of Georgia sociology professor Stephanie Bohon, "The state as a whole hasn't really adjusted to the fact that Latinos are here" (Bixler 2000).[3] In Rome and Floyd County, government officials have yet to address the issue in a directed, systematic way. In a 2001 editorial in the *Rome News-Tribune,* Pierre Noth urged locals to wake up—both to come to terms with the demographic changes that have been taking place in their communities and to assist their Latino neighbors in their efforts to assimilate. He stresses to his readers that "these are by and large good people. They are hard working, have strong family values and are still grateful for the freedoms that so many of the rest of us have begun to take for granted. We need them. We need their abilities and participation in building this community, we need their energy, we need their fresh perspectives just as, in another time, we needed all the other waves of immigrants from Ireland, Germany, Poland and dozens of other places to keep us going" (Noth 2001).

After emphasizing the importance of offering Latinos opportunities to learn the language skills they will need to be active, constructive participants in the area's economy, government, social life, schools, and health care system, Noth suggests that the city of Rome and Floyd County should "jointly form a task force to add to the [2000] census data and learn more about these new neighbors. That knowledge should lead to better serve them within the context of what government already provides to all the population" (2001). Although such a task force has yet to arise, certain sectors of the Rome and Floyd County community have begun to respond to the needs Noth highlights. More than a few churches now host Spanish-language services, and some provide limited education programs and social services to their Latino congregants. The Floyd County Health Department has employed several bilingual staff members to assist Spanish-speaking clients. From Wal-Mart and K-Mart to Kroger, shopping centers are filling their aisles and produce coolers with tortillas, jalapeños, and plantains. While Berry now trains all its education majors in ESOL (English for Speakers of Other Languages) instruction, another local college offers classes in both Spanish and ESOL to employees of the community's businesses and social service agencies. I designed the Applying Anthropology course in such a way that it might allow my students and me to complement such efforts while also providing feedback to local and regional leaders on how their efforts might be augmented or strengthened.

Applying Anthropology with
Berry Students: Experiment 1

The first time I taught the course, I began the term by taking students on a field trip to a trailer park populated by recent immigrants from Mexico and Central America. During this field trip, led by a local Latino church leader, we asked residents of the park about what it had been like to live and work in Rome, about how and why they had come, and about their future plans. The students were both fascinated and disturbed by many of the things they saw and heard that day, and they found themselves much more motivated to plan their research projects. Since the students' particular interests in the local Latino population varied considerably, I decided to allow each student (or team of students) to chose a specific research topic. Because of this, we had students scattered throughout the area—something that both enriched and limited our study in significant ways. Their field sites included a nonprofit social service agency run by and for Latinos, the Latino outreach program of a local church, schools in Rome and Floyd County, and finally, schools in Dalton—the latter providing a comparison case for the data collected at Rome and Floyd County schools.

Initially, I had planned for the students to report on their research in the form of term papers to be submitted at the conclusion of the course. However, as the students and I became more aware of the serious lack of attention that had been paid to Latino immigration by officials in the Rome/Floyd County area, we reassessed the original assignment and decided that instead of a term paper, each student would write an open letter to local and regional leaders. After the conclusion of the semester, I made copies of these letters, added a cover letter that summarized the students' main points, and mailed out the finished product. Our mailing list included the following:

- Rome city commissioners
- Floyd County commissioners
- Various other Rome and Floyd County officials, including those involved in city planning and community development
- Greater Rome Chamber of Commerce
- Floyd County Health Department
- City and County police forces
- Social service agencies
- Civic leaders
- Georgia senators and representatives
- Religious leaders
- Latino business owners
- Primary, secondary, and postsecondary educators
- Locally distributed newspapers—including both Spanish- and English-language papers.

Policy recommendations comprised a central feature of the students' letters. Those recommendations included

- Increasing support for the only Latino social service agency in the area
- Sponsoring communitywide, multicultural events to facilitate communication between Latinos and non-Latinos
- Improving legal services offered to Latinos

- Providing Spanish-language guides to the Rome public transportation system
- Providing Spanish-language translation and Spanish-language literature at social service agencies and government offices
- Advertising the services of local agencies and offices in the Spanish-language newspapers
- Improving and expanding ESOL programs in city and county schools
- Encouraging schoolchildren from different countries to share with one another their countries' distinguishing characteristics and customs
- Providing free or inexpensive tutorial programs for Latino students
- Providing free or inexpensive ESOL classes to Latino adults at convenient hours
- Forming a council of Latinos to work with non-Latino government and civic leaders
- Initiating and funding further research.

Local responses to our packet, while generally very positive, were sparse. I suspect this was due, in part, to some of the weaknesses of the packet itself—namely, the wide variety of topics addressed in the students' letters and the cumbersome length (the cover letter and the papers added up to forty-six pages). Among those we did hear from were the city commission, the county commission, and the county police. Another response came in the form of an invitation to me to join the fledging "Undoing Racism" committee, a group composed of city and county leaders concerned about ameliorating relations between blacks, whites, and Latinos. The students' research gained additional exposure when two of the students and I gave a poster presentation the following November at the American Anthropological Association's annual meeting in San Francisco.

Applying Anthropology with Berry Students: Experiment 2

During the next two years, Rome and Floyd County saw little progress in most of the areas the students had targeted with their recommendations. When I taught the Applying Anthropology course again in the fall of 2001, I left the basic objectives and structure of the course much the same as they had been in 1999. I had learned from the first experience, though, that undergraduate students need more training in ethnographic research methodologies than I had previously offered, so we spent more time on that than before. A more fundamental change was that instead of each student choosing an individual project, all the students collaborated on the same research. The reasoning was that if we more thoroughly probed one topic, then our feedback to local and regional leaders would be more rigorous in content and more digestible in scope and length. This change also allowed me to supervise more closely the students' work. The research project I assigned the students entailed working at a local middle school as tutors and mentors of Latino students, while also conducting interviews with those students.

I chose this assignment after having learned during the previous section of Applying Anthropology that education is one of the areas where the challenges presented by recent immigration trends have been most dramatically felt (see Bixler 2002; Moll and Ruiz 2002; Suárez-Orozco and Páez 2002). Between 1996 and 2000, the number of Latino students in Georgia's public schools rose by 98 percent. Growth rates are expected to continue their dramatic incline during the coming years.[4] To say that the educational system has been scrambling to keep up is putting it mildly. As Edmund Hamann noted in the late 1990s, "Latinos [in Georgia public schools] were less likely than their peers to finish school, more likely to struggle in the classroom, and less likely to have instructors from their ethnic background" (1997, 6; also see Education Trust 2001 and Hispanic Association of Colleges and Universities 2002). Similar patterns are visible on a national level as well.[5] So, too, is the fact that even as Latino enrollment in primary and secondary schools escalates exponentially, the rate at which Latinos are entering institutions of higher education remains dismally low (del Pinal and Singer 1997; Georgia Board of Regents 2000; Hispanic Association of Colleges and Universities 2002). According to the University System of Georgia, in 2001 only 2.1 percent of the students at its thirty-four universities and colleges were Latino (Prophet 2002). While many Latinos are kept away from colleges and universities by their legal status and/ or by a lack of financial resources, these hardly comprise a full explanation of the conspicuous lack of Latinos in higher education—particularly in states like Georgia, where the University System has publicly announced that the legal status of a student is irrelevant to college admission.

I hoped that through my students' work with local middle school students, we would gain a better understanding of some of the reasons for Latino underenrollment in higher education, while simultaneously improving the likelihood that the students with whom we were working would come to see higher education as a possible option for the future. Thus, my students' interviews focused first on asking the middle schoolers about their previous educational experiences, the education they were receiving at the time of our research, and their aspirations for the future. The Applying Anthropology students also were directed to share with the middle schoolers information about higher education, to describe their own college experiences, and to answer the middle schoolers' questions on the topic.[6]

To set up the research project, I contacted a middle school in the Floyd County school system. I was enthusiastically received by the school's assistant principal and guidance counselor. With their help, I paired each of my students with a fifth- or sixth-grader. Due to scheduling challenges at the school, the meetings of the pairs had to be limited to two thirty-five-minute sessions per week.

During each of our Applying Anthropology class sessions, my students were given a chance to share what they were learning and to work on solving problems they were experiencing. At the end of the term, each Applying Anthropology student submitted a report on the research she had conducted. Instead of the students writing individual letters to local and regional leaders, we (my students and I) decided that their final exam would consist of cooperatively drafting one letter that summarized the major points given in each of the individual reports. We hoped this would increase the readability—and therefore the effectiveness—of the students' input. While a number of the individuals and institutions on our mailing list differed from those on the 1999 list, the audience we pinpointed was basically the same. Based on what they had learned about the Latino students' educational experiences, their family lives, and their attitudes toward themselves and toward higher education, the Applying Anthropology students made a number of recommendations to this audience. Among them were the following:

- Current ESOL programs in the area's public schools should be strengthened. Recommended changes include
  - Soliciting Latino students' comments and suggestions on ESOL programs and, when possible, integrating those suggestions into the programs
  - Inviting Latino students who are proficient in both English and Spanish to tutor less-advanced ESOL students, thus providing extra help to beginning ESOL students while also boosting the self-esteem of the tutors and giving them opportunities to learn the value of service and leadership skills
  - Adding additional ESOL classes aimed at helping students who have good English-language skills but who need to refine their communication skills

- Hiring more bilingual teachers to assist Latino students with transitioning into English-speaking classrooms.

- Middle and high school students should be offered more information on higher education and on financial aid. To this end, school leaders might
  - Invite college representatives to visit middle and high school classrooms and offer seminars on the college experience, on academic requirements students must meet to get into different types of colleges, and on financial aid programs available
  - Recruit Spanish and education majors from local colleges to serve as volunteers in ESOL programs.[7]

- Latino parents should be welcomed to participate more actively in their children's education. This could be done by
  - Providing ESOL classes to those parents
  - Providing interpretation at PTA meetings and parent-teacher conferences
  - Providing Spanish-language versions of announcements and forms that are sent home to parents.

- More ESOL classes for immigrants and more Spanish-language classes for non-Latino locals should be offered in the community. Participation in already-existing classes, in the meantime, could be increased by creating a comprehensive listing of all such classes, and posting such listings in newspapers (both English and Spanish), at local churches, and at local businesses.

Once again, we received limited but valuable feedback to our mailing. Among the respondents were a county commissioner, an ESOL educator, several local professors, the editor of a Spanish-language newspaper, administrators of a local public school, and the editor of the *Rome News-Tribune*. Soon after the letter was circulated, I was recruited to co-organize a conference, "The Changing Face of North Georgia: Our Growing Latino Population." Held at Berry in March 2003, it attracted more than 100 participants from local businesses, churches, government, and education. I also worked with the newly formed Comite Latino de Rome y Floyd County (Latino Committee of Rome and Floyd County) to organize a town hall meeting and cultural fiesta, where more than 300 Latinos came together to celebrate their cultural heritage and speak with local government officials about their needs and concerns. Currently, I am working with administrators at several area schools to recruit Berry students as volunteers and interns.

Kevin Johnson (1998 [1997]) observes that even though Latinos are rapidly assimilating into communities across the United States, their adjustment is often marred by the stigmatizations they commonly face. This, he reports, has led to the increasing predominance of "separate and unequal Latino enclaves" in many cities and towns (428). Such enclaves already seem to be developing in Rome, Georgia. It is my hope that my work with Applying Anthropology students at Berry College may be used to strengthen efforts aimed at making this increasingly "Latinized" community a more unified, equitable, and welcoming one.

Notes

1. As David Kirp of the *Nation* magazine puts it, "While Hispanic migrant workers have long been an American fixture, this generation behaves very differently. Workers are bringing their families with them, and, more and more, are staying" (Kirp 2000, 27).

2. For the most part, Dalton's leaders have provided an exception to this tendency; see Duchon and Murphy 2001; Engstrom 2001; Hernández-León and Zúñiga 2000; Zúñiga and Hernández-León 2001; and Kirp 2000.

3. Georgia's overall Latino population is currently estimated at 475,000 and is expected to increase to around 825,000 by 2010 (Georgia Board of Regents 1999, 3).

4. Whereas the average age of all Georgians is 36.9, the average age of Latino Georgians is 26.4—meaning that an uncharacteristically high percentage of Latinos in the state are, and will continue to be, of school age (Georgia Board of Regents 1999, 3).

5. Lane points to unusually high dropout rates among Latino students, noting that "according to the National Center for Education Statistics, 37 percent of all Hispanic 18- to 24-year-olds did not complete secondary schooling in 1999" (2001, 2).

6. Originally I had planned to assign the Applying Anthropology students to a high school, but I quickly learned upon contacting secondary school educators that the decision of whether or not to go to college is best made when a student is in middle school, since college preparatory courses begin immediately upon entrance into high school.

7. In their papers, the Applying Anthropology students noted that Berry College is now requiring ESOL certification for all secondary and P–12 education majors before graduation. These future teachers, the letters stressed, could get practical experience for the certification by spending time in local ESOL classes. They pointed out that Spanish majors would also benefit greatly from working with native speakers and that, in some cases, these students might be able to gain course credit for such work.

References

Bixler, Mark. 2000. "UGA Study: Latinos Need Aid Adjusting." *Atlanta Journal-Constitution*, August 31.
———. 2002. "Latinos, Asians See Clout Growing." *Atlanta Journal-Constitution*, February 20.
Cornelius, Wayne A. 2002. "Ambivalent Reception: Mass Public Responses to the

'New' Latino Immigration to the United States." In Marcelo Suárez-Orozco and Mariela M. Páez, eds., *Latinos: Remaking America*, 165–89. Berkeley: University of California Press.

del Pinal, Jorge, and Audrey Singer. 1997. "Generations of Diversity: Latinos in the United States." *Population Bulletin* 52, no. 3. Retrieved February 27, 2002, from ⟨http://www.prb.org/pubs/bulletin/bu52-3.htm⟩.

Duchon, Deborah A., and Arthur D. Murphy. 2001. "Introduction: From *Patrones* and *Caciques* to Good Ole Boys." In Arthur D. Murphy, Colleen Blanchard, and Jennifer A. Hill, eds., *Latino Workers in the Contemporary South*, 1–9. Athens: University of Georgia Press.

Education Trust, The. 2001. State Summary of Georgia. Ed Watch Online. Reproduced by the Educational Resources Information Center (ERIC).

Engstrom, James D. 2001. "Industry and Immigration in Dalton, Georgia." In Arthur D. Murphy, Colleen Blanchard, and Jennifer A. Hill, eds., *Latino Workers in the Contemporary South*, 44–56. Athens: University of Georgia Press.

Georgia Board of Regents. 1999. "Regents Update Capital Priorities List." University System of Georgia System Supplement. Retrieved May 20, 2002, from ⟨http://www.usg.edu/pubs/sys_supp/june99⟩.

————. 2000. "Report of the Hispanic Task Force." Retrieved May 12, 2002, from ⟨http://www.usg.edu/pubs/annual_rep/2000⟩.

Guzmán, Betsy. 2001. "Census 2000 Paints Statistical Portrait of the Nation's Hispanic Population." U.S. Census Bureau press release. Retrieved January 12, 2002, from ⟨http//:www.census.gov/Press-Release/www/2001/cb01-81.html⟩.

Hamann, Edmund. 1997. "The Future Is Now: Latino Education in Georgia." Paper presented at the annual meeting of the American Anthropological Association, Washington, D.C., November 27. Reproduced by the Education Resources Information Center.

Hernández-León, Rubén, and Víctor Zúñiga. 2000. "Making Carpet by the Mile: The Emergence of a Mexican Immigrant Community in an Industrial Region of the U.S. Historic South." *Social Science Quarterly* 81, no. 1: 49–65.

Hispanic Association of Colleges and Universities. 2002. "Facts on Hispanic Higher Education." Retrieved May 15, 2002, from ⟨http://www.hacu.net/data_statistics/index.shtml?printer⟩.

Johnson, Kevin R. 1998 [1997]. "Melting Pot or Ring of Fire?" In Richard Delgado and Jean Stefanic, eds., *The Latino Condition*, 427–30. New York: New York University Press.

Kirp, David. 2000. "The Old South's New Face." *Nation*, June 26, 27–30.

Klein, Gil. 1999. "Hispanic Population Grows Rapidly in the South." *Tampa Tribune*, September 7.

Knight, Kacy. 2001. "Mexican Immigration, Poverty, and Policy." *Baptist Peacemaker*, Winter, 15.

Lane, Kristina. 2001. "Educating a Growing Community." *Black Issues in Higher Education* 18, no. 16: 28–31. Retrieved May 17, 2002, from ⟨http://vweb.hwwilsonweb.com/cgi-bin⟩.

Martin, Philip, and Elizabeth Midgley. 2003. "Immigration: Shaping and Reshaping America." *Population Bulletin* 58, no. 2. Population Reference Bureau.

Millman, Joel, and Will Pinkston. 2001. "Mexicans Transform Town, Carpet Industry." *Rome News-Tribune*, September 2.

Moll, Luis C., and Richard Ruiz. 2002. "The Schooling of Latino Children." In Marcelo Suárez-Orozco and Mariela M. Páez, eds., *Latinos: Remaking America*, 362–74. Berkeley: University of California Press.

Murphy, Arthur D., Colleen Blanchard, and Jennifer A. Hill. 2001. *Latino Workers in the Contemporary South*. Athens: University of Georgia Press.

Noth, Pierre-Rene. 2001. "Rome as a Nacho Grande." *Rome News-Tribune*, April 15.

Population Reference Bureau. 2002. "U.S. Hispanic Population Growing Fastest in the South." U.S. Census Bureau press release. Retrieved February 27, 2002, from ⟨http://www.prb.org/Template.cfm?Section+PRB&template=/ContentManagement/⟩.

Prophet, Tatiana. 2002. "The Bridge to Higher Education." AtlantaLatino.com. Retrieved July 7, 2002, from ⟨http://www.atlantalatino.com/02/06/05local1eng.htm⟩.

Suárez-Orozco, Marcelo, and Mariela M. Páez. 2002. "Introduction: The Research Agenda." In Suárez-Orozco and Páez, eds., *Latinos: Remaking America*, 1–37. Berkeley: University of California Press.

U.S. Census Bureau. 2000a. "The Hispanic Population." Census brief C2KBR/01-3.

———. 2000b. *United States Census 2000*. Retrieved March 4, 2002, from ⟨http://www.census.gov/main/www/cen2000.html⟩.

Willis, John M. 2001. "Hispanic Workers Up in Floyd, Other Counties in Region." *Rome News-Tribune*, September 2.

Zúñiga, Víctor, and Rubén Hernández-León. 2001. "A New Destination for an Old Migration: Origins, Trajectories, and Labor Market Incorporation of Latinos in Dalton, Georgia." In Arthur D. Murphy, Colleen Blanchard, and Jennifer A. Hill, eds., *Latino Workers in the Contemporary South*, 126–35. Athens: University of Georgia Press.

Civil Rights, Immigration, and the Prospects for Social Justice Collaboration

The U.S. South experienced phenomenal growth in Latino immigration during the 1990s. The 2000 census showed a 300 percent increase during the previous decade in Georgia's Latino population, the third highest percentage growth among southern states. In the region, only North Carolina (394 percent increase) and Arkansas (337 percent) saw higher rates of Latino population growth. Key counties surrounding Atlanta—Gwinnett, Forsyth, Cherokee, and Rockdale—experienced even higher growth rates, of 600 percent ("State Learning to Embrace Hispanics" 2001). The demographic changes in Georgia are not simply a metro Atlanta phenomenon. The carpet industry in Dalton, located in Whitfield County in the northwest section of the state, depends on Mexican immigrants in its low-paying jobs. Gainesville's poultry processing industry is staffed by Latino workers, as is agricultural production in Vidalia and Valdosta in the south.

The intersection between civil rights concerns and immigration issues is visible in each of these communities. In Dalton, for example, civic and business leaders promoted highly acclaimed exchanges with Mexico to build strong intergroup relations in the schools, yet white flight has taken place from the now majority-Latino public schools. Latino agricultural workers in south Georgia have been harassed by local law enforcement. White flight and profiling by law enforcement serve to racialize new immigrants, evoking parallel experiences of African Americans. In response, immigrants have turned to civil rights laws and programs to defend against harassment from growers and law enforcement. In Gainesville, local civil rights organizations united with the Hispanic Committee in northeast Georgia to oppose anti-immigrant billboards, which read "Amnesty for Invaders is Treason! (Stop the Illegal Alien Invasion)" and directed people to the ‹www.noamnestycampaign.com› website. This locally organized alliance linked support for new Latino residents to concern for racial justice to blunt these hostile expressions of anti-immigrant sentiment.

The evidence of disparate treatment and race-based animosity facing new as well as old populations raises key questions: Who can and should access civil rights remedies? Can understandings gained from examining immigrant rights issues serve to broaden, update, and enliven our understanding of civil rights? Even further, can new understandings energize ongoing attempts to implement effective remedies that yield full equality and justice?

The conservative-led campaign against race-specific remedies (such as affirmative action in education and minority business contracting or in establishing fair voting districts) during the 1990s resulted in rollbacks in specific programs originally designed to aid African Americans in overcoming the long and deep legacy of discrimination.[1] These rollbacks also adversely affected opportunities for other minorities. At the same time, federal immigration policy changes in 1986 and 1990 and the lowering of trade barriers through the North American Free Trade Agreement in 1993 led to increased immigration of both documented and undocumented entrants.

Immigrants from Latin America enter this color-conscious society self-identified by national origin. Often, less emphasis is placed on "race" than on identification with an ethnic group.[2] But national origin is "racialized" by the reaction of the majority-white community. Latinos experience problems commonly understood in the United States as racial discrimination: racial profiling and barriers to full access to education, political participation, and employment.

African Americans and Latinos share a history of discrimination in the United States, often at the hands of the same institutions. Historically, anti-immigrant sentiment was rooted in the same racial theories that buttressed segregation. Likewise, the easing of immigration restrictions paralleled the progress of the civil rights movement. Post–World War II anti-Nazism, a growing emphasis on human rights, and the emerging opposition to Jim Crow segregation led to a decline in acceptance of racial justifications for limiting immigration. The civil rights movement contributed powerfully to change in immigration policies (DeLaet 2000).

Yet despite this interwoven history, the struggle for racial justice at times meets immigrant rights uneasily. Competition surfaces in the context of a volatile economy, amid perceived or real job displacement of African American workers by Latino immigrants. Experiences with nonblack, often Asian immigrant store owners in African American communities or appearances of preferred treatment in schools, not only of whites, but also of Asian students, can produce tension. Perceptions are expressed that Latino immigrants can choose between racialization as "black" to enjoy targeted remedial programs or as "white" to increase their access to mainstream society. Stereotyping and competing interests must be acknowledged for progressive collaborations to be effective.

The increases in immigration and anti-immigrant sentiment that have paralleled a prolonged assault on hard-won civil rights gains characterized the final decades of the twentieth century. The dramatic increases in immigration to the U.S. South during the 1990s were accompanied by a rise in nativist activity, with organizations such as U.S. English opposing bilingual education and use of the Spanish language. This surge in anti-immigrant activity coincided with national campaigns that serve to undermine civil rights accomplishments—anti-affirmative action initiatives, legal moves to remove court supervision from deeply segregated school districts, and a pattern of racially motivated criminal justice practices. Recently, a worsening economic situation has put greater strain on African American, Latino, and Asian Americans in all walks of life, particularly workers, as well as low income whites, resulting in increased competition. In addition, especially in the aftermath of September 11, 2001, subtle pressure has increased to subordinate civil rights demands to the call for uniting as Americans. The situation—at the same time daunting and promising—calls for a clarification of civil rights objectives. Forging coalitions in these rapidly changing conditions is challenging but ever more crucial.

The appearance that members of immigrant groups progress easily to business ownership is another source of conflict. The role of new immigrant business owners in African American communities in employment practices, pricing policies, and customer relations has been noted as well. Alejandro Portes points out "hostility by domestic blacks and other domestic minorities at the 'exploitative' behavior of the foreigners" (Portes and Rumbaut 1966). African Americans have witnessed one ethnic group after another finding acceptance by whites—acceptance and opportunity that they continue to see denied to themselves.

The potential for increased competition between African Americans and new immigrant groups in the small business arena is illustrated by a legislative action in Georgia in 2001. In the context of a measure to amend a tax provision that gives a small tax break to companies with state contracts that subcontract with minority firms, the Georgia legislature was asked to redefine "member of a minority" as black, Hispanic, Asian Pacific American, Native American, or Asian Indian American. At that time, state law defined a member of a minority as "a member of a race which comprises less than 50 percent of the total population of the state."[3] The bill proposed to extend to companies with a state contract a tax break of up to $6,000 per year if they hire minority subcontractors for construction services, equipment, and goods.

When the measure came up for a vote, some members of the state Legislative Black Caucus, whose numbers in 2002 totaled 47 in the Georgia house and senate (out of 236, or 20 percent of the total), were among those whose votes initially thwarted the bill. Because it was designed to add Hispanic businesses to the list of those eligible for minority business status, the bill had been actively supported by the Atlanta-based Latin American Association, a group formed more than twenty years earlier when the majority of Atlanta's Hispanic population was Cuban American.

State Representative Stephanie Stuckey, a white legislator who represents progressive intown Atlanta neighborhoods, advanced the measure with help from Governor Roy Barnes's office, along with cosponsor Representative Roger Byrd (D-Hazelhurst), from more conservative south Georgia. Representative Jeanette Jamieson (D-Banks County), cosponsor of the bill that eventually passed, said it was "our intention to include other groups who have influence in our state . . . [but there was] concern on the part of certain groups [that] 'if you broaden the pie, their slice would be less.'"[4]

State Representative Robert Holmes (D-Atlanta) articulated the concerns of some African American legislators. Race, national origin, and immigrant status are distinct concepts, which can be accompanied by distinct forms of discrimination (Quiroz-Martinez 2001). "Many Hispanics are not people of color. They are a language group, an ethnic group," said Holmes. "These folks never experienced the same things we did." Holmes continued, "Why would a person [benefit] based on the language that they speak?" Several white legislators joined the Legislative Black Caucus in opposing the measure. "Many [white legislators] did oppose the bill because the black caucus did," said Holmes. "They were deferring to our judgment."

Not all African American legislators opposed the move. Longtime civil rights activist State Representative Tyrone Brooks (D-Atlanta), for example, was outspoken in favor of the measure. "We've got to expand the tent," said Brooks. Stuckey admits that her failure to consult black legislators before introducing the measure added to confusion over the intent of the bill. Rev. Jesse Jackson, in Atlanta for another purpose, held a press conference with Brooks, Stuckey, and twenty other legislators, calling for unity.

There was some opposition from conservative whites. Republican Earl Ehrhart, who represents a portion of Cobb County, Georgia, offered an amendment to the measure to keep the old language. His position was "completely different," said Holmes; "he wanted no local affirmative action."

Press reports focused on African American legislators for opposing inclusion of "Hispanic" in the list of groups to be specified. But before leaping to an easy condemnation of black legislators, one must understand the context —the limits to minority contracting in Georgia. A familiar array of mechanisms continues to preserve the economic status quo: bonding requirements prevent African American small businesses from accessing state contracts, and advertisers of bidding opportunities do not utilize minority media outlets, just to mention two examples.

Partisan interests were apparent in the debate as well. "The Republicans, including [house minority leader Representative Lynn] Westmoreland (R-Sharpsburg), were all over the bill," said Stuckey, a Democrat. Republicans "were very supportive, they were trying to woo the Hispanic vote," said Stuckey. "Plus they liked seeing the Black caucus fight with the other Democrats." Interestingly, few companies—about three per year, according to the *Atlanta Journal-Constitution*—access the tax benefit, but "symbolically, it's enormous," Sam Zamarippa, then-chairman of the Latin American Association in Atlanta, told the newspaper.

Demands for equity in state contracting have had limited impact and remain under challenge. The Advisory Committee on Minority Business Enterprise (MBE) in its January 1992 study reported that "while no comprehensive State records [are] maintained to precisely document what portion of these contracting dollars are awarded to MBE firms, however the Advisory Committee, using available documentation, estimates that minority contractors are awarded no more than one percent of the contracts issued each year by the studied agencies." It is important to note that these figures do not represent minority firms; these are businesses working with qualified minority subcontractors, which could be a small portion of their business. Still, this modest MBE program came under vigorous assault in the 1997 and 1998 legislative sessions.

The 1995 numbers show very slight increases. Many divisions of the state university system report less than 1 percent utilization of minority firms. Stone Mountain Park, that venerable monument to the antebellum South, comes in at a whopping 2.2 percent. The Georgia Department of Transportation, where big dollars are at stake and a vigorous and determined campaign has been waged, showed 5.3 percent minority participation in 1995. By 2002 the department's target minority percentage was at 8 percent, until a vote at a meeting in late summer lowered the percentage to 5. A furor ensued, with the result that the transportation board reversed itself in the following meeting, increasing the target to 10 percent.

A report by Georgia Tech economist Thomas D. Boston published in 2000 shows marked increases in 1998 and 1999 in the initial years of Governor Roy Barnes's administration (Boston 2000). But attorney Rodney Strong, who prepared an unpublished 2002 report on MBE progress, suggests that after an initial "bump" in 1998 and 1999, when Barnes took office, little additional progress has been made. The limit on actual progress for African American economic interests lays the foundation for African American reticence to expand access to an already pitiful pie.

When the initial house bill was blocked, the governor took the extraordinary step of lobbying personally to include Hispanics in the definition in another bill before the senate. Barnes, sensitive to a growing Latino electoral presence in the state, was also aware that the National Hispanic Chamber of Commerce Convention planned its convention of 10,000 to be held in Atlanta in the fall of 2001. Barnes anticipated the need for Latino votes and financial backing in a tight 2002 gubernatorial race. That bill passed; the whole process was concluded within a couple of weeks. As a result of the debate in the 2002 session, the state has an inclusive definition of "minority."

This debate over Georgia's minority business policy illustrates potential difficulties for social justice coalitions—and shows why deliberate attention to coalition building is necessary. "This kind of opened things up in a way," said Holmes. But despite the positive outcome of this legislation, perceptions of different interests between African American constituencies and other minority groups persist.

Attempts to roll back civil rights gains continue as a nationally coordinated strategy, begun in the Reagan administration (actually a continuation of the opposition that had characterized the civil rights period itself) and stretching from Ward Connerly's anti–affirmative action initiatives in California and Washington state to Jeb Bush's One Florida campaign. In Georgia, one form that the opposition to affirmative action took was an effort in 1997 by Earl Ehrhart. Ehrhart introduced legislation to eliminate modest programs that created opportunities for African Americans and other minority groups in housing, education, and employment.

While this region and this nation have witnessed much progress, the debate over affirmative action in Georgia highlights the limits of progress toward full equality. After much struggle, the equal justice goals of the African American community stand unrealized. This is the environment in which inclusion of Latino businesses is taking place—businesses that, in our still-race-conscious society, may face less overt discrimination.

Teodoro Maus, former Mexican consul general in Atlanta, who moved on to head the national Mexican-American Chamber of Commerce, points out that Latinos can learn much from civil rights struggle. Maus applauds the political power and political savvy that African Americans have gained. "They have been struggling for a long time and have a great understanding of how things should be moved and . . . how pressure could be applied" (*Dialogue for an Inclusive Democracy* 2002). Latino strength in numbers and in the labor force brings a powerful strength to the coalition table, he notes.

"This notion of a shrinking pie is a myth," said Leticia Saucedo, a Mexican American Legal Defense and Educational Fund representative from Texas, at a Georgia meeting to examine the need for building bridges between African American and Latino leaders. "We have shown in other places that where you do coalition building that the pie does expand," Saucedo continued, "and there is an increase in the level of well-being for all parties" (*Dialogue for an Inclusive Democracy* 2002).

First-generation immigrants tend to focus on U.S. policy toward and issues in the country of origin (Portes and Rumbaut 1966, 354–38). Even when political participation is defined far more broadly than simply voting, to include contacting a public official, protesting, campaign work or contributions, informal community activity, or voluntary service on a local board, Latino participation is substantially less than that of whites, and African American participation rates are slightly less than those of whites (Verba, Schlozman, and Brady 1995, 370).

But naturalized citizens and second-generation immigrants tend to be more involved in U.S. politics. In potentially razor-thin elections, the national political parties and candidates are vying for Latino votes. In the political firefight during the 2002 midterm congressional elections and leading up to the 2004 presidential race, Republican and Democratic parties were attempting to set the terms of multiracial coalition building. This context, however, also provides bargaining leverage for coalition building.

Encouraging signs of an emerging coalition at the national level include discussions begun in late spring 2002 by the congressional Legislative Black Caucus, the Asian and Pacific Islander Caucus, and the Hispanic Caucus. Civil rights organizations, including the leadership of the National Association for the Advancement of Colored People, are establishing national alliances, building on state-based collaborations, such as one between Texas's League of United Latin American Citizens and the Texas Conference of Branches announced in 2001.

Coalition-building efforts are emerging in local communities. In Gainesville, Georgia, for example, where nearly a third of the population is Latino, members of the African American activist group, the Newtown Florist Club, have partnered with El Puente, a Latino community organization, to challenge racial profiling and cosponsor youth activities. A statewide project of the Southern Regional Council, the Georgia Partnerships Network focuses on strengthening combined African American and Latino political clout, supporting efforts to allow undocumented immigrants to obtain driver's licenses.

Coalition building is needed at the federal, state, and local level around specific demands. Increasing the pool of MBE financing, improving workplace and wage policies, bettering education, ending racial profiling in the context of criminal justice, and implementing fair immigration policies are necessary. "We must find a way of working together in close unity," said civil rights veteran C. T. Vivian, "and depending upon each other for the greater good of all of us" (Vivian 2002). A combined voting bloc of more than 25 percent in key communities—African American and Latino voters, together with Asian Americans and Native Americans, where they represent substantial numbers, along with progressive whites—could have a substantial impact in expanding and reinvigorating the civil rights agenda.

Notes

A version of this essay appears in the report *Across Race and Nation: Building New Communities in the South*, prepared by the Memphis Center for Research on Women (CROW), the Highlander Research and Education Center (HREC), and the Southern Regional Council (SRC). Based on a collaborative project between the three institutions, *Across Race and Nation* examined demographic changes in key southern states and assessed the prospects for collaboration between new immigrant groups and long-standing residents. The essay draws on interviews conducted by Blanca Rojas and Dwayne Patterson, as well as those conducted by the author. Thanks also to Barbara E. Smith, Dwayne Patterson, Wendy S. Johnson, and Luz Borrero for comments on the manuscript.

1. Here we must acknowledge the inadequacies of language and difficulties with the term "minority." In addition to its problematic use as a marginalizing term, it can be applied incorrectly. In many cities and in some rural areas, formerly disfranchised African Americans are the majority. The situation leads to confused constructions, including the unwieldy term "majority-minority." Such linguistic difficulties further complicate the tasks facing social justice collaborations.

2. See discussion of race and ethnicity in Smith 2001, 6.

3. Ga. Code. Art. 2, Chap. 7, Title 48, Sect. 1(a)(1).

4. Quotes are from interviews with the author, except as otherwise noted.

References

Boston, Thomas D. 2000. *State of Georgia Minority Business Utilization FY 2000*. Atlanta: Boston Research Group.

DeLaet, Debra L. 2000. "From Nativism to Nondiscrimination: U.S. Immigration Policy in Historical Perspective." In DeLaet, *U.S. Immigration Policy in an Age of Rights*, 23–48. Westport, Conn.: Praeger.

Dialogue for an Inclusive Democracy. 2002. Video produced by George King for the Southern Regional Council's Partnership for Racial Unity.

Portes, Alejandro, and Ruben G. Rumbaut. 1966. *Immigrant America: A Portrait.* Berkeley: University of California Press.

Quiroz-Martinez, Julie. 2001. "Missing Link." *ColorLines,* Summer, 17–21.

Smith, Barbara Ellen. 2001. "Demographic Overview." In Smith, *The New Latino South: An Introduction.* Memphis: Center for Research on Women.

"State Learning to Embrace Hispanics." 2001. *Atlanta Journal-Constitution,* April 3.

Verba, Sidney, Kay Lehman Schlozman, and Henry Brady. 1995. "Race, Ethnicity, and Political Participation." In Paul E. Peterson, ed., *Classifying by Race,* 354–78. Princeton: Princeton University Press.

Vivian, Rev. C. T. 2002. Interview with Dwayne Patterson, January 30.

Part Six

Tripartite Epilogue

Donald M. Nonini

Critique
Creating the Transnational South

The Humanities and Social Sciences
Confront Globalization

Recent theoretical developments in the humanities and social sciences have
led to a fundamental reconceptualization of nation-states, regions and areas,
cultures, ethnic groups, identities, and subjectivities. Three to five decades
ago, the dominant approaches in these disciplines emphasized the existence
and persistence of discrete cultural areas of the world; relatively stable and
uniform cultures identifiable with specific regions; clearly delineated nation-
states whose national economies and polities were coextensive with national
territories; ethnic groups who were identified with and indeed defined "their"
nation-states, regions, and locales; and languages and dialects mapped unambiguously onto groups and their spaces. Since then, however, these emphases
have in part given way to, if not been entirely displaced by, interdisciplinary
theoretical approaches that focus on the processes of globalization and transnationalism associated with diasporas, international labor migrations, and
border crossings and the making of borderlands; on the cultural formations of
multiculturalism, hybridity, creolization, and displacement; and on the spa-
tialities of hyperspaces, fuzzy and overlapping zones of sovereignty and control, and deterritorialization. These interdisciplinary approaches to globalization and transnationalism have begun to produce promising insights into both
past and contemporary social, cultural, and political phenomena throughout
the world.

Whereas before such reconceptualization, humanists and social scientists
tended to emphasize cultural uniformity and stability, unambiguous borders,
national and regional "units of analysis," and the equivalences of nations to peoples to cultures and to territories, now such notions are quite rightly viewed
as limited, simplistic, and reductionist. Area studies programs have been challenged as no longer adequately organized to study the contemporary processes
of globalization. New theorizations in cultural anthropology and social history

have critiqued previously assumed direct connections between social systems, culture, and territories. Anthropologists, historians, and scholars in women's studies, ethnic studies, and cultural studies have sought out the voices of those marginalized by structures of racial, gender, and class oppression, and this has led to the critical and fundamental rewriting of histories and interpretations of national and regional cultures and characters. Accounts by Michel Foucault and others of relations of power, normalization, discipline, and knowledge have challenged prior theorizations of colonialism, imperialism, racism, and gender domination.

To summarize a large recent literature, two major interdisciplinary approaches to the study of transnationalism and globalization have emerged out of these developments. First, anthropology, qualitative and demographic sociology, women's and ethnic studies, and social history deal with *the social relations of transnational migration*—for example, studying the demographics of international migrant populations; reconstructing the histories of socially marginal groups (e.g., slaves, smugglers, and undocumented laborers); describing and analyzing the migration networks and circuits of laborers, tourists, students, refugees, and other transmigrants; and investigating the interactions between migrants and the "native" residents of "host" societies, in zones and sites of overseas labor, residence, and landing.

Second, anthropology, cultural and media studies, women's and ethnic studies, and cultural history have focused on *the cultural formations of diasporas*—for example, interpreting the cultural productions of diasporic intellectuals, studying the circulation of electronic and media imagery and the emergence of consumption-based ethnic and gender identities, and attending to expressive cultures associated with hybridity, border crossing, and creolization.

These two major approaches to transnationalism and globalization are at times complementary; at other times, productively in tension. In any event, the shift in theory is, for the most part, well under way within many fields of humanistic endeavor.

The American South as Exception

The American South has long been viewed by some scholars, and certainly in popular depictions, as a quintessential exception—a region all to itself, uniquely defined vis-à-vis the rest of the United States, with a distinctive heritage, history, and character—singular and locatable from its cuisine, race relations, manners, dialects, folklore, and customs.[1] In fact, however, the American South has been multicultural since at least the sixteenth century. There has also been no time during which the modern American South has not participated in larger global structures, and there have been few periods during which it has not experienced influxes of migrants from Europe, Latin America, the Caribbean, Asia, and elsewhere. However, only during the last three decades have changes associated with globalization in the regional economies of the Americas called forth new flows of people and capital between the North American South and Mexico, Central America, the Caribbean, and Asia. For instance, Dominican laborers work seasonally on contracts in the orange groves of Florida, Mexicans are employed in large numbers in the poultry processing industries of North Carolina, and Puerto Rican professionals in Atlanta and Houston remit funds between the continental United States and San Juan. Unlike the highly publicized mass influx of Latino migrants into southern California and the Southwest, these movements have gone largely unnoticed. They are also both more recent than and qualitatively different from earlier migrations into the United States associated with the bracero program from the 1940s through the 1960s, with the Mexican–U.S. Border Industrialization Program and maquiladoras, or with the flight of Cubans to southern Florida after 1956. Since the 1960s, immigration by groups from beyond the United States into the American South has accelerated, with the formation of new transnational circuits made up of labor migrants, businesspeople, professionals, political refugees, students, and tourists, which connect southern locales to specific "offshore" communities in Latin America, the Caribbean, and Asia. These developments have accompanied the increased globalization of the southern economy in this period.

Three Decades of Globalization and Economic Transformation in the American South

During the last three decades of the postwar process of economic restructuring in the United States, the American Southeast region has emerged as a major growth pole within the reconfigured North American economy.[2] While the "industrial heartland" of the American Midwest and the Atlantic Seaboard has deindustrialized, the Southeast has shown rapid growth in the financial sector, in business services and media, in new forms of high-tech industrial production (e.g., in armaments, electronics, and pharmaceuticals), and in specialized agro-industries such as poultry and swine rearing and processing. At the same time, the small-scale agricultural and rural character of the South has been irreversibly changed by the loss of small farms and the rationalization of agriculture. New financial centers—Atlanta, Georgia; Charlotte, North Car-

olina;[3] and Houston, Texas—have become nationally prominent, while North
Carolina has developed the third largest film industry in the nation after New
York and Los Angeles. The downsizing of the federal government and its
functions (e.g., the military) has benefited the Southeast disproportionately,
given the political dominance of southern representatives in Congress and the
executive branch. Foreign-owned corporations have invested heavily in the
region compared with other areas of the United States.

Rapid economic growth, albeit very uneven, has drawn large numbers of
people to the South, with the populations of the region of fourteen southern
states growing by 47 percent compared with the national average of 28 percent for the years 1970 to 1994. There have been substantial in-migrations of
retirees, tourists, professionals, technicians, and managers from outside the
South—drawn to the scenic and cultural amenities of these states and to their
attractive employment opportunities. The historic out-migration of rural
African Americans from the South to the cities of the Northeast and Midwest
has been decisively reversed, as middle-aged African Americans return to the
South to find new work, care for aged parents, and flee the dangerous and im-
poverished inner cities of urban areas elsewhere.

As part of these changes in the postwar South, there has been a large influx
of transnational migrants from Mexico, Central and South America, the Caribbean, and Asia. They have come to the South to work in the agricultural fields
of its rural areas and in its factories and construction sites, to establish new
businesses, to study in its universities, and to find employment as domestic laborers, professionals, janitors, and restaurant cooks.

The Multicultural South and
Transnational Connections

As a result of these changes, the populations of the American South have become more culturally diverse. The American South now falls more clearly
within the ambit of transnational diasporas—of Mexicans and Central Americans, South Asians and Southeast and East Asians (Hmong, Montagnard, Chinese, Vietnamese, and Korean), and peoples from the Caribbean (e.g., Puerto
Ricans, Cubans, and Dominicans).

These transnational connections have led to the contemporary South being
transformed in numerous ways. New modes of dislocated living, new daily practices associated with expatriation and exile, and qualitatively distinct forms of
mobility in crossing national boundaries (e.g., Mexicans being smuggled in by
"coyotes" or Chinese by "snakeheads," versus entering as university students
on J-1 visas) have come into existence. New cultures arising from residing in

and passing through borderlands and "border-seas" have emerged.[4] Not only have people moved between the American South and offshore locales; so, too, has there been circulation of printed and electronic media images associated with ethnic-, race-, and nationality-based forms of consumption and identity, as in images of middle-class male machismo conveyed by the youth programs of Univision, a Spanish-speaking television network broadcasting throughout the urban and rural South. As transnational migrants to the South and their children have appropriated and reworked these images, as well as those of the English electronic media of television, videos, and films, they have produced distinctive imaginaries of what it means to be "modern," that is, alternative modernities contrasted to that envisioned by the majority of self-ascribed "local" or "native" Americans. When transnational immigrants have congregated in communities in the American South, they have created new social institutions, whether Apostolic Protestant churches or labor unions among Central American migrants in small southern towns, native-place associations among Hmong factory workers, or Theravadic Buddhist temples among Vietnamese Americans in Atlanta or Raleigh. It is important to note that these changes have not taken place in a social or cultural vacuum but are increasingly challenging the self-perceived conditions of the majority populations of the South —whites and African Americans—some of whom claim autochthonous status because their ancestors have lived in the South "for generations." Responses by these majorities to the new migrants have ranged from hostility to indifference to welcome, although scholars as yet understand little about the causes for this variation.

When pointing to the emergence of a transnational American South, it is necessary to follow through on the theoretical and methodological implications of this change. Not only can the South no longer be seen as a bounded geographic region with a distinctive mono- or even bicultural identity. More than that, it is only one geographic terminus for a multiplicity of transnational itineraries of persons, groups, and images moving back and forth between southern locales and offshore communities. In this sense, the necessary unit of analysis is not the American South or the offshore communities to which it is connected, but *precisely* these itineraries, the sites along them, and the processes of mobility of people and images they trace out.

Globalization and the Making of the Transnational South

These historical reflections on recent changes in the American South lead to a consideration of the essays in this book, which are oriented by three pivotal questions about the region. First, although it is evident that the American South has been transformed by globalization, it is yet worth asking, What indeed is globalization, and what are the contours of globalization in the American South, particularly as it has affected the multicultural, transnational dimensions of this region? Second, in light of globalization, what new ways are needed to think of the American South as a region and of the identities of southerners? Third, what are the processes by which the southern United States has been made both global and transnational in the last three decades and continues to be made so?

To start with, as we consider these three questions, we need to keep in mind the valuable distinction that James Peacock in his essay makes between the South's oppositional identity within the United States and its integrative identity with respect to the rest of the world beyond the boundaries of the United States. The South's oppositional identity, if I understand Peacock's point correctly, can be a foil to understanding its integrative identity, that is, its prospective relationship with the rest of the world. In other words, how can the integrative, global identity of the South be illuminated by the unique historical experience of the southern region: the bitter defeat of the Civil War, the world-turned-upside-down conditions of Reconstruction, followed by the imposition of terror and Jim Crow with the emergence of a regional identity deemed poor and backward by the rest of the country, and then, leading to the present, the triumph of the civil rights movement and the integration of its victories into new efforts and new forces for making racial and more broadly civic equality? The South's history of opposition points to defeat; tragedy; drastic shifts in reputation and self-image; the disappearance and emergence of old and new forms of pride in and identifications with people, place, and region; and the fashioning of the nation's leading forces for renewal. This history not only points to the imperatives for a historical and, indeed, self-reflexive consciousness about the position of the South with respect to the rest of the United States, but it also suggests that this consciousness can be a model for reflecting historically on the position of the United States in relation to the rest of the world. It intimates that the future history of U.S. encounters with globalization may be, like that of the South itself, one of surprises, reversals, and ironies. Indeed, the events of September 11 and their aftermath may precipitate the first such nuanced re-envisioning of the future history of America's experience with globalization.[5]

Globalization: Realities and Rhetorics

I shall begin with the question of what globalization is. For a first cut, we can ask, To what extent does globalization consist of reality—that is, a convergence of demographic, economic, cultural, political, and other conditions that, taken together, add up to more than the sum of its parts—or of rhetorics, or discourses of persuasion? Quite clearly, globalization consists of both realities and rhetorics and, moreover, of rhetorics about realities and of realities about rhetorics. On one hand, over the last three decades, the different regions and nation-states of the world have become increasingly interconnected through the movement of people, ideas, capital, commodities, weapons, microbes, media images, rumors, and legal and financial regimes.[6] Put less abstractly, the operations of transnational corporations; of multilateral organizations such as the United Nations, the International Monetary Fund (IMF), and the World Trade Organization (WTO); and of global nongovernment organizations like Greenpeace, the World African Federation, and Amnesty International; the movements of armies internationally (and notably, U.S. military campaigns abroad); and the illicit trades in narcotics, human beings, arms, and endangered animal and plant species are all real processes that have transformed the world irreversibly. On the other hand, in the United States, including the South, there are multiple, massively funded and supported industries of persuasion—lodged in the business and popular press, academia (particularly in the discipline of economics), the electronic media, government at different levels, and elsewhere —devoted to persuading a vast number of Americans that such globalization is inevitable, natural, and desirable. The very existence of these industries points to the rhetorical dimensions of globalization—that is, that it is not a thing but a concept that can be accepted, rejected, debated, challenged, yielded to, made into truth, or discarded as fiction. In anthropological terms, globalization is a cultural construct. Another way of putting this is to say that there are multiple contentions, even struggles, over globalization as a hegemony (as witnessed since 1999 in Seattle, in the large demonstrations of protest against the WTO, the World Bank and IMF, and the World Economic Forum) and that, more than ever, the rhetorical dimension of globalization is salient. Still, having said as much, we must recognize that the dominant ideological stance on globalization in the South, as elsewhere in the United States, is neoliberalism —the ideology that globalization is inevitable, natural, and desirable, for it implies the expansion of markets that provide optimal solutions to social and economic problems, while in contrast, governments are corrupt, ineffective, and inefficient.

That globalization is both reality and rhetoric in the ways indicated resonates with the current condition of the American South. Clearly, the American South is enmeshed in the processes that make up the reality of globalization: world trade, the movement of investment capital, the transmission of ideas and images, and most visibly, the migration of people across national borders. Equally clearly, the South participates in the debates, arguments, and duels of persuasion regarding the inevitability, naturalness, and desirability of these processes. Witness, for instance, controversies in North Carolina about the status of the North American Free Trade Agreement (NAFTA) and the loss of textile and other manufacturing jobs in the state that it has entailed, and its prominence in foreign policy issues connected to "free trade," U.S. commercial relations with East and South Asia, and much more (Rives 2002). There are, therefore, research imperatives for scholars in the humanities and social sciences to know more about both the processes constituting globalization *and* the "language games" regarding globalization that are being played, and played out, in various settings, both everyday and extraordinary, within the American South. Of course, it is important to acknowledge that the distinction between rhetoric and reality is at best a heuristic one. That is, we need to know more about the political realities of the rhetorics of globalization. For instance, how do men and women, natives and immigrants, and factory workers and farmers living in the factory towns of the South talk about and generate the reality of a politics of debate about the inevitability and desirability of globalization that resonates more broadly with public issues in their communities (Holland et al. in press)? Equally, humanists and social scientists need to know more about the neoliberal rhetorics that local elites in the South employ in setting out the realities of strategies development and economic growth in communities throughout the South—and to investigate alternatives to these rhetorics incorporated in activism by natives and immigrants in the South.

Globalization and Southern Identities

A second question, indeed the crucial one, is What is the American South and who are southerners? What does it mean to call oneself a southerner today and make certain claims in invoking that label? Of the many possible ways of posing this question, it may be rewarding to ask it diacritically: What does it mean to be a nonsoutherner residing in the South, and how long does it take (and what conditions must prevail) before such a resident becomes a southerner, and a genuine one at that? Asked ethnographically or historically, What are the cultural traits that genuine southerners claim to have and that nonsoutherners lack but might acquire and thereby change their identities to become southerners? The American South as a region has long been transformed by the economic, political, and military engagements of the United States with the rest of the world, particularly as this has affected the South's historically specific racial, class, and gender dynamics. These engagements have accelerated over the last thirty years—whether we are thinking about the emergence of Charlotte as a world financial center, the migration of Koreans as shopkeepers and professionals to Atlanta, or the labor circuits of Dominicans and Mexicans that have become crucial to the profitability of southern agriculture. These engagements, and the contributions they have demanded in the forms of labor, innovation, and creativity from immigrants to the building of the transformed South, must surely matter in some measure in determining who counts as a genuine southerner?

In the discussions of the relationship between the South and globalization, I am forcibly struck by how these discussions, including most of the essays in this book, show a crucial lacuna—indeed, an oversight of what until recently provided a definitive definition of the American South and southerners: the rural character of both. What has happened to rural life in the American South, and why has it largely been ignored in much of the humanistic and social science literatures that now treat the transnational South, with a very few exceptions, such as southern folklore? Can most of us actually bear to look? What perhaps most closely links the American South to globalization is the urbanization of its people. Yet this experience of the last thirty years is composed of a multiplicity of narratives of trauma, loss, and injury to the rural economy, of the disappearance of rural lifeways and styles of living, and of the destructive transformation of its rural landscapes. This is so, even if we forgo any sentimentality or nostalgia about an idyllic rural southern past but consider the massive contemporary changes—whether we are thinking of the devastation of ✳ the West Virginia mountains caused by mountaintop removal by coal companies described in Bryan McNeil's essay, or of the conversion of cucumber growers in rural North Carolina from independent family farmers into combined petty labor bosses (of sweated Mexican laborers) and virtual employees of a pickle processing corporation that precisely dictates every step in the cucumber growing cycle, as described in Sandy Smith-Nonini's essay. Although Harry Watson in his essay tellingly reminds us of the older southern themes of home, family, faith, and place, where are we to find these in most of the modernist narratives of progress and development in the transnational South focused on urban spaces?

Political-Economic Shifts and Cultural
Production under Globalization in the
American South

This takes me into the third question: What are the processes by which the
South has been made global and transnational in the last three decades? To
start with, the essays in this book provide ample evidence of the full involvement of the southern economy in the commercial and financial institutions of
global capitalism. In fact, this is an understatement. The South is no longer,
nor has it been for some time, a residual region, for in the last three decades
it has pioneered nationally many economic institutions and practices that now
go by the name of post-Fordism or flexibility (Harvey 1989). As the essays by
Sandy Smith-Nonini on the H2A program for cucumber growers in North
Carolina and by Barbara Ellen Smith on contingent labor in Memphis's distribution sector suggest, the South historically may have led in constructing,
and its elites certainly anticipated and led in creating, the design of the features of the neoliberal political and economic order that currently prevails
more widely in the United States. These features include the use of contingent and casual labor, the active state promotion of "a good business climate"
that privileges such an arrangement over stable unionized employment, the
promotion of conditions for employing nonfree labor (e.g., convicts and undocumented immigrants), and the condemnation of "big government" by
creating a "no new taxes" pocketbook state, even as certain sectors (e.g., armaments and finance) have developed a parasitical (i.e., corporate welfare) relationship to it. Indeed, one is left wondering whether Ronald Reagan's pay-
back to his southern conservative supporters for their decisive votes for him
in the 1980 national election was basically to facilitate the spread to the rest of
the United States of these "southern" features of political economy—some
of which (e.g., semi-unfree labor, as in African-American sharecroppers, and
anti–federal government rhetorics) had ample precedent in southern history?
That the South plays a leading role in the globalization processes within the
United States may be difficult for those who still dwell on southern victimiza-
tion to accept—as indeed it may be for those nonsoutherners who still hold
prejudices about southern backwardness.

The new conditions of flexible industrial production can be observed up
close in Steve Striffler's essay on poultry processors' employment of Latino
labor, and in Sandy Smith-Nonini's essay as well. In both instances, immigrant laborers are treated in culturally distinctive ways that partition them
into lines of production by their race, nationality, and evident in Striffler's Ar-

kansas production line, gender as well. Such division of laborers along unspoken but nonetheless obvious racial, national, and gender lines, only occasionally articulated in the discourse of managers, allows for their intensified exploitation, even to the point that this is self-defeating, as in the case of Striffler's description of sabotage and production line breakdown at the Tyson poultry plant. One wants to know whether in the case of the contingent laborers in the large distribution sector in Memphis studied by Barbara Ellen Smith, managers fostered similar divisions among workers and, through implicit practices rather than overt categories, expressed them as well; this would be in addition, as Smith's study shows, to contingent workers being cast in managers' discourse as reliable, flexible, and productive, compared, that is, with permanent employees of FedEx and other Memphis corporations. In each of these cases, moreover, there is no natural relationship between the qualifications of these immigrant and contingent laborers and their wages and working conditions dictated by the magic of the labor markets. Instead, in each case, state and federal governments fail to regulate rigorously, if at all, working conditions by enforcing labor and occupational safety laws, often on the neoliberal grounds that governments can not afford inspectors and the apparatuses of law enforcement, while undocumented immigrants accept low wages, few benefits, and dangerous working conditions not only because of their eagerness for work but also because of their fear of being reported to and then deported by the Immigration and Naturalization Service.

Other essays in this book warn us that the features of the new southern economy extend beyond the production line to include the global research and development sector and the service sector—the fastest-growing part of the southern economy—and to the sphere of consumption in which so many in service are involved. Guldbrandsen, in his portrait of Durham, North Carolina, points to the influx of large numbers of professionals into Research Triangle Park, nearby universities, and high-tech companies. Ajantha Subramanian and Sawa Kurotani, in their essays, also discuss the circulation of diasporic high-tech professionals and managerial elites throughout the South. When urban professionals in the South manifest refined values committed to the consumption of ethnic cuisines, books, recorded music, sports events, health clubs, vacation resorts, and New Age experiences, they have come to constitute the principal customers of numerous small businesses. Moreover, Guldbrandsen emphasizes the large number of entry-level, minimum-wage laborers who serve these professionals as salespersons, waiters, domestic workers, hotel cleaners, security guards, gardeners, and so forth. Both trends—an influx of professionals from outside the South, including transnational professionals (cf. Subramanian and Kurotani essays), and a movement of large numbers of workers to service them—indicate changes in urban areas throughout the American South, particularly in the growth poles of new wealth and employment associated with centers of finance, high technology, and petroleum-related and research-based employment, such as Austin, Atlanta, Houston, and Charlotte, among others. Since many minimum-wage service workers have left rural areas of the South for jobs in large cities and suburban areas, they have participated in the massive migrations from rural to urban areas in the South that I note above, while a vast number of others have come from Mexico, Central America, and the Caribbean. The presence of cosmopolitan professionals served by very large numbers of contingent workers distinguishes the globalized southern economy with a new and extreme form of economic and social inequality. Taken ensemble, the influx of certified professionals from elsewhere in the United States and from overseas; the hypertrophy of the service sector based on large populations of poorly paid, nonunionized, contingent workers, including those migrating from abroad; the proliferation of consumption experiences often connected to virtual associations with specific locales (e.g., Austin with high-tech research and education, the Blue Ridge mountain towns with scenic beauty, and Orlando, Florida, with middle-class Disney World fantasies); heightened socioeconomic inequalities exacerbated by elite fears of crime, filth, and the threat of "outsiders"; and local and regional governments committed to low taxes and minimal public services make up a distinctive pattern that, although national in scope, is pervasive in major urban areas of the South.

In their essays, Subramanian and Kurotani analyze in different ways the transnational circulation of new kinds of elites in the South who are immigrants inserted into labor and other markets within global capitalism quite differently from the service classes, and to whom neoliberal state elites turn a far more welcoming face. At the upper end of the immigrant class hierarchy can be found Kurotani's corporate Japanese managers and, somewhat lower, Subramanian's South Asian professionals. Kurotani illuminates the ways in which state officials sought to lure Japanese investors during the 1990s in the global competition for capital not only by offering investment incentives and discouraging labor unions, but also by luring them with consumption amenities deemed cosmopolitan and suitable to the self-cultivated global images of Japanese managers and their family members. Kurotani also reconstructs how high-tech Japanese corporate managers, in light of the bursting of the speculative bubble in Japan in the mid- to late 1990s, sought to diversify, decentralize, and become more flexible by relocating from the Northeast to the South, precisely during the same period that the South's experiment with post-Fordist flexibility was in full swing. The South Asian professionals discussed by Subramanian followed more diverse paths, yet they still moved in authorized elite circuits bringing them to the South: employment links to corporations, universities, and research institutes. Subramanian relates how her informants employ racialist discourses that employ their educational capital, spatial separation, and religious affiliations to differentiate themselves from African Americans, with which many majority Americans confuse them. For both Japanese managers and Indian professionals, it is remarkable that their class-specific residential enclaves isolate them from people of "the real South." As one of Kurotani's informants put it, "There are no southerners in my neighborhood." Instead, garrisoned and spatially separated ethnic enclaves combined with access to homeland consumption commodities that allow them to establish middle-class lifestyles that simulate life "back home" convey to them a sense of comfortable class homogeneity combined with diasporic community. Both groups, interestingly, also have life narratives focused on extraterritorial sovereignty. While Kurotani's expatriate Japanese managers speak of their tour in the South as "being sent down from the capital"—the power of the corporation extending from Japan to touch them overseas—Subramanian's professionals aspire as nonresident Indians to exert strong influences over India's domestic, that is, Hindu, politics through their monetary donations to the homeland. It is worth asking of both Subramanian and Kurotani how more local, southern conceptions of sovereignty might intersect with these extraterritorial ones. For instance, what happens when the wives of *sarariiman* form allegiances to southern friends and to American kinship norms and do not wish to go back to Japan and the subordination to their husbands' parents that will follow, even as their husbands see themselves as finally being delivered from American exile when they receive the word summoning them to return? And will the grown children of South Asian professionals feel the same allegiance to political Hinduism in India as their parents once they have lived as adolescents and adults in the South?

I noted above that globalization in the American South has been tied to global capitalism, particularly in its post-Fordist or flexible phase in the United States. But as I also intimated, capitalist enterprises in the South have never had an unmediated relationship with economic markets; that relationship has always been mediated by the practices and policies of states. Governments in the South have for some time taken an active role in the managing and disciplining of an immigrant labor force on behalf of employers, as Smith-Nonini compellingly demonstrates in her historical analysis of the federal government's H2A program for Latino farmworkers in the southern states. Such state interventions in markets on behalf of private interests and contrary to neoliberal doctrine are evident in the essay by Rachel Willis and, in a strongly contrasted way, in the essay by Meenu Tewari. Willis writes of the successful internationalization strategy by firms in the hosiery industry of North Carolina that continue to flourish vis-à-vis their global competitors elsewhere. Her article provides a counterexample to the gloomy generalizations regarding deindustrialization in the United States and, in particular, the decline of the U.S. and southern textile industries. Willis finds the secret of success in the cooperation between the owners and managers of hosiery enterprises; the Hmong, Vietnamese, and Latino immigrant labor force; and the state, manifested in government-sponsored training of immigrant hosiery workers in North Carolina community colleges and technological innovation in the industry made possible by targeted state-funded research in a public university. Similarly, Tewari points to how Chinese furniture manufacturers formed linkages with U.S. furniture buyers in High Point, North Carolina, in part through technological innovations in shipping but also through China's state sponsorship of the Chinese furniture industry, and the partnerships that state officials formed with Taiwanese investors already firmly established in furniture production in concentrated industrial zones in the People's Republic. In both cases, against the doctrine of neoliberalism, certain forms of active state guidance and the favoring by states of certain industries over others prove effective in supporting and protecting private enterprise—through state-subsidized technological innovation, in Willis's example, and state-generated agglomeration advantages of scale (in China), in Tewari's example.

In both cases, the presence of skilled immigrants, in part, accounts for competitive success. As a manager in one factory studied by Willis said, "These immigrant workers have saved our industry." The engagement of the two industries with their immigrant workers differs, however, depending on the globalized structure of the industry in question. In the case of the hosiery industry, managers and technicians treat immigrant workers as if they were U.S. nationals and harness them to a southern place-based nationalist strategy that allows the industry, with the help of government, to sustain itself in place, that is, in the South. In this case, be it noted, the Hmong and Vietnamese workers had acquired a quasi-American status because they were political refugees allied to Cold War U.S. military adventures. In the case of the furniture industry, however, skilled Mexican furniture makers who have immigrated to High Point, North Carolina, form only one element in a larger denationalized commodity-chain ensemble dominated by buyer-driven strategies. Here what matters is the South-based logo, or front-end brand name, while the actual location of manufacture depends on comparative advantage cultivated by state practices elsewhere, that is, in China, rather than, as Tewari notes, in Mexico, as one might predict given the provisions of NAFTA. Here, given the global dispersion of supply-chain steps created by buyer-driven strategies within the furniture industry, it is worth asking Tewari to give us a more complete depiction of how U.S. southern managers, technicians, and workers view the nationality of skilled Mexican workers vis-à-vis not only themselves but also their Chinese counterparts.

Levengood's essay shows the virtues of comparative history for clarifying globalization by examining the radically different histories of migration by Latinos to two southern U.S. cities—by Cubans to Miami and Mexicans and Central Americans to Houston. He credits the disparities in relative political power by Latino populations in the two cities to the regional specializations of each locale. On one hand, Miami rapidly emerged as a gateway entrepôt for trade to Latin America and the Caribbean, one in which Cubans played a crucial intermediary role within an enclave that concentrated their political power in space. On the other hand, Houston grew as a regional materials-processing and manufacturing center to which Mexicans migrated for decades to form the lowest level of an expanding labor force dominated by preexisting antagonisms between blacks and whites, while a well-ensconced white urban power elite maintained its political dominance by annexing middle-class suburbs while dispersing Latino political power. Levengood suggests that the latest influx of Latinos to the American South will far more likely recapitulate the patterns found in Houston rather than in Miami—spatial dispersion throughout the region during a period of slow economic growth within racialized labor markets that situate them as members of the most insecure elements of the labor force—precisely, as I note above, what the South's vanguard commitment to post-Fordist flexibility calls for.

Thaddeus Guldbrandsen's essay on Durham, North Carolina, employs the example of one city to suggest the emergence of what can be called a neoliberal governmentality in the urban South—a cultural logic of governing by the state in structuring relations between specific populations and markets. Guldbrandsen points to a new hybrid institution—the public-private partnership—which manifests the new mode of governance. Public-private partnerships take either of two forms. One consists of market-oriented partnerships of corporations, businesspeople, and local governments, which are an attempt to provide profit-driven solutions to public problems that government alone is deemed too corrupt, lethargic, or inefficient to solve. The other form—where the profit calculus cannot be applied—is comprised of community-oriented partnerships of governments and citizens in the nonprofit sector. These partnerships are outcomes of the reorganization of local government arising from the Reagan revolution and the Contract with America that followed—in which, as I intimated above, southern political elites played a central role in movements to downsize, privatize, and marketize the public functions of the state at all levels. It is important to note that the Reagan-impelled backlash against Big Government was by no means confined to Washington, D.C., and the federal government but also registered in southern cities and towns in the form of two decades of experimentation and elaboration of both kinds of public-private partnerships. Guldbrandsen's essay invites us to explore further how neoliberal governmentality among local political elites has been manifested elsewhere in the South.

A set of essays illustrates how citizens' practice and discourse in the South has contested the various features of neoliberal globalization I have described in this essay. Of all the articles, Bryan McNeil's study of mountaintop removal in West Virginia and citizens' response to it most clearly formulates a fundamental conundrum of place-based politics in the South. How can residents of communities reorganize themselves adequately to resist or impede the mobility of corporations that (it is argued inevitably) accompanies the globalization of the southern economy? What is to stop the sheer physical destruction of local environments, the appalling loss of livelihood, and the elimination of ways of making a living that, although oppressive in a variety of ways (for example, to women), still sustained a way of life? Where labor unions have never developed, or where (as in the West Virginia example McNeil reports) they have been eclipsed by the mobile maneuvers of corporations, can they be revived, or are there other collective alternatives feasible for creating what David Harvey (2000) calls "spaces of hope" and resistance?

Finally, the essays by Barbara Ellen Smith, Jennie Smith, Ellen Spears, Lucila Vargas, and Gregory Stephens all, in quite different ways, speak to the imperative for an open-ended, hopeful approach toward activism and organizing by people and groups in the South now being marginalized by globalization—an approach based in interethnic, interracial, cross-class, and bigendered dialogue and mutual respect for differences. This is an approach that takes language and discourse seriously as one (crucial) means by which personal and group identities are fashioned—and subjectivities all too often created. Therefore the relationship that those who are marginalized have to it must be transformed. Intimations of the problem and a solution to it can be read, for instance, in the examples Vargas discusses in her review of how Latina youth read the popular media representations of them—and may do so either creatively or self-destructively.

I think that the challenge for activists is how to use the language of dialogue and the skills of "critical media literacy," as Vargas calls it, to empower those who are dispossessed as long as they lack ownership of these tools.[7] And wherever and whenever they are so empowered by their access and start to organize, it is imperative for the rest of us to listen respectfully to their words, then join them in solidarity when they speak and act.

One of the aims of this book has been to address the urgency that originally prompted the formation of the Transnational South Project. The causes, logics, affects, and effects of globalization and transnationalism have currently outpaced public comprehension, and this public need must be addressed. There is, then, the challenge of promoting public knowledge about transnationalism in the South. This is imperative not only or primarily because of the worthwhile goal of achieving academic understanding of remote phenomena, but also in light of the tragic events of September 11 and their aftermath. For majority citizens and residents of the American South and for Americans in general, the condition of transnational immigrant America is not a remote matter but one crucial to their understanding of their neighbors or the classmates of their own children; or of works of religious transcendence such as the Koran, by which many of their coworkers or neighbors live; or of the meaning of nearby "exotic" places of worship (such as mosques and Buddhist temples), frequented by people who, to many of the ill-informed among the majority group, appear strange. Increased public knowledge of the transnational South is therefore essential in the period of risk and danger that Americans have collectively entered. The essays that make up this book, I hope, will constitute an important step in contributing to this public knowledge.

Notes

1. What other region of the United States, for example, has had the quiddities and oddities of its customs as exhaustively inventoried and normativized, as in *The Encyclopedia of Southern Culture*?

2. Reportedly, if the South were considered a nation, its economy would be the fourth largest in the world.

3. Charlotte is reported to be, in terms of total bank assets, second only to New York within the United States.

4. At the risk of coining a neologism, I hold that "border-seas," like borderlands (Alvarez 1995), can be seen as transition zones for persons moving between different nation-states, e.g., connecting the southern United States with the Caribbean islands

(Puerto Rico, Dominican Republic, etc.) or with South America, rather than being conventionally as no more than zones of separation.

5. These include not only the traumatic losses of September 11 broadcast world-wide via the electronic media but also new obsessions with homeland defense against terror, that distinctively modern form of violence associated with globalization, and with these, the mobilization of the U.S. military, new commitments to regulating im-migration, and the reemergence of racial and religious animosities—all of which af-fect the American South disproportionately compared with other regions.

6. Arjun Appadurai, for instance, argues that various kinds of scapes have come into existence that have organized movements of different things across the globe—ethno-scapes, financescapes, mediascapes, ideoscapes, etc. While this is an important insight, his further claim that disjunctures exist between the logics of movement of these dif-ferent kinds is subject to serious challenge.

7. Thanks to John Pickle for pointing this out in his comments.

References

Alvarez, R. R. J. 1995. "The Mexican-U.S. Border: The Making of an Anthropol-ogy of Borderlands." *Annual Review of Anthropology* 24: 447–94.

Appadurai, Arjun. 1996. "Global Ethnoscapes: Notes and Queries for a Transna-tional Anthropology." In Appadurai, *Modernity at Large: Cultural Dimensions of Globalization*. Minneapolis: University of Minnesota Press.

Harvey, David. 1989. *The Condition of Postmodernity*. Oxford: Basil Blackwell.

————. 2000. *Spaces of Hope*. Berkeley: University of California Press.

Holland, D., D. Nonini, C. Lutz, L. Bartlett, M. Frederick, T. Guldbrandsen, and E. Murillo. In press. *If This Is Democracy: Public Interests and Private Politics in a Neoliberal Age*. New York: New York University Press.

Rives, K. 2002. "The High Price of Free Trade: No End in Sight to N.C. Job Losses." *Raleigh News and Observer*, August 18.

Wilson, Charles Reagan, and William Ferris, eds. 1989. *The Encyclopedia of Southern Culture*. Chapel Hill: University of North Carolina Press.

James L. Peacock

The South and
Grounded Globalism

What have we learned about the globalized South? What might we learn further?

I propose that we have learned, if we did not already know, first, that the globalization phase is a distinctive and significant aspect of the South and, second, that recognizing this aspect provides a special perspective on the South; we have also learned some particulars about this process.

Is globalization new? The question has been debated in general and can be debated regarding the South. Of course it is new and not new, in general and regarding the South. Building on the work of David Moltke-Hansen, George Tindall, Jack Green, and many others, one might distinguish three phases, almost a cycle in southern history. In the first phase, during the seventeenth and eighteenth centuries, the South was a node in a network stretching from Europe through the Caribbean to the coast of what was still being colonized. Charleston was an example, exporting rice and importing peoples—at least fifty languages, of Native Americans, Africans, and Europeans—were spoken there during this early quasi-global period (Nichols 1988). During the second phase, around 1830, the South as a region was invented, as people migrated inland and formed a regional identity that turned inward, in opposition to the new nation. This regional identity resulted in secession, the myth of the lost cause, and diminished global connection and migration during the nineteenth and twentieth centuries. This was the period when the South gained its identity as an isolated and exceptional region, problematical and mysterious to other Americans, defensively cherished yet frustrating, even to many southerners. Globalization emerged in new shape in the twenty-first century, affecting the South and also fueled by it. The South exported information (CNN), dollars (Bank of America), and culture (from Coca-Cola to blues and bluegrass) and received a new influx of immigrants from Asia and Latin America. Certainly one should not exaggerate the changes, for much has remained constant throughout these centuries, yet one could argue that this new global phase is an important turning point for the South, equal in significance to the previous watershed when the South turned inward in the nineteenth century to adopt a distinctive and oppositional regional identity within America.

Whatever the long-term change, even a superficial impression shows dramatic short-term change as well. So many features of the South today are strikingly different from those of quite recent times, as a few experiences illustrate. A decade ago, when I would return home to the South from Asia, fellow passengers from Hong Kong or Singapore would disembark at New York or Los Angeles, while I continued to North Carolina. Now a fair number continue with me, migrating to Atlanta to live on Buford Road or to Raleigh to work in the Research Triangle. Several decades ago my wife and I lived with a family in Surabaya, Indonesia. This was during the Sukarno era, on the eve of the Year of Living Dangerously, when Indonesia really was at the other end of the world, isolated economically and politically even from near neighbors such as Singapore and both opposed to and distant from America and Europe. Yet today the grandson of the family with whom we lived resides in Chapel Hill, born and raised in North Carolina and a remarkable citizen who is a catalyst for changes here.

Of course, the South joins and fuels the wider process of globalization — greatly increased volume and speed of interaction, primarily due to electronics and air transportation, so that information, goods, ideas, and peoples ricochet around the world, crossing national and regional boundaries with speed unimagined even a decade ago, before the advent of e-mail, for example. To send a telegram from Indonesia in 1962 was a major operation, while now we constantly interact via e-mail with friends in Asia. This is what most refer to as globalization or globalism, though some emphasize, too, the driving force of capitalism: "Dollars make the world go round and go round the world" (Massey and Jess 1995). The South is obviously part of this world trend and process, economically, electronically, and culturally. Yet while recognizing these forces, we should recognize, too, the changes in our daily lives and experience.

Even as I write, the Swedish consul calls to say Sweden is opening a new consulate in Raleigh and is planning an opening reception at Exploris, the global museum there, which is itself new. All of this reflects one impact of globalization, namely immigration and a resulting cultural diversity.

Contrast this with the recent South, which was pretty parochial.

Remember the South, those of you who are old enough, forty or more years ago. The cars on the road were Chevrolets, Fords, and other American brands; there were no Toyotas or Mazdas and few Mercedeses, BMWs, and Jaguars. Restaurants were American, mainly southern, serving iced tea and corn bread. There were no Chinese, Mexican, Japanese, Indian, or Mexican restaurants, except in large cities. If you worked in agriculture or construction—and I did both—your fellow workers were black and white, not Hispanic, unless you lived in border states such as Texas. But today Jennie Smith, a scholar discussing the influx of Hispanics into Rome, Georgia, refers to the Latinization of Rome. Evidence of such migration and diversity is everywhere around us: cars with Texas tags bear migrants from Mexico, mosques and Hindu temples are being built, and a columnist from Cairo, Samia Serageldin, writes about both southern literature and Middle Eastern affairs for a Chapel Hill newspaper. External signs such as these reflect deeper experiences of families and individuals, whose journeys and struggles to get here resonate with immigrants everywhere. For example, Long Vo and Yung Le, two graduate students in Chapel Hill, share a history of migrating via boat from Vietnam, he to North Carolina and she to Australia, each prevailing over similar challenges.

The Atlanta Olympics marked a milestone in southern globalization, a world event held in a southern city, exemplified by an experience I had there. While my wife and I were attending the Olympics, our car battery died, and we got a jump start from an African immigrant now living in Covington, a small town where my wife grew up in a time when such immigrants were unheard of in such places.

Such impressions and experiences are telling but demand more systematic and focused studies—demographic statistics, labor economics, and community studies—to explore the structures and processes reflected in our new social and cultural landscapes. The approach of this volume is not to attempt an exhaustive overview but, rather, to present strategically selected case studies: of FedEx in Memphis, of global partnerships in Mobile, of sock manufacturing in Hickory, and of Asian professionals and Hispanic farmworkers. Such studies document the larger point that the South is globalizing, and they reveal some of the patterns that this process entails.

Our second proposal is that recognizing the impact of globalization provides a special perspective on the South. That is, not only do we learn some facts about what is happening, but we also perceive them through a distinctive lens. The majority of views of the South come from national and regional, not global, perspectives. This is true of scholarship, of journalism, and of popular opinion. "North Carolina seems more northern than South Carolina," states a northern visitor, implying that this is a compliment; northern is better, more efficient, effective, and modern, so North Carolina is a little more like us, us northerners. For a century or more, since the Civil War, this view of the South from the standpoint of the North has been shared by many citizens of the United States, northern and southern alike. We live with this perspective, which affects attitudes about education, business, sports, and just about everything: How many southern children think of Christmas in terms of snow and sleighs, or of Thanksgiving as Plymouth, Massachusetts, pilgrims? In recent years, of course, the South has risen, some assert, in economic, political, and cultural strength within the nation. It has been almost half a century since a Democrat from the Northeast was elected president, and recent presidents of both parties as well as some Senate leadership come from the South. Country and western music, partly a southern invention, has spread from Nashville (Johnny Cash is on the cover of *Time* magazine, and Canada has a country and western music competition). Such trends lead to phrases such as "the Americanization of Dixie and the Dixiefication of America" (Egerton 1974), which do capture important trends. However, these views stem from a national perspective. A global perspective differs. Instead of viewing the South in relation to the nation, which in many ways has been defined by the North since the Civil War, we see it in relation to the world. What does this entail? Consider several examples.

In Birmingham, Alabama, next to the African American church that was bombed some years ago, is a civil rights museum. Next to that is a human rights extension. This extension shows global resonances of what were usually seen as regional and national issues.

In Durban, South Africa, a few days before September 11, 2001, a conference was held regarding racism. The Durban conference was a landmark—despite U.S. defection—in defining slavery as a global issue, for which Europe professes responsibility vis-à-vis Africans. Not long before, Yale historians pointed to their university's implication in slavery—including naming Calhoun College after John C. Calhoun, slaveholder and secessionist from South Carolina. These steps generalize the issue of slavery from a region, the American South, to the American nation, including New England, and to Europe and Africa and the world. Regardless of whether President George W. Bush, who represents both New England and the South or Southwest, and Colin Powell, who represents African Americans and the Caribbean, joined this conference led by Irish human rights and United Nations leader Mary Robinson and held in South Africa, the event illustrates the globalization of a regional issue.

In addition to museums and conferences, scholarly efforts that frame the South in a global perspective can be cited. For example, see the syntheses of Peter Kolchin (2003), the comparative work of Peter Coclanis (1989) and Emiliano Corrales (in preparation), and various products of our Rockefeller seminar on the South in comparative perspective—for example, Manisha Sinha's study of South Carolina and Shinobu Uesugi's study of Alabama. The examples cited happen to focus on the past, but comparison can be useful with regard to current situations as well, and in disciplines such as anthropology and religious studies in addition to history. For example, see Miles Richardson's study of Spanish America and the U.S. South (2003) and Peacock's and Pettyjohn's comparison of fundamentalists in Indonesia and the U.S. South (1995). Also, there is a growing body of literary studies positioning the South globally and comparatively—for example, Deborah Cohn's and Jon Smith's edited volume *Look Away! The U.S. South in New World Studies*, forthcoming from Duke University Press, and the paper by John Matthews, "The U.S. South, Modern American Empire, and Post-Colonial Studies" (2004).

Comparatively, how unique is the South? How is it similar to and different from other places or identities? The southern plantation system displayed strong similarities to practices of Russian and Prussian estate owners and Junkers of East Germany, as well as to Caribbean, Latin American, and other colonial plantation-based societies. James E. Crisp (1985) defines the South as a unique overlap of a white majority and a plantation society. More elaborately, he would say that the South is the northernmost extension of the plantation system of South America and the Caribbean and the southernmost extension of a dominant Northern European culture. Still others compare the South with South Africa: Alistair Sparks's *The Mind of South Africa* (1990) is explicitly modeled after Cash's *The Mind of the South* (1941). So the South is one example of more general patterns, a perspective developed at length in a previous Rockefeller institute and conference.

What is added, then, by a global perspective? A global perspective provides a greater framework within which the regional and national particulars assume broader and different meanings. For example, some features of the South that have been regarded as odd from a northern or national standpoint turn out to resemble common patterns around the world, while within a global perspective it is the U.S. North that is odd and exceptional in some ways. Examples range from general to specific: emphasis on family and manners may seem greater in the South than in the North, but it is common among many societies, and words or sayings in the South that seem odd stem from British origins. Regional features are simply interpreted differently when perceived as expressions of and linkages to world processes rather than as parts of national processes. In fact, just about everything in the South can be reinterpreted, because we are accustomed to experiencing everything, either implicitly or explicitly, as regional or national—either particularistically, as part of our local experience, or in comparison with the North. Everything looks different when viewed as part of the wider world. One purpose of this volume is to introduce such a view.

Granted this general point, what specific information does this volume provide, and how might our inquiry go further?

What does it not do? The comparative approach, just mentioned, is not prominent here; that is, little effort is made to compare patterns in the South to patterns elsewhere in the world. Little attention is given, for example, to patterns of farm or industrial or electronic work in the South as compared to India, China, or Singapore, or to the role of women or minorities in such an array of places. Comparison of patterns or types is not a favored approach. Instead, the emphasis here is on process—ways the South is engaged in, part of, contributing to, and affected by global processes. How is this explored?

Consider two crosscutting distinctions: foreign/domestic and objective/subjective. "Foreign" refers to the South in the world—the region's impact and engagement abroad, outside the region and nation—and "domestic" pertains to the region within. The first tells about the South in the world; the second, the world in the South.

The foreign reach of the South includes myriad streams and elements: CNN, Bank of America, blues and bluegrass, William Faulkner, Edgar Allan Poe, Toni Morrison, Cajun cooking, or German infatuation with Native Americans. This aspect—the outreach of the South—is not emphasized in this volume. Rather, emphasis is on the in-reach of the world, the world in the South —immigration and the lives of immigrants in the South, for example. However, the foreign/domestic gap is bridged throughout, notably through interplay of world and regional economics; Willis, for example, focuses not on the South's sending out of the items mentioned above but on socks: Hickory, North Carolina, manufactures most of the socks worn around the world.

The second distinction is between objective and subjective. This volume emphasizes the objective: the demographics, economics, and to a degree, sociology of the South as it globalizes. While exhaustive information is not provided, we receive snapshots strategically placed to highlight key features of the contemporary southern "face." This objective description is the main contribution of the volume, and it sets the stage for inquiry into subjective aspects.

Consider the subjective aspect of the South—the emotions, ideas, and ethical understandings of southerners as they encounter global forces. To do this, one must push beyond the data and analyses in this volume or, indeed, in any extant study. An overriding concept relevant here is identity,[1] which is used as in Erik Erikson's classic studies, for example, of Germany (1950), providing a subjective definition of a collectivity. What do southerners proclaim as "We are" or "I am" in terms of southernness, identity with the region?

What impact does globalization have on southern identity? I propose three hypotheses:[2] first, that the South is moving from dualism to pluralism, that globalism has moved the South from a black/white dualism toward a more pluralistic society and identity; second, that the South is moving from opposition nationally to integration globally, that southern identity now depends less on opposition to the nation than on integration with the world; and third, that global can synergize with local, specifically that a sense of place could be preserved under globalism, creating a sort of grounded globalism that might resonate with yet also transform the South's traditional emphasis on place.

Consider the first hypothesis, dualism to pluralism. Demographically the trend is clear; Hispanic, Asian, and other migrants enrich the predominantly black/white spectrum of the older South. What is happening subjectively?

Behaviors—external actions—of the various groups are noted, some in this volume but also elsewhere. In particular, the media report conflict, such as attacks on Asian restaurants or muggings of Hispanics, but one can observe also more positive actions—for example, the election of an immigrant to an important position, such as president of a civic club. "Mr. Cucumber" is the nickname of an Indian migrant serving as president of the Lions Club in Tifton, Georgia; he is an expert on cucumbers at the Georgia Coastal Plains Experiment Station, and although the nickname may seem demeaning, his election reflects the respect in which he is held. Such anecdotal observations are deepened by the essays in this volume. Ajantha Subramanian shows how Indian professionals in Research Triangle Park, North Carolina, recoup any loss of identity by creating an essentialized Indian identity adapted to American norms of upward socioeconomic mobility. (On the other hand, Sawa Kurotani illustrates how Japanese professionals migrating to the South risk losing status because the South is not defined as a central place within the American hierarchy as viewed by Japanese.) Going beyond the essays, one observes external clues such as southern accents, body language, manners, and styles that are differentially adopted by various migrants. Such observations indicate sometimes surprising degrees of assimilation by immigrants into regional identities, sometimes none at all; notice differences between parents who arrived as adults and children who were born in the United States or arrived before adolescence, for example, and differences according to class and ethnicity.

What about pathologies? Alcoholism, psychiatric problems, and other signs of the obvious stresses on immigrants are reported in the news and in research (Akhtar 1995). Familiar and classic literary portrayals can be seen as reflecting older but similar histories of the psychology or psychopathology of migration. Take Tennessee Williams's *The Glass Menagerie*. The mother is a migrant (from the mannered Delta of Mississippi to the city of St. Louis), and her children are second-generation migrants. The children are somewhat alienated from their mother and her old world and struggle to transition to the new one; the daughter retreats into her toy zoo, the glass menagerie.

Informal culture, jokes, dreams, and other materials show attitudes and perspectives reflecting the influx of migrants. In a joke among Hispanics, Jesse Jackson and Jesse Helms argue about whether God is black or white. Both die and meet God, who greets them with "Buenos días." I dream that our dog Sophie runs away and I find her inside the house of Latino neighbors. Such jokes, dreams, and other elements express the experience and perception of migrants, migration, and the diversifying host society.

Let us turn now to the second hypothesis: that the South's attitude of opposition to the nation is giving way to a sense of integration with the wider world. This implies a Copernican revolution: the South, oppressed and depressed for more than a century, frees itself by broadening its perspective. The universe no longer rotates around the North, against which one must rebel or cringe, but around the world, with the North as merely one element. The burden of history is lifted, it seems.

Consider data from the 2001 Southern Focus Poll, administered by the Odum Institute and sponsored by the *Atlanta Journal-Constitution* and the Center for Study of the American South. Results suggest that while some southerners see themselves oppositionally—as different from nonsoutherners—a majority of those surveyed focus more on global ties. In this poll southerners were asked whether they saw themselves primarily as different from nonsoutherners or as linked to people around the world. Nearly 50 percent of respondents answered that they felt "connected to people around the world." Fewer than a third of those surveyed viewed themselves primarily in terms of their difference from nonsoutherners.

These results are striking, though of course open to debate. Beyond survey data, however, observations are at least suggestive. An example is the World Motel in McCrae, Georgia.[3] Why would one name a motel that in such a small, out-of-the-way place? Apparently the owner is Pakistani, and he cleverly labeled his establishment not according to a generic American or an ethnic category but, rather, to make it global. By identifying with the world, in effect he transformed his own identity from that of ethnic immigrant to world citizen. Similar identifications could be cited for native southerners, ranging from claims of global business (CNN and Bank of America) to global causes (Human Rights and the Carter Center) and global events and displays such as the Olympics or Exploris museum.

Finally, the third hypothesis reveals partial effects of the second: a feeling of integration with the world alters southerners' experience of place. Sense of place gives way to a sense of constructed place, entailing not only history and memory but also ecology, community, and preservation within a recognition of global forces. The South is famous for a sense of place, though this entails cultural construction and mental as well as physical definition. Also, much of the South's sense of itself as a place is of recent history, since the early nineteenth century, and it is somewhat defensive and oppositional. (Roy Blount asserts, "The North isn't a place . . . its just a direction out of the South" [qtd. in Cobb 1995, 16].)

Such a distinctively southern sense of place mixes reverence for ancestry and defensiveness against outsiders. Today this can mix with ecology and preservation movements, though these often arise as much from outsiders as from insiders. (Sunset Beach, N.C., vacation home owners, many of whom are migrants from elsewhere, lead movements based in ecology against local developers; Loudon County, Virginia, boasts a historical society supporting preservation against developers, and the preservationists seem to include those from elsewhere as well as natives.) Retirees seeking escape from globalization meet locals who seek to profit from it. My prediction is that a dynamic mix will entail both aspects, a particularized sense of place in memory and history and a more global concern about place based on ecology. The combination I term "grounded globalism."

What does grounded globalism entail? It entails a possible mix of ecological and historical sense of place, and perhaps other dimensions as well.

In this scenario, the South would emerge as a unit different from others, and hence distinctively useful or viable, yet integrated into global currents. Note the example of the European Community (EC). The EC has decided that nations are often too small for globalism and too big for viable localism, so regions sometimes serve better than nations within an integrative system such as the EC. The EC has thus created the Committee on Regions. The South might emerge as such a region in the world, or part of the world.

The South expresses strengths of popular and folk culture, such as African American and Appalachian, its landscapes, and historic places. Its history includes these varied strands. How can they be configured as part of a globalizing process in cultural guise?

The special role of the South could be a positive, integrative side of its oppositional identity. Ambivalence does not undercut the South's cultural distinctiveness, for that is its distinction. The South is in but not wholly of America the Beautiful, the U.S.A. that is the City on the Hill—the perfected utopia —but also the world bully, the most powerful nation, one that bombs, in-

vades, colonizes, and exploits. The South, owing to its somewhat marginalized and oppositional history within the United States, can and in some ways
does provide a link to the rest of the world that the nation as a whole, and
specifically the triumphalist North, cannot, at least not in the same way. The
North, for example, might connect to other places through ethnic links, but
the South's connection to the world is grounded in a regional identity that has
a special history, troubled to be sure, but also inspiring and inspirited.

As I noted earlier, the South is only one case. There are many Souths. However, globalization as a world phenomenon is transforming Souths everywhere.
"I am a world citizen, not an Indonesian!" proclaimed a young nephew of two
old friends in Yogyakarta, Java. They were disturbed by his declaration, which
they talked about for days after. It violated a national identity that they had
fought for during their own secession, from Dutch colonization, and the regional and ethnic identity as Javanese, which is as deep as that of southern, was
lost, or so it seemed to the aunts of the older patriotic generation.

Globalism itself is a species of broader processes, the most comprehensive
of which Max Weber termed rationalization (1947). Weber's characterization
usefully includes an action aspect and an ideational aspect—the forging of
new means/end relationships (as when capitalism turns "tallow into candles
and men into money") and of new configurations of consciousness (for example, the "spirit of capitalism" that engendered and affirmed the practice of it).
Both aspects see light in the present volume within the context of globalization, which some see as simply extending Weberian rationalization globally
(cf. Peter Beyer). Within the world context, the globalization of the South is
merely one of many Souths; within the context of the South, global impact is
huge.

Notes

1. For a discussion of identity, see Jacobson-Widding 1983.
2. I first explored these three hypotheses in Peacock 2002b.
3. See my discussion of the meaning of motels in Peacock 2001, 33.

References

Akhtar, Salman. 1995. "A Third Individuation: Immigration, Identity, and the
Pyschoanalytic Process." *Journal of the American Psychoanalytic Association*
43:1051–84.
Applebome, Peter. 1996. *Dixie Rising: How the South Is Shaping American Values,
Politics, and Culture*. New York: Times Books.
Beyer, Peter. 1994. *Religion and Globalization*. London: Sage.

Cash, W. J. 1941. *The Mind of the South.* New York: Knopf.

Cobb, James. 1995. "We Ain't Trash No More!" *The Future of the South: National Humanities Center, American Issues Forum I.* Occasional Papers 1.

Coclanis, Peter A. 1989. *The Shadow of a Dream: Economic Life and Death in the South Carolina Low Country, 1670–1920.* New York: Oxford University Press.

Corrales, Emiliano. In preparation. "Casting Steel: Region and State, Mexico and the American South, 1910–1920." Ph.D. diss., University of Chicago.

Crisp, James E. 1985. *History 243: The United States, 1845–1914.* Chapel Hill, N.C.: Independent Study by Extension.

Egerton, John. 1974. *The Americanization of Dixie: The Southernization of America.* New York: Harper's Magazine Press.

Erikson, Erik H. 1950. *Childhood and Society.* New York: Norton.

Greene, Jack P. 1992. *Imperatives, Behaviors, and Identities: Essays in Early American Cultural History.* Charlottesville: University Press of Virginia.

Jacobson-Widding, Anita, ed. 1983. *Identity: Personal and Socio-Cultural.* Uppsala: Almqvist and Wiksell.

Kolchin, Peter. 2003. *A Sphinx on the American Land: The Nineteenth-Century South in Comparative Perspective.* Baton Rouge: Louisiana State University Press.

Massey, Doreen B., and Pat Jess, eds. 1995. *A Place in the World? Places, Cultures, and Globalization.* New York: Oxford University Press.

Matthews, John. 2004. "The U.S. South, Modern American Empire, and Post-Colonial Studies." Keynote address at the Southern Intellectual History Circle meeting in Charleston, South Carolina, February 26.

Moltke-Hansen, David. 2000. "Regional Frameworks and Networks: Changing Identities in the Southeastern United States." In Lothar Hönnighausen, ed., *Regional Images and Regional Realities,* 149–70. Tübingen: Stauffenburg.

Moltke-Hansen, David, and Michael O'Brien, eds. 1986. *Intellectual Life in Antebellum Charleston.* Knoxville: University of Tennessee Press.

Nichols, Patricia C. 1988. "English as a Bridge between Cultures: Scotland, Carolina, and California." *Catesol Journal* 1:5–15.

———. 1989. "Storytelling in Carolina: Continuities and Contrasts." *Anthropology and Education Quarterly* 20 (September): 232–45.

Peacock, James L. 2001. *The Anthropological Lens: Harsh Light, Soft Focus.* 2d ed. Cambridge: Cambridge University Press.

———. 2002a. "Action Comparison: Efforts towards a Global and Comparative yet Local and Active Anthropology." In Andre Gingrich and Richard Fox, eds., *Anthropology, by Comparison,* 44–69. London: Routledge, Kegan, and Paul.

———. 2002b. "The South in a Global World." *Virginia Quarterly Review* 78, no. 4 (Autumn): 581–94.

Peacock, James L., and Tim Pettyjohn. 1995. "Fundamentalisms Narrated: Muslim, Christian, and Mystical." In Martin E. Marty and R. Scott Appleby, eds., *Fundamentalisms Comprehended,* 115–34. Chicago: University of Chicago Press.

Richardson, Miles. 2003. *Being-in-Christ and Putting Death in Its Place.* Baton Rouge: Louisiana State Press.

Sparks, Alistair. 1990. *The Mind of South Africa*. New York: Knopf.

Tindall, George. "Native and Newcomer: Ethnic Southerners and Southern New-comers." In Valeria Lerda, ed., *From Melting Pot to Multiculturalism*, 205–18. Rome: Bulzoni Editorie.

Tindall, George Brown, and David E. Shi. 1984. *America: A Narrative History*. 3d ed. New York: Norton.

Weber, Max. 1947. *The Theory of Social and Economic Organization*. Trans. Talcott Parsons and A. M. Henderson. New York: Oxford University Press.

Harry L. Watson

Southern History, Southern Future

Some Reflections and a Cautious Forecast

Reflecting on the question of southern identity in a justly renowned essay of nearly half a century ago, the late C. Vann Woodward mused on the forces of change that were already ripping up the structures of poverty, inequality, and regional isolation that had classically marked the region of his birth. The distinguished historian called the wave of post–World War II transformation the Bulldozer Revolution and remarked how industrialization, urbanization, population mobility, and economic development were putting an end to a long roster of peculiar southern institutions, including "the one-horse farmer, one-crop agriculture, one-party politics, the sharecropper, the poll tax, the white primary, the Jim Crow car, [and] the lynching bee." If "the great machine with the lowered blade" could banish all these woeful but unmistakable markers of distinctiveness, Woodward (1968, 18–19) asked, could the South continue to exist as a separate region with its own unique identity?

Woodward's famous answer to the prospect of a vanishing South was that everything about the South might change but its history, which he defined as "the collective experience of the southern people" (1968, 25). He went on to elucidate several humbling aspects of southern history that he thought other Americans would do well to remember. The experiences of poverty, defeat, and moral failure, he thought, gave southerners more in common with the world's other people than with the innocent and affluent triumphalists who seemed to prevail to the north.

Perceptive as it was, Woodward's forecast of enduring southern identity rested on the hidden assumption that "the southern people," black and white alike, would continue to connect with their "collective experience" in much the same way that family members retain a common identity by passing along memories and legacies from their forebears. At least in 1958, apparently,

Woodward could scarcely imagine a South inhabited by newcomers with little or no personal connection to the region's past, and thus removed in all but mythical or academic ways from the wellsprings of traditional southern identity. In this respect, at least, Woodward joined forces with W. J. Cash (whom specialists tend to think of as his polar opposite) in assuming a perpetual and continuous quality to the region's character and population (1941).

But a South that seems disconnected from its past is exactly the region that the essays in this volume describe. Public schools teaching English to Latino immigrants, gated suburbs housing Japanese and Indian scientists, and factories staffed by Hmong knitters were all beyond the imagination of most observers less than a generation ago but now dot the southern landscape like the cotton gins or tobacco barns of past decades. These newcomers bring their own histories, and there is little reason to think that the intricate family stories of who married whom Before the War (and everything that such conversations represent) will ever have much meaning for them. Aside from the frippery affected by a handful of reenactors, it is hard to detect among them the hoofbeats of Jeb Stuart's cavalry that Cash found among an earlier generation of southern leaders. The transnational South has become a reality, forcing all of us to take new stock of the question of southern identity and the meaning of globalization in a formerly isolated region.

As we prepared this volume, the editors repeatedly confronted two questions. Is globalization a more-or-less uniform process that has occurred in much the same way in the South as elsewhere, or is it a more protean experience that has different features in every location it touches? To put it another way, we asked if globalization has a southern identity. Is there a *southern* globalization that differs from similar developments elsewhere? Or does this revolutionizing process so flatten traditional distinctions that regional variations are irrelevant?

Without always addressing these questions directly, the essays in this volume make clear that the answer to these questions must be "yes" or "both." On one hand, the South today is subject to the same rapid movements of people, capital, and technology that characterize globalization everywhere. The region faces many of the same disorienting changes as coastal China or post-Communist Poland, as nearly instant investment and development in one sector brings equally rapid disinvestment and decline somewhere else. Dramatic changes in markets, production decisions, migration patterns, and demographic features are common facts of life from Hong Kong to High Point.

Despite these universal characteristics, however, globalization is a complex process and does not strike every locality with equal force. Where C. Vann

Woodward pointed to the bulldozer as the symbol of postwar economic change, globalization reminds me of a misshapen asteroid, approaching the earth with a tumbling motion. Some of us may be hit by the blunt end and some by the point, and others will face various combinations of the two. The asteroid's impact will also be affected by differences in its target landscapes. Some locales boast convenient hollows to absorb the force of a blow, while others feature delicate protrusions that may shatter from the force of an approaching object. The same globalizing process can thus have very different effects, even inside the same county. The North American Free Trade Agreement, for example, has contributed to the migration of hundreds of southern textile plants to the developing world, even while Meenu Tewari finds that it has drawn highly skilled Latino immigrants to domestic furniture factories virtually next door.

Veteran storm-watchers know that the same hurricane can demolish one building while leaving its next-door neighbor no more than jostled, depending on the history, the structure, and the environment of the buildings involved. So it is with globalization. History and social structure have shaped distinctive environments in every human community that inescapably affect the inhabitants' experience of the present, often regardless of whether the participants fully understand how those influences operate. What are the legacies on the southern landscape that shape the region's experience of the worldwide phenomenon of globalization? What is globalization's southern identity?

If the impact of the storm or the asteroid depends on the structure and history of what is being hit, forecasting the future impact of globalization requires a detour into the southern past, and inevitably to the legacy of slavery and the plantation. An earlier transnational economy virtually created the historical South, as seventeenth-century demand for popular commodities like sugar and tobacco powered European colonization, the conquest of Native Americans, the enslavement of Africans, and the creation of an enduring biracial population. The plantation was an institution that the southern colonies of British, French, and Spanish North America shared with similar outposts in the Caribbean and Latin America, as the economies of scale associated with mass production of tropical crops encouraged the formation of landed estates and large communities of enslaved workers. As long as slavery prevailed, plantation strongholds like St. Domingue and the Carolina Sea Islands were among the wealthiest portions of the globe (particularly if their inhabitants were counted the way their rulers preferred to count them, as property) and enriched their metropoles with some of the most opulent commerce the world had ever known. Today, the old plantation belts are among the poorest regions of the Americas, whether in Mississippi, Haiti, or Brazil. Slavery had discour-

aged education, diversification, technological improvement, capital formation, and the development of domestic markets, and freed workers resisted a
superhuman pace of production when finally released from their chains. Where
sharecropping preserved a semblance of the plantation order well into the
twentieth century, the South's plantation belts perpetuated slavery's preference for low taxes, weak school systems, and hostility to outside influences,
while relying on racial animosity and systematic terror to keep blacks and poor
whites ignorant and quiescent. To say the least, this was hardly a promising
platform for successful economic development, and the Deep South festered
as the nation's "economic problem number one" until well after World War II
(Wright 1986; Coclanis 1989).

The plantation also left its legacy in the upland South, where slaves were
a minority of the population but where white yeoman farmers fed their families from their own farms and cherished their independence from those they
regarded as swindling merchants and overbearing gentry. In the North, a similar inland population was gradually attracted to urban markets and the division of labor, embracing the values of Benjamin Franklin's Poor Richard and
fostering America's industrial takeoff as a population of Yankee tinkerers and
small-time entrepreneurs. In the South, the plantation system discouraged the
growth of cities, transportation systems, and interior markets, keeping the upland regions isolated and underdeveloped until after the Civil War. The result
was a white yeoman population that celebrated its independence from outside
domination but lacked the necessary skills and capital to protect that independence when commercial expansion eventually appeared along with Re-
construction-era railroads. By the end of the nineteenth century, most of these
families had lost their lands. Imprisoned by debt to merchant-landlords, they
eked out a bare living by sharecropping cotton or tobacco on fields where they
had once produced much of their own food and clothing (Hahn 1983).

Industrialization eventually took hold in the upland South, as merchants
and landlords invested their profits in factories to spin the region's cotton into
yarn and poor whites exchanged the known hardships of sharecropping for
the promising allure of "public work" in the mills. When indigenous investors
had proved the profitability of these efforts, outside firms followed and brought
the bulk of the American textile industry from New England to the southern
Piedmont by the 1920s (Hall et al. 1987, 183–236). Even so, industrialization
came late to the South, and the abundance of native white workers discouraged the entrance of European immigrants after the Civil War, just as slavery
had done before that time.

The South's economic isolation thus bred cultural homogeneity and ethnic uniformity. The South had been ethnically diverse in the eighteenth century, but the end of immigration and the slave trade flattened most ethnic distinctions into two simple categories: black and white. More ethnically uniform than northerners, southerners also faced industrialization with less formal education and fewer nonfarm skills and attracted companies that offered no more than unskilled, low-paying jobs, often performed by children in the early mills. Dependent on cheap labor for survival, leaders of these industries tended to support the South's tradition of low taxes, weak public services, poor schools, and low wages. Taking their factories into the countryside, first to exploit waterpower sites and later to tap the hinterland's seemingly inexhaustible supply of rurally based workers, southern industry fostered a diffuse pattern of urbanization. With the exception of a few major marketing centers like Atlanta, small towns and rural, nonfarm employment inhibited the rise of a southern, urban culture. Southern workers reacted to their low wages with protests, strikes, and union drives in the 1920s and 1930s, but national political considerations and a regional tradition of violent repression of dissent intersected to crush their efforts (Hall et al. 1987, 289–357). Eventually, the mobility of southern industry, the dispersion of mill villages, and gradually rising living standards combined with continued bare-knuckle techniques by employers undermined the union movement, leaving the South with the nation's weakest institutions of organized labor.

Unlike the twentieth-century demographic profile of most of industrial America, the South's remained biracial rather than multiethnic, and the region was more homogeneous and culturally isolated than any other part of the Union. John Shelton Reed has remarked that the U.S. South and the Afrikaner provinces of South Africa are the only places in the world where evangelical Protestants constitute the majority of the population and command the cultural heights of the society. Religious change made headlines in North Carolina recently when the 2002 census revealed that Roman Catholics had barely replaced Methodists as the second largest denomination in the state, with Baptists still in a commanding lead.[1]

The South's traditional biracial society created a strong tendency to soften ethnic differences well into the late twentieth century and often forced nonconforming individuals and groups into its established racial polarities. American Indian groups like the Lumbees of North Carolina have struggled for more than a century against a white preference to define and segregate them as black people. When I first moved back to North Carolina some twenty-five years ago, I met a Chinese American from California who said that the South was the first place he had ever lived where he was socially defined as a white person. Today, if he wished, such a newcomer could join any number of campus clubs and organizations that would define him much more precisely, even differentiating him from another student I saw recently with a tee shirt listing ten reasons why "You Know You Are Vietnamese if . . . ."

The South's cultural isolation and homogeneity have not entirely disappeared, but they are rapidly changing. As recently as 1950, the American state with the highest proportion of residents who had been born in that state was Mississippi, at 88.5 percent. The next top-ranking states were Alabama, South Carolina, North Carolina, Kentucky, Georgia, Louisiana, and West Virginia. Not until Pennsylvania and Maine entered the list at ninth and tenth place, respectively, did any nonsouthern states join the top ten in this category. At midcentury, in other words, the southern states were the least likely to attract migrants from other places and thus (presumably) were the most likely to perpetuate their own established customs without challenge from outsiders. Fifty years later, in the federal census of 2000, Pennsylvania's raw percentage of in-state natives was 80.77 percent, only three points lower than in 1950, but this proportion now gave Pennsylvania the nation's second-highest percentage of its own natives, and evidently a corresponding tendency to repel migration from elsewhere. The remaining states in the top ten were Louisiana, Michigan, Iowa, Ohio, Mississippi, West Virginia, Kentucky, Wisconsin, and Alabama. The Deep South and the Mountain South were obviously still represented, but stalwarts of the nation's industrial heartland had joined the so-called Rustbelt and were now exporting instead of attracting residents. As a measure of the overall change, South Carolina was once the cradle of secession and ranked third in native residents in 1950, but it jostled for twenty-second place in 2000, between Tennessee and Arkansas (*U.S. Census of Population* 1954; "Place of Birth by Citizenship Status" 2000).

If the southern past has been marked by poverty, racial conflict, and relative ethnic homogeneity, what are the implications for its global future? A few lessons are obvious. The South is attracting low-wage and low-skilled immigrants today because many of its native-born workers have found better opportunities, while its traditional industries continue to demand cheap labor. In this context, owners will inevitably move their factories to the workers, by going offshore, or will move the workers to the factories, by encouraging legal or illegal immigration.

It might also seem intuitively obvious that the South's established cultural uniformity will lead to outbursts of nativism and ethnic hostility as its population diversifies. In 1995 the Southern Focus Poll asked representative numbers of southerners and nonsoutherners, "Over all, do you think that recent immigrants have improved the quality of life in your community, hurt the quality of life, or made no difference?" Contrary, perhaps, to expectations, southerners were *less* likely than nonsoutherners, by the slight margin of 28 percent to 33 percent, to say that immigrants had hurt their quality of life. By a striking margin of 46 percent to 37 percent, southerners were *more* likely to say that immigration had made no difference to their communities. A year later the same poll found that southerners were less likely than nonsoutherners to complain that "current laws and regulations go too far in protecting the rights of immigrants."[2] Episodes of ethnic conflict have certainly cropped up, but the record so far is that southerners have made their traditional values a selling point rather than a flashpoint, by reinterpreting them as devotion to home, family, faith, community, and place. Chambers of commerce and economic development agencies have instinctively absorbed Woodward's insight that history has given the South much in common with the rest of the world, particularly the developing, postcolonial world, and turned it to their advantage. I was particularly struck by the reference in Ajantha Subramanian's essay to North Carolina governor Jim Hunt's address to a group of Indian business leaders, in which he stressed that, as "southerners," Indians and North Carolinians shared a common commitment to "the sanctity of the family, of religion, of education, and of hard work." The governor passed silently over the fact that most southern churches have traditionally held up Indian religions as archetypes of what their Protestant missionaries ought to eradicate. For the purposes of attracting foreign investment, it was enough to say that religion drew southerners and Indians together against the unnamed godless from somewhere else.

Will the South's historical substrate always shape what globalization builds here? Surely not. The particulars of place will not always override the fundamentals of capital flows, trade shifts, immigration concerns, and the re-creation of infrastructure. The fact that North Carolina was in the Confederacy and California was not thus contributes to a difference in resources and experience between the two states, but the practical need to provide translators and health care is much the same in both places.

The new wave of immigrants may not be as interested in established regional differences in the United States as older Americans are, and there is no inherent reason why they should be. To use myself as an example, I lived in France for nearly a year and enjoyed it thoroughly; but I never thought of myself as a Frenchman, and certainly no one ever mistook me for one. While I was a sojourner and not a permanent immigrant, the fundamental point still holds: newcomers to the South bring their own historical identities that they may not want to lose, and they certainly do not need lessons in "southern-ness" to make them good citizens of Georgia or Tennessee or Texas.

Moving to Cary, North Carolina, has evidently done little to foster a new southern identity among the Japanese families that Sawa Kurotani interviewed. The manager who joked that "there are no southerners in my neighborhood" thus made a sound point. Indeed, the transnational South can occasionally foster group identities that are not even American, as Steve Striffler found in an Ozark chicken plant when multiethnic workers decided that mutual exploitation made them "all Mexicans here. Screwed-over Mexicans." It will make more sense to call these newcomers southerners when they decide for themselves that something "southern" distinguishes them from former compatriots who now live in California or New York.

If globalization will bring entirely new population groups to a formerly homogeneous region, what will be their impact on the southerners who are already here? This aspect of the transnational South remains the least explored by contemporary scholars. Conventional discussions usually begin and end with economic developments like plant closings and competition for jobs between natives and newcomers. The realities of industrial job losses are undeniable, but the exact contribution of free trade agreements to these matters (as distinct from obsolete technology or other problems) is still uncertain. According to Rachel Willis, Hmong and Latino workers did not migrate to North Carolina's Catawba Valley to take the jobs of old-timers but because expanded opportunities for native workers had created a *shortage* of low-skilled workers there. Willis and Barbara Ellen Smith describe instances where Latino immigration has put downward pressure on southern wage levels, but even this fact may create less resentment than we might expect. If black and white native southerners leave jobs that paid $8.00 an hour for jobs that pay $12.00, immigrants leaving $2.00 jobs in Mexico may replace them at a new wage of $7.00. Statistically, the average southern wage rate may go down in this scenario; but everybody is better off than they used to be, and initially at least, no one is likely to complain.

The record is likewise ambiguous in areas of cultural competition. Barbara Ellen Smith also describes a series of ethnic stereotypes that employers use in Memphis to justify their preference for Hispanic workers: honest, hardworking, reliable, willing to work overtime and on weekends, and so forth. These compliments sound suspiciously like inverted stereotypes of native southerners, especially blacks, so the employers seem to be saying that they prefer Hispanics because they perceive them to be harder workers than the black workers they may have replaced. If Latino immigration has thus led to massive unemployment among native blacks, then Memphis may be ripe for explosive conflict between displaced black workers and their hated Latino rivals.

Tension between blacks and Hispanics certainly exists, but so far the atmosphere in Memphis and similar places is reasonably placid, and perhaps the situation is less dire than we think. If black workers now have the freedom to desert employers who remind them of plantation overseers, who can blame them for changing jobs? If Hispanic workers are now willing to replace them, is it because their white supervisors bring less racial animosity into workplace relationships, making these difficult jobs less humiliating and more bearable? Such questions will require careful study to answer accurately, but so far, there seem to be enough jobs for everybody, natives and immigrants alike. If that remains true, economic and cultural conflict in the transnational South is likely to remain manageable.

The one area where cultural resentment of outsiders has clearly increased is in the resurgent neo-Confederate movement. Throughout the South, battlefield reenactors and genealogical groups such as the Sons of Confederate Veterans have enjoyed increased memberships and greater cultural visibility, while fringe groups like the League of the South have come forward with quaint demands for a new southern secession movement. Observers of reenactment report that many participants tend to be politically conservative but lack strong ideological commitments to white supremacy or separate southern nationhood. Tony Horwitz (1998) finds whole families involved in the movement, and many of them are more nostalgic for antique gender roles than for racial purity or vanished plantations.

Rejection of outsiders is much stronger among the secessionists of the League of the South. In its position papers, the league stiffly acknowledges black membership in southern culture and rejects racism in what it calls a spirit of Christian charity, but it insists on traditional homogeneity when it comes to more exotic influences. Its website pledges "to protect the historic Anglo-Celtic core culture of the South because the Scots, Irish, Welsh, and English have given Dixie its unique institutions and civilisation. Should the Christian, Anglo-Celtic core be displaced, then the South would cease to be recognisable to us and our progeny."[3]

More widespread evidence of neo-Confederate sentiment appeared in recent struggles to retain Confederate emblems in the state flags of Mississippi and Georgia and to keep the Confederate battle flag flying above the South Carolina statehouse. While these incidents may well owe some of their force to native white resentment of outside cultural influences, there is little reason to suspect that they presage any larger cultural struggle that would seriously interfere with continued immigration or participation in global economic activities.

If there is little danger that the League of the South will dominate regional response to globalizing change, what will be the southern face of globalization? Forecasting the future is presumptuous and unreliable, but history and the trends reported in this volume suggest that the global South will be distinctively southern without remaining unchanged. Several likely developments stand out.

First, an economy based on low-wage manufacturing will come under steadily mounting pressure, leading to continued job losses or increased immigration or both, depending on specific local conditions. Leaders will face a sustained responsibility to devise a more stable foundation for the regional economy that draws effectively on the skills and preferences of the newcomers as well as those who have been here for generations.

As immigration continues, the arrival of newcomers from outside the classic boundaries of Protestant Christianity and black/white racial polarity will generate unprecedented demands for pluralism, tolerance, and mutual respect. Established racial categories will expand to recognize a wide variety of nontraditional ethnic groups. The white South's gradual acquiescence in the leading demands of the black civil rights movement will be valuable preparation for the challenges ahead. Even so, black southerners will continue to press for the unfulfilled demands of that movement, perhaps in the face of incomprehension or indifference on the part of the newcomers as well as established white southerners.

As the South adapts to its new residents, southerners may mobilize long-established conservative values to smooth the process of change. Without rejecting family, faith, tradition, and respect for social hierarchies, southerners are likely to interpret them as reassuring verities that legitimize tolerance for superficial differences and make the newcomers feel welcome.

Finally, long-established black and white southerners, whom history forged into linked but dual ethnic groups, will no longer comprise the entire body of the southern people. This will not make their cultures extinct, as the League of the South seems to fear, but it will reconfigure them as two large subpopulations among several smaller ones, entitled to their private identities but without the right to control all public symbols. The search for new symbols of community will demand increased attention from citizens and their leaders.

If something like this forecast comes to pass, it will not happen effortlessly. There will be much work to do, not only for economic planners and ESL teachers, but also for scholars, artists, and citizens of goodwill. The white heritage of defensiveness and grievance still flourishes in many places and calls out for informed critiques (Swain 2002). Popular misunderstanding of slavery, the Civil War, and Reconstruction is widely entrenched and feeds white affection for Confederate symbolism and resistance to cultural inclusiveness. Southern poverty and racial inequality have not disappeared. Many old issues fester from the days of the civil rights movement and still cry out for redress. We will often need to remind ourselves that a just, diverse, and democratic South is in everyone's long-term best interests. Globalization's southern identity is not foreordained; it will take imagination and determination to make it diverse, prosperous, democratic, eco-friendly, and transcendent of its history.

Notes

1. See, for example, *Raleigh News and Observer*, February 14, 2002.
2. Southern Focus Poll Data accessed via ‹http://cgi.irss.unc.edu/tempdocs/16:38:04:2.htm› and ‹http://cgi.irss.unc.edu/tempdocs/16:38:04:4.htm›.
3. "On Defending the Anglo-Celtic Culture of the South," 2004. The league prefers English-style orthography as more traditional and thus more authentically southern.

References

Cash, W. J. 1941. *The Mind of the South*. New York: Knopf.
Coclanis, Peter A. 1989. *The Shadow of a Dream: Economic Life and Death in the South Carolina Low Country, 1670–1920*. New York: Oxford University Press.
Hahn, Steven. 1983. *The Roots of Southern Populism: Yeoman Farmers and the Transformation of the Georgia Upcountry, 1850–1890*. New York: Oxford University Press.
Hall, Jacquelyn Dowd, James Leloudis, Robert Korstad, Mary Murphy, Lu Ann Jones, and Christopher B. Daly. 1987. *Like a Family: The Making of a Southern Cotton Mill World*. Chapel Hill: University of North Carolina Press.
Horwitz, Tony. 1998. *Confederates in the Attic: Dispatches from the Unfinished Civil War*. New York: Pantheon.
"On Defending the Anglo-Celtic Culture of the South." 2004. League of the South website. Retrieved from ‹http://www.dixienet.org/positions/free-ac.htm›.
"Place of Birth by Citizenship Status." 2000. Census 2000 Summary File 3, P21. Washington, D.C.: U.S. Government Printing Office. Retrieved from ‹http://factfinder.census.gov/servlet/DTTable?_ts=81870009238 ›, ‹http://cgi.irss.unc.edu/tempdocs/16:38:04:2.htm›, and ‹http://cgi.irss.unc.edu/tempdocs/16:38:04:4.htm›.
Swain, Carol M. 2002. *The New White Nationalism in America: Its Challenge to Integration*. Cambridge: Cambridge University Press.
U.S. Census of Population: 1950. 1954. "Special Reports." State of Birth. Vol. 4, pt.

4, chap. A, tab. 7. Washington, D.C.: U.S. Government Printing Office. Retrieved from ⟨http://factfinder.census.gov/servlet/DTTable?_ts=81870009238⟩, ⟨http://cgi.irss.unc.edu/tempdocs/16:38:04:2.htm⟩, and ⟨http://cgi.irss.unc.edu/tempdocs/16:38:04:4.htm⟩.

Woodward, C. Vann. 1968. *The Burden of Southern History*. 2d ed. Baton Rouge: Louisiana State University Press.

Wright, Gavin. 1986. *Old South, New South: Revolutions in the Southern Economy since the Civil War*. New York: Basic Books.

Contributors

Catherine Brooks speaks French, Spanish, Hindi, and Urdu and has taught English as a Second Language at Kodaikanal International School in Tamil Nadu, India. She is currently working as a travel director for a company specializing in international travel.

David H. Ciscel is professor of economics at the University of Memphis. He is also a faculty affiliate with the Center for Research on Women and the School of Urban Affairs and Public Policy. He is a labor economist and has published frequently in the *Journal of Economic Issues*.

Thaddeus Countway Guldbrandsen is research assistant professor of anthropology at the University of New Hampshire and director of the Center for the Study of Community at Strawbery Banke. He is coauthor of *If This Is Democracy: Public Interests and Private Politics in a Neoliberal Age* (forthcoming). He is currently completing a book-length manuscript titled "Bull City Futures: Transformations of Political Action, Inequality, and Public Space" and is involved in two major research projects that examine contemporary transnational migration in New Hampshire.

Carla Jones is assistant professor of anthropology at the University of Colorado, Boulder. Her research focuses on the intersection of new class and gender identities in urban Indonesia.

Sawa Kurotani is assistant professor of anthropology at the University of Redlands. Her first book, *A Long Vacation: Transnational Mobility and Domesticity among Japanese Corporate Wives in the United States*, is forthcoming from Duke University Press.

Paul A. Levengood is the managing editor of the *Virginia Magazine of History and Biography* at the Virginia Historical Society in Richmond. His *Boom Town: Houston, Texas, during World War II* is forthcoming from Texas A&M University Press. He has published an article in the *Southwestern Historical Quarterly* and reviews in several historical journals. His essay here is part of a long-term study that examines migration to the South in the second half of the twentieth century.

Carrie R. Matthews is a Ph.D. candidate in comparative literature at the University of North Carolina at Chapel Hill.

Bryan McNeil is a Ph.D. candidate in the Department of Anthropology at the University of North Carolina at Chapel Hill.

Marcela Mendoza is a researcher at the Center for Research on Women and an affiliate faculty member at the Department of Anthropology, University of Memphis. She has published a book, many articles, and book chapters about indigenous peoples of the South American Gran Chaco and about Latino immigration in the United States.

Donald M. Nonini is professor of anthropology at the University of Toronto. He is also coauthor, with Dorothy Holland, Catherine Lutz, and others, of *If This Is Democracy: Public Interests and Private Politics in A Neoliberal Age* (forthcoming). He is the author of *British Colonial Rule and the Resistance of the Malay Peasantry, 1900–1957* (1992); editor, with Aihwa Ong, of *Ungrounded Empires: The Cultural Politics of Modern Chinese Transnationalism* (1997); and the author of numerous articles on the cultural politics of Chinese ethnic identity and citizenship in Malaysia.

James L. Peacock is Kenan Professor of Anthropology at the University of North Carolina at Chapel Hill. He served as director of the University Center for International Studies at UNC from 1996 to 2003 and as president of the American Anthropological Association from 1993 to 1995. His publications include *The Anthropological Lens* (rev. ed., 2001). He is a Fellow of the American Academy of Arts and Sciences and recipient of the Franz Boas Award of the American Anthropological Association.

Barbara Ellen Smith is professor of sociology and director of the Center for Research on Women at the University of Memphis. She is the author or editor of three books and numerous articles, including *Digging Our Own Graves: Coal Miners and the Struggle over Black Lung Disease* (1987) and *Neither Separate nor Equal: Women, Race, and Class in the South* (1999).

Jennie M. Smith founded the anthropology program at Berry College in Rome, Georgia. Until recently she served as the chair of the Department of Sociology and Anthropology at Berry. During the 2002–3 school year, she cofounded the college's Latin American and Caribbean Studies Program and is now its director. She is the author of *When the Hands Are Many: Community Organization and Social Change in Rural Haiti* (2001; reissued 2003).

Sandy Smith-Nonini is assistant professor of anthropology at the University of Toronto. She has done research on the cultural politics of public health in El Salvador and Peru as well as on the occupational health and labor struggles of Latino migrants in rural North Carolina. She received the Peter K. New Award for applied anthropology in 1995.

Ellen Griffith Spears is a doctoral candidate in American studies and A. Worley Brown Southern Studies Fellow at Emory University. She was associate director of the Atlanta-based Southern Regional Council from 2000 to 2002. She is the author of *The Newtown Story: One Community's Fight for Environmental Justice* (1998). Her most recent article, "Making Illnesses Visible: Negotiating Justice in Contested Environments," appears in *Defining the Public Health: Emerging Illnesses and Society* (forthcoming).

Gregory Stephens is lecturer of cultural studies and film at the University of West Indies-Mona. He is the author of *On Racial Frontiers: The New Culture of Frederick Douglass, Ralph Ellison, and Bob Marley* (1999). Many of his online writings and radio shows can be accessed at ‹http://www.gregorystephens.com›.

Steve Striffler is associate professor of anthropology and Latin American studies at the University of Arkansas. He is the author of *In the Shadows of State and Capital*

(2002) and coeditor of *Banana Wars* (2003). He is currently finishing a book titled *The Triumph and Tragedy of Chicken* (forthcoming).

Ajantha Subramanian is assistant professor of anthropology and social studies at Harvard University. Her work concerns the historical processes through which national minority identity and citizenship are constituted. She has conducted fieldwork and archival research in South India and the United States, among Indian Catholics and Indian Americans.

Meenu Tewari is assistant professor of economic development in the Department of City and Regional Planning at the University of North Carolina at Chapel Hill. She is a member of the Research and Training Advisory Committee of the Institute of Small Enterprises in India and has consulted for several international organizations.

Lucila Vargas is associate professor at the School of Journalism and Mass Communication at the University of North Carolina at Chapel Hill. She edited the anthology *Women Faculty of Color in the White Classroom* (2002) and wrote *Social Uses and Radio Practices: The Use of Radio by Ethnic Minorities in Mexico* (1995).

Harry L. Watson is professor of history at the University of North Carolina at Chapel Hill. He is the author of four books, including *Liberty and Power: The Politics of Jacksonian America* (1990) and *Andrew Jackson vs. Henry Clay: Democracy and Development in Antebellum America* (1998). He is currently at work on a history of the United States. Since 1999 he has served as director of the UNC Center for the Study of the American South.

Rachel A. Willis is associate professor of American studies and economics at the University of North Carolina at Chapel Hill. Her recent research has focused on the North Carolina hosiery industry.